The Path of a Baby Boomer

DOWN FROM THE MOUNTAIN

BRIAN VICKERY

SWEETSPIRE LITERATURE
——— MANAGEMENT ———

CONTENTS

FOREWORD

BRIAN VICKERY WAS born in 1945, a post-war baby with a birth date that qualified him as a 'baby boomer'. Much has been written about those born in this era with most suggesting that this was an age of free spirit, good music, and business success. It was also an age of drug taking, dysfunctional families, and more importantly, the Vietnam War.

This is the story about a young man who was caught up in most of the complexities of the time but negotiated his way through life with the help of a good upbringing, a supporting family, and a strong resolve for achievement. Brian was raised and educated, like many of his friends, without privilege and as a student should be classed as a borderline failure. His mind was never on his studies, and he clearly demonstrated all the qualities of an underachiever. Academically, he had nowhere to go but down.

Brian's life changed with the death of his mother and the call-up for National Service. He served a thirteen-month tour of Vietnam; spent two years in the Northern Territory, a year in Hong Kong, a year in Brunei with the Brigade of Gurkhas; and had a career spanning twenty-three years in the Australian Army. Brian and his wife, Carole, ran several businesses over a ten-year period, not all successfully. Brian 'chanced his arm' when the opportunities presented themselves, enabling him to achieve things in life which should never have been possible-he is a person thankful for his achievements and philosophical about his failures. Brian was never likely to die wondering whether 'he could have made it'. Such is the path of one 'baby boomer'. Brian did, indeed, lead an extraordinary yet fulfilling life.

CHAPTER ONE

THE EARLY YEARS

MOUNT WARNING HAS always stood out as the signature feature of the Tweed Valley in northern New South Wales. It dominates all before it and was named by Captain James Cook for the warning it offered to ships. It was named Wollumbin by the local aborigines. It was the place of my birth, well, the place where my parents were living when I came into the world at the local hospital of Murwillumbah. I was the first son, although the second child, of Catherine May and Norman Axford Vickery. My sister's name was Helen. My father was a banana grower on the steep slopes of the eastern side of the mountain. Banana growing has always demanded hard work for little return, and my parents escaped neither. Bushfires, bad weather, obscure plant diseases, and continually fluctuating prices kept my parents from reaping any significant financial reward for their hardship.

Norm was born in Tenterfield in NSW and moved to Tumbulgum, a small township north-east of Murwillumbah on the Pacific Highway when my grandparents moved there for work in establishing what was then known as Oaks Avenue. My grandfather, Jim, was employed cutting and laying a corduroy surface of logs to improve the quality of the highway north of Tumbulgum. When this task was completed, he gained employment in the sugar mill at Condong as a labourer and rode his bicycle from Tumbulgum to Condong (a distance of about twelve kilometres) and return every day for the rest of his working life. Both my father and two of his brothers, Bill and Les, worked at the mill at various stages in their lives.

Catherine, my mother, was born and schooled in Murwillumbah and met Norm when she was living in River Street, South Murwillumbah. The period of courtship embraced 1939 when war was declared. A young man, Bill Huggins, living next door to the Andrews family (Cath's maiden name was Andrews) married Cath's sister Elsie in 1934. Bill, Norm, and Cath's brother Les all joined the army together with Bill, having been a soldier previously in Britain. Les and Norm were both called to Newcastle on the same day and were allocated successive service numbers (NX47578 Private N. A. Vickery and NX47579 Private L. Andrews). After initial training in Tamworth, Norm and Les were accompanied by Bill Huggins and they joined 2/4th Pioneer Battalion in Greta, NSW, on 24 February 1941. Norm and Cath were married during leave from Greta on 12 April 1941.

After six months' training at Greta, the trio was posted to Darwin but was required to undergo a further six weeks' training en route to Alice Springs. In Darwin they were allocated their companies and began further training. Around 14 February 1942, their unit was advised that they would be going to Timor. The RAAF fighter planes, however, that were to provide the unit's air cover did not arrive, so the passage was delayed. After two days, 2/4th was ordered to proceed to Timor on the USAT 'Meigs' without air cover. Approximately twenty-four hours after they sailed, forty-four high-level Japanese bombers spotted the vulnerable troop ships and attacked. The Japanese fighter squadron was from the same fleet air arm that attacked Pearl Harbor the previous December.

An escorting cruiser maintained a tremendous rate of anti-aircraft fire as the ships zigzagged to avoid the bombs. Fortunately, none of the convoys was sunk although the ship that Bill and Norm were on was damaged pretty badly. Based on the evidence that a trap had been set by an enemy naval squadron, General Wavell, from his headquarters in Java, ordered the convoy to return to Darwin.

Information was received that the Japanese had landed in Keopang harbour, which was the destination of the convoy transporting 2/4th Pioneers. It is interesting to reflect that had the RAAF turned up on time, the convoy probably would have landed in Keopang harbour about the same time as the Japanese.

On the afternoon of 18 February, the convoy entered Darwin harbour. The harbour was full of ships waiting for orders. On the steamy, tropical morning of 19 February, the history of Australia was changed forever. Seventeen Japanese bombers, fifty-four dive bombers, and eighteen zero fighters attacked the city of Darwin. So suddenly did the attack occur that Darwin was completely surprised. This was the first time bombs had fallen on Australian soil, the first time Australians had been killed in their own homes by an act of war. The war had come to Australia. The raid was short, some fifty minutes in duration, but the devastation for an unprepared city was enormous.

Japanese attacks continued in decreasing frequency over the next few months until, with the help of American air support, supremacy was regained in the air over Darwin. It was during this time, probably helped by the direct hit on his ship on its way to Timor, that Norm decided to join the medical corps as a male nurse. He joined 121 Australian General Hospital and was sent to Katherine to assist with the wounded and the refugees who were flooding out of Darwin. The three brothers-in-law were separated at this stage and, to my knowledge, did not see each other again until they were discharged in 1943/44.

Norm returned home to Murwillumbah in 1943 and bought a small banana plantation on the lower slopes of Mount Warning and had two children—myself and my sister, Helen. The remote location alone provided the newlyweds with enormous hardships as Murwillumbah, although being only about thirty kilometres away, was accessible only by a poor-quality dirt track across a large creek and a low bridge over the Tweed River. Norm had purchased himself a Dodge Fast Four truck, which for all its reliability didn't possess four-wheel drive. Chains were needed when it was wet and had to be put on and taken off every time a major mud patch was to be negotiated. A simple trip to town could often take three to four hours. The road also provided many sharp objects which continually caused punctures. Norm was not blessed with a cool temperament, and repairing punctures on the Dodge was, to say the least, testing. Although very young, I recall well sitting on the side of the road for long periods of time while Norm cussed and cursed as he repaired a tyre. I remember also on one occasion that he stuffed a tyre full of grass just so that he could get the family home.

My personal memories are vague, but I know we lived on the mountain until I was about 4 years of age and my sister, 5. The living conditions were sparse as there was no electricity or sanitation service.

The work was hard, and the elements ensured that few ever made money out of bananas. Bushfires, heavy winds, and torrential rains seemingly complimented the birds and pestilence that made my father's life difficult. Our schooling requirements provided the impetus for my parents to move closer to town. The move into town must have been difficult financially for Norm and Cath as the house they purchased was of timber construction, unlined and measured only three metres wide by twelve metres long with a small bathroom attached and an outside toilet. This provided only one bedroom for the four of us (I slept in the same bed as my sister), one cupboard (built-in) between the four us, and a kitchen where we cooked and ate. The total inventory of furniture was two beds, one table and four chairs of wooden homemade construction, and a galvanised bathtub. A fair indication of the size of the house can be gauged by the fact that when it was sold, a local solicitor placed it in his front yard as an office. We did, however, have electricity for the first time, although no water heater. The house was situated on a large block of land, and from a kid's point of view, that was the main thing, very little else seemed to matter. I don't ever really remember being unhappy.

Norm had to re-establish his life and was able to do this by securing a partnership in a smallgoods business with a long-time friend, Mr Stan King. Whereas Cath seemed content for both of them to assist in running the business with and Stan and his wife Beryl, Norm was anxious to try something different. He re-arranged the shop and installed a cooking vat with extraction fans and started selling fish and chips. Norm was an experienced cook and took great pride in producing a quality product. Before long the business was doing very well with the smallgoods section complimenting the fish and chips and vice versa. Norm and Cath decided now would be the time to make use of Norm's war service homes loan and construct a house more suitable in size, particularly for two children who would soon be entering high school. No sooner had the plan been formulated than disaster struck. The year was 1954, the occurrence was the worst floods ever to hit the Tweed Valley and, for that matter, most of New South Wales and Southern Queensland. Whereas Stan and Norm had been good at what they did, neither was particularly experienced at business. The building was insured, the stock and equipment weren't. Both families had their own houses to worry about as well, as they were both living in flood-prone areas. The floodwaters lapped the floor of our house, and as the house was built on the banks of the river, there was some concern that it might float off its stumps and be caught up in the torrent of water that was previously the Tweed River. This was a frightening time for us all. Fortunately, the flood peaked at this point, and little damage was done to our private property. Our pet duck, however, couldn't resist the opportunity the river had given him to escape.

As the flood receded some days later, the impact of the devastation hit home. In effect, Norm and Cath again were broke. Enough was salvaged from the shop for Stan and Beryl to begin again, but there was insufficient stock or trade to support two families. This was not an era for governmental flood relief, and as all their money had been invested in the business, Norm and Cath immediately began to search for work.

Norm, recalling the training and enjoyment he gained as a male nurse in the Northern Territory during the war, immediately applied for a vacant position at the local hospital and was accepted. Cath, still longing for her dream of a sizeable house in which to raise her children, accepted a job with a local cafe opposite the railway station and, in fact, remained there until her death in 1963. She rode her bike, in all weather, three kilometres each way, each day for the nine years. It always used to pain me travelling past her on the school bus and observe her peddling to work. I was embarrassed only for her as even in those days, few ladies of her age were required to cycle to work. My father had purchased another car at this time, a 1934 Dodge sedan, and when his shifts allowed, he drove Mum to work. This generally meant that he placed her bicycle on the passenger's side of the car (which she had to hold) and dropped her at work. She then had her bike to ride home in the afternoon.

The effort of both my parents working eventually paid off. Norm's application, based on permanent employment, for a war service homes loan, was approved, and Mum's dream was at last realised. The house was built, and Helen and I at last had our own bedrooms. Mum quickly turned the house into a home and, with regular income, gradually introduced a modicum of modern furniture and, before long, a television set. The television set, to Mum, was the reward for all those years of hard work. To her, television was the most relaxing medium she had ever experienced. I cannot recall anything that gave her greater pleasure—on reflection, it was less than she deserved but more than she ever expected. Norm and Cath, it would seem, had both found their place in life. Nothing in life is perfect for long, however. Norm discovered that with the extra money in his pocket, he could call at the local hotel on the way home from work each day/night and there was still a bit left over for his days off. His drinking became a regular event, and he began to get defensive whenever Cath shortened him up about it. On his days off, if I was available, he would ask if I would like to go to town with him, and then I would spend five or six hours sitting outside one of several hotels waiting for him to finish his session. It was during these boring, senseless sessions that I vowed and declared that no child of mine would ever sit and wait outside a club or hotel whilst I sat and drank alcohol. To this day, I have honoured that vow.

Chapter Two

ADOLESCENCE

PRIMARY SCHOOL WAS one of the most pleasant experiences of my life. The Murwillumbah Public School (which is now celebrating 125 years of existence) boasted some of the best teachers any pupil could expect. The pressure to succeed was not evident at that stage in my life, and I was very good at practical subjects such as drawing, painting, and wood carving. It is interesting to note, however, that I finished second (overall) in all subjects in sixth class (the final form), although I was not made aware of this until many years later by my father.

I should also point out that it was a segregated school, in that the results to which I refer did not include the equivalent girls' class next door. The greatest bonus to emerge from primary school was that I made many lifelong friendships, mainly male because of the segregation, although I had attended the early classes with a number of the girls.

High school, in 1958, I was to find out, was a totally different kettle of fish. I managed to find myself in the 'A' class with some pretty smart students. At this stage in my life, I was six foot four inches in height (approximately 193 centimetres) and weighed less than seventy-five kilos. I had big ears and a baby face. I was extremely shy and had an inferiority complex a mile wide. The one really telling talent that emerged during my primary school days was that I could box, perhaps 'fight' might be more an appropriate term, and this proved to be very useful in my early days at high school. In order to cover a basic shy personality, I, like most of my ilk, resorted to being boastful and crude to cover my deficiencies. This did little else other than attract unnecessary attention to myself from teachers and students alike. I was one of only two males in my class not to wear long trousers in winter. This was not because I didn't choose to wear them, but because Mum and Dad simply had nothing left to spend. This did not concern me as I had spent the whole of primary school without even wearing shoes, so I believed the high school had already made significant gains by getting me to wear shoes, let alone long trousers.

Most of the teachers found that I was disruptive and had no genuine interest in education. Two options were tried in an endeavour to allow the rest of the class to learn unhindered. One was to place me right up the front of the class where the teacher could lean over and whack me every time my attention wandered. The other was to isolate me up the back right-hand side of the class and ensure that no one sat within two seats of me; this was probably the most successful. These solutions were not applied in music where the teacher found me intolerable and refused to allow me into his classroom. It was pretty challenging standing outside the music room every week as it was on the same floor as the deputy headmaster's office, and if he happened to be wandering the halls of power and spied me, it was six of the best. This became such a regular event that I began to get a complex about it. I started to think that going to school on Mondays was a waste of time.

The punishment metered out by the headmaster, however, was much worse for me as he was a little man and seemed to take great delight in dishing out his form of justice. I recall on one occasion five of us were sent down to the headmaster for causing some form of disruption. He gave the others six on each hand and sent them back to the classroom. He saved me for last and stood on his chair to ensure maximum effect; he also aimed for the extreme end of the fingertips which felt like an electric shot every time he landed the cane on my hands. He also didn't count those he missed, so it was of little benefit to breathe a sigh of relief as I watched the cane go sailing past the fingertips occasionally.

The only element of pride that I took from these occasions was that I never, ever pulled my hand away (as some did). I always knew that I would pay an extra price if I did this.

By the time I returned to my classroom, the other boys had told the rest of the class that 'it didn't hurt', unfortunately that wasn't the case for me. I was feeling the effects of the extra effort put into my caning and, in fact, had gone quite white (according to my classmates), the automatic assumption being that big boys feel pain the most. Nevertheless, I went quiet for a long time, and whereas I do not condone standing on a chair when executing corporal punishment on a 13-year-old, I do concede that I got what I thoroughly deserved and to this day do not believe that anything but good came out of this event. The greatest punishment was my loss of face to the rest of the class for seemingly being the only one affected by the caning. I didn't really feel up to explaining the extra attention I had received.

At the start of high school, I took on a paper run which required me to get up at four o'clock each morning, Monday to Saturday, pick up the papers from the local newspaper office, and prepare them for delivery. The delivery was then done on my bike over an area of about six kilometres before riding to school. Initially, payment was eight shilling per week (approximately eighty cents), but this increased to sixteen shillings per week (approximately one dollar sixty cents) in my second year when

I changed newsagents. This doesn't seem like a lot of money now, but it meant a lot to me at the time. It is interesting to note that the smart students never did paper runs. The big downside the paper run held for me was that every time the bell rang for class, at school, I used to jump thinking it was the alarm clock going off—I became gun shy at a very early age.

Between the ages of 13 and 14, I doubt that I developed or matured at all. I recall one of my math teachers yelling at me one day and concluding that 'Vickery, to my knowledge, no one is perfect, but you are the closest I have come to a perfect idiot'. Sadly, I took this as a form of compliment. The tragedy of this was, first of all, not recognising what the teacher was saying, and secondly, not having the wherewithal to rise above it.

I was fortunate, however, to have maintained some friendships from my primary school days, and these friends prevented me from becoming a total lost cause. Paul Cosgrove and Trevor Mitchell convinced me to join the school cadet corps and also learn to play a musical instrument with the local Army Reserve (then the Citizens Military Forces) band. Trevor and Paul both opted for the bagpipes, and I became interested in the side drum. This was an unfortunate decision for me as I was not a naturally talented drummer but could have succeeded had I had a consistent teacher. My teacher, however, was a talented drummer but seldom remembered to turn up for practice.

Week after week I turned up at the local drill hall for practise; week after week I went home disillusioned. My two mates, however, were a little better served and became quite proficient at their task; somehow this was enough for me. Once a month we would join the band as it marched down one of the local streets in Murwillumbah. I seldom had the confidence to join in but gained great enjoyment from watching Paul and Trevor taking their place amongst the seasoned pipers. Eventually, I stopped chasing the dream and resigned myself to being a private soldier in the cadet corps.

Left to Right: Les Andrews, Thelma Vickery, Norm Vickery,
Catherine May Andrews, Jean Ward, Bill Huggins

Cadets produced some useful results. Knowledge, new skills, a basic view of military discipline, and the chance to wear a uniform all provided me with enough interest to tolerate the education process. Despite my intense dislike for school, I did not miss a day for other than genuine reasons such as mumps or chickenpox, although I somehow suspect this was more out of respect for my parents than for school. Annual cadet camp was always an event to look forward to. In fact, it really was my first exposure to male bonding, although I didn't recognise it at the time. Living under tents on palliasses filled with straw isn't exactly what the modern camper would visualise, but to us in our early teens, it was a big adventure and one that only those who went on the camps could share. Firing the .303 Lee Enfield rifle, the Owen sub-machine gun, and the Bren gun all provided memories that we would live on for months into the future.

I recall on one occasion being tasked to accompany a senior officer, presumably a general, although in those early days, they all seemed the same to me, to a firepower demonstration. I had no idea what I was supposed to do, so I just shadowed the officer and sat with him in the well-appointed stands and watched the demonstration. All the other cadets, and there were thousands of them from all over NSW, were crowded together, rather uncomfortably I thought, on the side of a hill. I had a magnificent view and the officer explained everything that was happening to me. When we returned to the lines, I was bubbling with excitement about the events surrounding the demonstration. My mates enjoyed the demonstration but were far less enthusiastic about it than I was. I gained great kudos by explaining some of the things that we had witnessed and eventually was forgiven for being randomly chosen to sit in the best seat in the house. Nonetheless, it was an event that I recalled many times over the succeeding months to ensure that I, good-humouredly, maintained some measure of elevated status amongst my peers.

Sport has always been the love of my life. High school provided the opportunity to play rugby league, tennis, and cricket, and I took up all of them. Again, I was not blessed with natural talent, but with a bit of coaching, I quickly got the drift of all of them and was at least competitive. My favourite sport was rugby league. Keith Kennedy and Tom Tanner were our woodwork and technical drawing teachers, respectively, and also keen rugby league followers and past players. Every Wednesday afternoon in winter, we would play at school. On Saturday mornings, we would be graded into divisions and play in a junior league, and every month or so, we would get the opportunity to play against other schools.

My father, unfortunately, did not like me playing league and restricted me to playing with the school. I found this very disappointing as he was a keen rugby league follower and was happy for me to sit with him on Sunday afternoons at the local park watching the senior teams go around. This did not blunt my enthusiasm, and I was able to take it up again in a few years' time.

Girls did not play a big part in my life at this stage. I enjoyed their company but was never comfortable that they enjoyed mine. Whereas I attended parties and dances, these usually concluded by me going home by myself. I was partly to blame for this situation as I was particularly shy and would have felt very embarrassed if refused by a girl, therefore, I thought it better not to ask.

Weekends in the main were, in retrospect, fairly dull affairs, although I don't recall being unhappy during this time. A bunch of us would go swimming in the river or at the local swimming pool. Sometimes we would go grass sledding on a hill behind my auntie's place. Often we would attend the cattle auctions and make plans and practice at being auctioneers. Christmases were always great times as my mother and father always pitched a tent at Kingscliff, a local beach resort, for at least two weeks and sometimes longer. As the years progressed, they purchased a second tent, and we actually had a living room and a bedroom and invited my cousin to join us. Finally, Dad had a prefabricated hut built, and we were no longer worried about being blown over by the occasional summer southerly wind. We spent the summer holidays playing in the bush and swimming until we were exhausted.

In 1960 I entered my third year of high school. The first signs of maturity were starting to emerge. I was beginning to understand that I had to apply myself a lot more if I wanted to achieve my intermediate certificate. I had already decided that I wanted to become a carpenter, and all that I needed was a basic qualification to get an apprenticeship. Mum had greater ambitions for me and wanted me to stay in school and work at becoming an architect. She acceded to my argument that I was not interested in staying in school and that I was pretty sure I could get an apprenticeship with the father of our next-door neighbour, with whom I had been working (on weekends) for some months. Somehow I had managed to stay in the 'A' class, although finishing last or second last in each of the previous two years, and I thought that I had a good chance of passing the examination and finally quitting school. The examination quickly approached.

I gained a pass in the intermediate certificate but failed mathematics. By my standards, this was good enough, so four days before my fifteenth birthday, I bid farewell to my class and left. My memory suggests that there were only a couple from our class who did not continue on to leaving certificate and matriculation.

Two events now occurred that had a profound effect on my future. Firstly, my mother was wise enough to realise that I would get nowhere in life without a mathematics qualification and paid, although God knows how, for me to have one-on-one tuition and resit mathematics the following year. This I did and excelled at the subject when I was not able to grandstand in front of a class. Secondly, it was 1961 and Australia was entering a recession. The builder with whom I was hoping to acquire an apprenticeship was suffering a downturn in business and an upturn in unpaid debts, so he could offer me no employment. I was therefore left to ponder my future.

Again it was my mother who took the initiative and suggested that I contest the public service examination for the position of junior postal officer at the Murwillumbah Post Office. This was considered to be a pretty lowly position, and few young people, including myself, were keen to apply. My mother insisted I apply on the basis of job security, superannuation, and regular promotion and made it all sound rather worthwhile. I sat the exam, along with about ten others, and took a job at Woolworths whilst awaiting the results.

Brian as a 'telegram boy' making a delivery as part of a local festival

A week after I started at Woolworths, the results came through, and I had achieved the best results of all candidates and was offered the position. The additional tuition that Mum had arranged for me in mathematics was the key factor in my achieving such a good pass. I was given a uniform and a bike and told to report to the Telegrams Office. Though often subject to light ridicule from my friends for wearing a post office uniform and peaked cap, I thought this was the most wonderful of times: working outdoors, riding around the streets, getting fit, earning an income (albeit a very small one), and meeting the local residents. The major benefit was that I often saw the contents of the telegrams before they were placed in the envelopes, so I was able to gauge my approach to the recipients. I was never very good at handling bad news, so I delivered those respectfully and beat a hasty retreat. When the news was good, however, I hung around a bit longer in the hope of getting a tip. It seldom worked; making money was never going to be my forte.

This was an important time in my life. This was the time when I first became associated with the demon drink, alcohol. As most of my peers had stayed in school, I quickly found new friends in and around work and through the local church group that I attended. Unfortunately, most of these young people were all older than I was, probably by two to three years, meaning that they were legally entitled to frequent and drink at hotels. I wasn't old enough, but I was six foot four inches tall at this stage, and my friends assured me this would help if my age was queried.

My first attempt at entering a hotel was a complete disaster. A friend and I decided to go to Coolangatta to the dance at Danceland on a Saturday night. I was still 15 years old. My friend owned a utility and decided we would go to the Dolphins Hotel at Tweed Heads and prepare ourselves for the dance. I was apprehensive and obviously showed it. I continually checked the door for any casual police presence, and of course, this action did not go unnoticed by the publican.

Logically, we were thrown out and told not to come back until I became of age. My friend was pretty unimpressed with my performance and admonished me for the rest of the night. It did, however, show me the ropes and, because it took so long for the publican to actually determine the fact that I was underage, convinced me that by reviewing my actions, I probably could get away with it. This I did, and although we had to drink at other hotels, I was never again asked to leave prematurely. About six months later, I went back into the Dolphins Hotel and drank there all one Saturday afternoon right in front of the publican, and he neither recognised me nor asked me to leave. Maturity takes many different forms.

It wasn't long before I progressed into the position of postman. This was another job that I enjoyed enormously (wet weather and dogs notwithstanding), but it was short-lived as I was selected to attend the Postal Clerk-in-Training School at Strathfield in Sydney, NSW. At 16 years of age, my mother handed me a bunch of grapes and put me on the train for 'the big smoke'. The postmaster general's department had arranged boarding house accommodation at Ashfield for me. Somehow I managed to find my way to the boarding house and booked in. Five other trainees had also moved in on the same day. At first, we were all a bit apprehensive about each other, but as the six of us had to sleep, in fact, live in two rooms, we very quickly became close friends. On the following Monday, we caught the train from Ashfield to Strathfield (three stops away), walked up the boulevard to the training school, and commenced our training.

This was another exceptional period in my life. Although homesick for the country and my friends, I was doing well at the school and had made many new friends. Somehow I had successfully blown the bottom out of the boarding house gas washing tub and was ordered to pay for it. This did not suit me as I was unused to gas and had no money to buy a replacement anyway, so the five of us decided it was time to quit Ashfield and move closer to Strathfield. We found another cheaper, bigger boarding house at Strathfield, which meant we could walk to work. There were also a number of other trainees staying there, which meant that we settled in very quickly.

The school provided us with a chance to view some of the rest of Sydney by sending us on detachments to various post offices in the city and allowing us to work the counter as trainees. Again, this was an enlightening and enjoyable experience. I was sent to Crown Street in Darlinghurst. This was the time when Woods Lane and Bourke Street were the popular brothel areas in Sydney, and logically most of the prostitutes would visit the Crown Street Post Office for their stamps and child endowment payments, etc. During the daytime, the prostitutes were chatty and cheerful and not 'wired' like they are today. Serving and speaking to these ladies was an extraordinary, perhaps sexual experience for a 16-year-old. Fortunately, each afternoon, immediately after work, I would walk down to Central Station and catch a train back to Strathfield, my testosterone once again in check.

I gained excellent experience working at Crown Street because it was a big post office which was generally very busy. The postmaster was an extremely good fellow who allowed me a lot of latitude in what I did, which helped me to learn the full range of my duties. The staff was also good to me, and even though I was very junior, they treated me much like an equal. By the time my detachment was completed, I felt like I could run any counter in any post office in the country.

The training school lasted six months, and I was lucky to get an early mark of a couple of weeks. The teleprinter was the most difficult part of the course to pass because unlike electric typewriters and computers, it had a very stiff keyboard and was capable of only forty-four words per minute. This meant that any attempt to race beyond the maximum capacity of the machine meant that some letters would not reproduce. The exam was to type as many telegrams in thirty minutes as you could; there was a minimum number that you had to reach, and you were allowed to make only five mistakes. I think I managed to get through forty-seven telegrams, which was well above the required number, with nil mistakes. All trainees who thought they could pass the exam were tested; the rest were allowed another two weeks.

The next morning, after the exam, it was announced that four of us had passed and we could leave immediately. All other trainees had to wait for the subsequent exam in two weeks' time; this included those that failed the first attempt. I was delighted; even though I knew that I had done well in the exam, in terms of my typing speed, I could only guess as to whether I had made any mistakes or not. I was also advised that I was to be posted back to Murwillumbah as a fully qualified postal clerk (un-allotted), which meant that I would relieve other staff whilst they had holidays, long service leave, etc.

Prior to leaving Murwillumbah to attend the school, I was advised by the senior officers at the post office to take the opportunity whilst in Sydney and gain my Third Division Public Service Certificate. Night school was provided by the PMG Department and was free. I could see that my future was limited because I didn't have my leaving certificate, and if I wished to pursue the PMG Department as a career, I would need some further education.

Part of the course at the training school was regular English classes at which I did surprisingly well. The instructor quickly realised that I had the ability to pass the exam and was quick to reinforce the advice that I had been given in Murwillumbah, 'Get your Third Division Exam out of the way whilst you are there!' Memories flooded back of the difficulties I had experienced over school studies. The instructor quickly pointed out that the reality of it was that it was only two nights per week and lasted only for six months. Reluctantly, I agreed and started night classes almost immediately. I almost faltered at this point as I was quite a regular drinker, thus I turned up somewhat inebriated for many of the classes (but always on time). Fortunately, my time in the 'A' classes at school proved its worth, and I cruised through the course probably to the chagrin of the teachers.

This was a major step in the right direction as I was to find out, as most of the postal clerks who were then currently in the postal service were from the old school and did not bother to sit for the examination, which, in the long term, gained me enormous seniority.

I remember vividly being sent on relief duty to Lismore. The senior postal clerk (SPC), he was the clerk who worked in the glass cage at the end of the counter and paid child endowment and handled money orders, had gone on leave for three weeks. The most senior postal clerk, who I recall as being about 40 years of age, automatically assumed he would fill the vacancy and therefore be paid higher duties allowance, which was a significant lift to his wages. He went absolutely bereft when I, still 16 years of age at this stage, turned up and advised the postmaster that I held my Third Division Public Service Certificate. Fortunately, I had worked at Lismore before and had good reports from the postmaster. However, everyone believed that Lismore was far too busy for the senior role on the counter to go to a 16-year-old. The experience of Crown Street, however, came to the fore, and even though I recall I had a few problems over sending a money order to Pakistan, I finished the job without any major problems. I even managed to win the respect of the person I so heartlessly deprived of the extra take-home pay. I also managed to gain an excellent rapport with two of the mailroom workers because I had been a postman. The interesting thing about these two guys was that they had been prisoners of war in Changi jail in Singapore during the Second World War, a fact that I found fascinating then but retain in solemn memory now.

The other members of the un-allotted list (relief staff) were a great bunch of guys, and we became very well known throughout the Northern Rivers of NSW. 'Badger' Maher was from Byron Bay and possessed the most superb handwriting I had ever seen. Ted Kennedy was a big rugby league player from Alstonville, and Barry Robinson, like me, came from Murwillumbah and somehow managed a local rock and roll band in his spare time. We rotated all over the place for both short and long terms. We all opted for three-week stints because the allowances were phenomenal. However, after the first three weeks, the department believed that relief staff had had enough time to find cheaper, long-term accommodation and, as such, reduced the allowances dramatically.

I recall, on one occasion, I was posted to Kingscliff, a small coastal village south of Tweed Heads. I was only there for three weeks, so I claimed the allowances and then stayed in the surf club (I was a member) across the road for nothing. This was a fortunate time as Les Johns, the legendary Australian and Canterbury rugby league player, walked into the post office one day and asked if there was any chance he could stay at the surf club. I offered to show him the ropes, and he stayed on for about ten days. Some years later, I re-acquainted myself with him in the Top of the Moon at the Oceanic Hotel in Coogee. This was also a coincidental occasion as the bouncer at the Top of the Moon on that particular night was Jim Christian who was a policeman at Murwillumbah in my earlier days. He told me he was 'moonlighting' for the extra cash.

I was working at the post office at Kyogle during the weekend of the Tony Madigan–Athol McQueen fight for the Australian heavyweight boxing championship. Athol McQueen lived just outside of Kyogle and somehow had convinced the promoters that the fight should occur in his hometown. I had decided not to stay for the fight and was heading back to Murwillumbah for the weekend.

On Saturday morning, as usual I looked at my watch at twelve o'clock, balanced my account and took my advance, and locked it in the safe. Without saying anything, I stepped out the door of the post office, a bit surprised that it hadn't been closed by this time and walked across the road to start hitchhiking to Murwillumbah, a distance of about 130 kilometres. A car stopped almost immediately and picked me up. The driver told me they were going to the airport at Casino and would drop me there. I noticed that the person in the front seat had huge shoulders and was occupying most of the passenger seat. It was Tony Madigan; they were going to pick up his gear for the fight off a plane. Whilst sitting in the back seat in absolute awe of the guy who took Cassius Clay the distance in the 1960 Rome Olympics, I chanced a look at my watch and saw with absolute horror that the time was only shortly after eleven o'clock. I had misread the time when I closed down my counter. I immediately screamed out for the driver to stop the car, which he did with alacrity although some surprise. I thanked them and walked across the road and began to hitch a ride in the opposite direction. Luckily, I did not have long to wait and was quickly delivered back to the post office. The irony of the story is that I walked into the post office, reopened the safe, replaced my account, and no one even realised that I had been missing. I guess what saved me was the fact that no customer had needed my services during my absence. Luck's a lottery.

In those days, hitchhiking was great fun, but it also had considerable drawbacks. Firstly, it was really hard to get a ride when it was raining, and secondly, I seemed to spend most of my weekend hitchhiking just to get to and from work. I decided to buy a car. Initially, I bought a Morris Major, but soon found that it lacked a bit of grunt and didn't fit the image that a successful young postal clerk should exhibit. So I bought an FC Holden. What a great car—shape, power, and style—could there be anything more to life?

One of my first tasks after buying the car was to provide relief whilst the postmaster at Ballina (another coastal town) took some well-earned long service leave. This meant that I would be in Ballina for some considerable months. Logically, I booked into a long-term boarding house and got to know the other tenants reasonably well. One afternoon about three weeks after I arrived, an attractive young lady came into the post office and bought some stamps. As it was a quiet afternoon, I started to talk with her and soon found out that she was a model from Canberra, staying in Ballina for a couple of days.

The longer I spoke, the more we seemed to enjoy each other's company, so I asked whether she would go to the movies with me that night. She agreed and we set a time and a pickup location. I was ecstatic. It was unusual for me to be this forward, normally I was too shy to approach any girl so directly. This was shaping as the best night of my life—mind you, I had just turned 17 years of age.

No sooner had the girl left the post office than the acting postmaster called me in and advised me that the plans had changed and I was to be in Tweed Heads to start work the next morning at 7.30. It was about an hour-and-one-half drive and I had to arrange accommodation. What was I going to do? Option one was to take the girl out and then drive to Tweed Heads in the middle of the night and sleep in the car—I discarded this option because I would have nowhere to shave and clean up before work. Option two was to ask at the boarding house to see if anyone would be interested in taking out a beautiful young model. This I did and caught most of the guys in the television room prior to the evening meal. They thought I was having 'a lend' of them. Eventually, a reserved young apprentice butcher said that he would do me a favour and take the girl out, but if she turned out to be a dragon, he would look me up and 'get even'. Although still hugely disappointed, I felt that I had done the best I could and packed up, had my evening meal, and headed for Tweed Heads. I had the chance to run into the young butcher about six months later and was curious as to how the night had proceeded. I asked him 'how he got on'. 'Great', he replied, 'we get married next Saturday!' There was no sense in me carrying that conversation any further.

The posting to Tweed Heads was great. The southern end of the Gold Coast still got a lot of visitors in the winter, so the job was busy and satisfying. The postmaster's son, Bill Buckley, was a rogue of the highest order, and we became great friends—quite unashamedly chatting up all the girls who came to the counter, knowing full well that they were Victorians and were unlikely to accede to our bold offers. In fact, Bill was married and would have been in extreme trouble had any of them accepted.

As life leads you to believe things cannot get any better, you are suddenly and heavily reminded how human you really are. On returning from Tweed Heads to Murwillumbah one Friday afternoon, my next-door neighbour advised me that my mother had had a stroke and was taken to the local hospital. My father and my sister were already there when I arrived. It was a disheartening scene seeing Mum in enormous discomfort but nonetheless alive. Dad, of course, was working at the hospital at that stage, so he was kept fairly well informed. During the night, however, Mum suffered a further stroke and went into a coma from which she never recovered.

I recall that, during the week that Mum was in the coma, much soul-searching took place. Dad was asking himself should he arrange for her to go to a Brisbane hospital for more up-to-date treatment or would she be just as well off where she was. My sister and I were contemplating life without a mother—would it be a great life without restraint, or would it be a monumental wrench in our lives from which we would spend a long time recovering? Realistically, we dared not think about the final outcome. My mother and I were great mates, and she was always thankful that I came home most weekends even if only briefly. My sister, on the other hand, was almost totally dependent on my mother and all that she provided. Helen was not ready to leave home. Inevitably, the call we all feared came at two o'clock in the morning exactly one week after she had had the first stroke. Dad's best mate and our mother had passed away. The future immediately became a total blank.

None of us handled the situation well. I lost all sense of direction and became confused about life in general—I had great difficulty coming to terms with the whole situation. Helen was distraught and couldn't conceive any logical path her life was likely to take. Dad sought refuge in the bottle, although we could sense his extreme sense of loss and his inability to cope with the pain. We tried to resign ourselves to the inevitable task of organising a household consisting of three not four adults, but with me being away from Murwillumbah for much of the time during the week and Dad spending all his spare time at the local hotel, Helen's life became one of abject isolation. I was able to secure a long-term posting to Murwillumbah Post Office, but even this didn't help resolve the problems of a now-dysfunctional family. We laboured this way for about nine months when I was posted away again.

During one week, I was advised that there was a rumour that Dad had remarried. I rang Helen, and she knew nothing about it. I headed home on the Tuesday night and tracked Dad down and confronted him with the rumour. He confirmed it and advised that he would be leaving Murwillumbah with my new stepmother to follow the fruit-picking season in Shepparton in Victoria. Helen was now in even a greater state, not only had she not recovered from losing her mother, but her father had remarried without advising her, and her home was about to be sold. Her life was probably at its lowest point. This situation was only resolved by the good grace of some wonderful neighbours and the support of some caring relatives (aunties, uncles, and cousins). John and Barbara Prosser, who had been living next door to us for at least six years, offered for Helen to go and live with them. I now know this to be one of the most generous gestures imaginable. I arranged to find accommodation at a small boarding house in town.

Helen stayed with the Prossers until she married Roly Young in 1965. Roly was a local carpenter and joiner and had been going out with Helen for some time. They purchased an old home in Murwillumbah and had one son, Stuart. They have since moved to live in Queensland.

The immediate years after my mother's death were unsettled ones for me. My mother's funeral was the first funeral I had ever attended. I missed her badly. I felt also that my father had betrayed my sister and me, but I chose not to make an issue of it. Weekends became harder to fill, my intake of alcohol increased dramatically, and I took up smoking.

A number of things occurred, however, which helped reshape my life. Firstly, I found a girl who shared some common interests with me and enjoyed my company. She was raised in the country, was attractive, and was unpretentious. We had been seeing each other for a couple of months before my mother died. She continued to see me during my downhill slide and, in fact, probably prevented me from self-destruction. On Saturday nights, we would go to the dance at Byron Bay, and on Sundays, we would go to the beach or for a drive in winter, sometimes to visit her parents who lived just out of Murwillumbah. We experimented with sex and found it to be as enjoyable as it was exciting, although she was always reserved about it, fearing pregnancy. I recall pursuing a few moments of pleasure in my car beside a secondary road near her parents' place one night. As the windows began to fog up, a young policeman shone a torch in the window on us and politely asked us if we knew the owner of a cow that had just been killed on the highway. Words were at a premium, so I curtly replied, 'No!' I had great difficulty regaining focus after the interruption particularly as the cow belonged to the girl's parents.

The second profound influence on my life at this time was my decision to join the Cudgen Headland Surf Lifesaving Club. I was never much of a swimmer but was a useful beach sprinter and enjoyed enormously the ethos of the lifesaving movement. Several of my schoolmates were members and encouraged me to join. My girlfriend wasn't happy about this as it meant more opportunities for me to 'be with the boys'.

The surf club presented me with my first glimpse of public attention. We were on the beach about 300 metres north of the public surfing area doing a mock surf rescue for our instructor's certificate. One of the other members of the squad was the person in trouble and was sitting on the buoy about 200 metres out to sea. I was the rescuer and took the belt and commenced the swim out to do the rescue. During the swim, a large stingray cruised along the gutter between ourselves and the beach. It was big and black in the water, and we all assumed that it was a shark. The siren sounded for everyone to clear the water, and the 'patient' and I both tried to balance on the buoy, an impossible task. Logically, everyone on the beach came down to watch, and we continued with the rescue. We were absolutely terrified as the R & R team pulled us through the water to the beach and prepared for the resuscitation phase. The public, however, thought that this was a real rescue after a shark attack and gave us a rousing round of applause as we came out of the water only to be disappointed when neither of us showed any signs of bleeding. The 'patient' and I couldn't have cared less about their disappointment; we were just relieved and happy to be in one piece.

The surf club provided me with endless weekends of fun and excitement attending surf carnivals up and down the coast and introduced me to some of the community's greatest characters. Although I was still very immature at this stage, the loose but ever-present discipline of the club reinforced the principles which I had learnt at school cadets and helped develop in me a personal set of standards which were to become very important in later life.

Free from the restrictions placed on me by my father, I joined a local rugby league club and gained many similar enjoyments to those that I was achieving through the surf club in the summer. My girlfriend again objected to this distraction and demanded more of my attention. The result was foreseeable. Perhaps, in those days, I found it more demanding to chase sex than I did to score a try (fortunately, I was able to correct this unbalanced defect in my character within a couple of years). I decided to call off the relationship rather than pursue a course which was becoming untenable. We agreed to disagree and went our separate ways. The big benefit that came out of my joining the South Murwillumbah Rugby League Club was my friendship with the first-grade coach, Les Duncan. Les was recruited from Ipswich as captain/coach of South Murwillumbah. He was given the task of taking the team that ran last in 1964 in the Group One Rugby League Division to making the semi-final in 1965. Such was his stature and leadership ability that he not only made the finals, but also took his team on to win the game that mattered most, the Grand Final. He gave his age as 28 but was in fact 32. I was only playing reserve grade during 1965, but Les knew everyone in both the A and Reserve teams and took a special interest in me because he could see that I was a young man who needed a mentor. He knew that with some guidance, I would mature rapidly and find my place in life. Les had a veranda added to his house and asked me to live with him and his wife, Delores. My life was again beginning to take shape.

CHAPTER THREE

NATIONAL SERVICE

I N DECEMBER 1965, just when I thought that I had my life sorted
out, I received my National Service call-up notice. National Service
was introduced in 1965 to assist the Americans in their fight against
communism in South-East Asia. It was for two years in duration. It was
commonly referred to as 'The Draft'. My disregard for a worthwhile
education was now starting to become obvious. I did not know where
Vietnam was, I did not understand the 'domino theory', and I had
absolutely no interest in joining the army or any of the services for that
matter. To my way of thinking, this conflict had nothing to do with me,
and I therefore resented being drafted to help solve it.

Desperate situations, however, require desperate measures, and my
mates were not short on suggestions as to what these were. One friend
suggested that drinking neat scotch the night before my medical would
raise my blood pressure to unacceptable levels. Another advised that
consuming a tube of toothpaste immediately before examination would
achieve the same result. Distasteful as both these measures were, I tried

them. The interesting thing is that I was still very drunk from the scotch when I tried the toothpaste (bloody hell); surprisingly it seemed to sober me up. My blood pressure levels were reported as normal. The doctor, who was a personal friend of my father, listened to me complaining about my eyesight, my flat feet, and my sore back until he could take no more. 'Brian', he said, 'I watched you play rugby league last season and thought you played well—I think you are fit enough to join the army, and what's more, I think you will love it—Pass!'

Sadly, this seemed to be the attitude of almost everyone who I spoke to: 'You will love it', 'It will be a great experience for you', 'Good on you, Brian'. I didn't need this; I wanted to get out of this commitment and get on with what was shaping to be a good life. Fortunately, the other five or six to get their draft cards at the same time as I had no better luck. I think one of them was discovered with flat feet, something which he previously knew nothing about, but was quite relieved to find that he was not going to make the train trip with us to Sydney. I did not particularly enjoy my previous trip to Sydney to attend the postal school; I was expecting to enjoy this one a lot less. I noticed that not one of our mates who had missed out on their call-up came to see us off at the station. Lucky bastards!

The Postmasters-General's Department was very good to me on being informed that I was to do my compulsory service. They, in fact, provided me with my first-ever plane ride and flew me to Sydney for a day to brief me on where I stood in the scheme of things, how my seniority would be affected, and what was being considered for me when I returned. They offered me a position as inspector-in-training on return, which I think was a year-long course for a selected few. I was flattered and returned to Murwillumbah knowing that my future was not being destroyed by National Service, merely stalled.

Saying farewell to friends was a lengthy process and, as it turned out, an expensive one. After a fortnight of drinking and shaking hands, my last night in Murwillumbah was a memorable one. After leaving the hotel at about 10.30 p.m., we repaired to a friend's home where we set up a poker game. There were five in the school, and we decided to play blind poker, so we removed 4s down from the pack to make it a faster game. The game went well, and I was confident I could take a few quid with me to Sydney the next morning.

The clock rolled around to about 1 a.m., and I knew it was time that I got some sleep. I had three sixes in my hand, which I assessed to be a winning hand if I could pick up a pair to go with it. I discarded both remaining cards and hoped to replace them with a pair. Bingo, a fourth six. Now, this was an unbeatable hand. Betting was steady and I held my cool, not letting on that I had four of a kind. Betting continued to be strong, and I was thinking that this could be a big pool—there was well over 100 pounds in the kitty.

Two players dropped out; I still kept my cool, giving away nothing. Betting was strong, but I was running out of money—I advised the other players that I was betting the last of my money and would appreciate it, as a farewell gesture, that they 'call' me. The other two players were clearly ready to quit also and acceded to this request with great alacrity—both thinking they had winning hands. I knew I had a winning hand, so I just wanted the winner to be declared so I could go to bed. The first player showed, and he had a very good full hand, queens and kings. I had him beaten—the second player threw down three jacks and held two cards; logically I expected that he was full on jacks, so I started to reap in the kitty. All of a sudden, the second player threw in a fourth jack; this defied logic, two sets of four of a kind with five in the school and forty-four cards in play—impossible. All of a sudden, I knew that my first weeks in the army were going to be very lean.

I, in fact, had spent every penny I possessed. The only money I had was two shillings my mother's ex-boss had given me to tip the porter on the train. Bugger that, I needed it more for food; I never did work out what the porter would have done for me anyhow. I had all my worldly possessions in one suitcase and nothing in my pocket—hardly the ingredients for a successful future.

On arrival in Sydney, we were picked up at Central Station. Central Station was also the rendezvous point for anyone who travelled in by car. This was a fascinating half hour. New recruits rolled up in a variety of cars (one in a Rolls-Royce) and on motorbikes. What a sight to us boys from the country. Many bought excess luggage and had girlfriends who were all over them, weeping and crying. Most of the guys had shoulder-length hair, which was the fashion for the time. Us country boys, sitting on the bus, thought this was all unnecessary particularly as we hardly had a person to see us off on the train and we all had fairly short hairstyles.

Eventually, the driver had to round up all the draftees off the footpath, herd them inside, and lock the door so they would stop getting back off the bus. He then proceeded to drive us to the local drill hall in Marrickville, a nearby southern suburb where we were all inducted. This was a boring process that took hours and involved a lot of waiting around. During this time, we were issued a very unsatisfying cut lunch, which confirmed every rumour we had ever heard about army meals.

At about two o'clock, we were told to leave the hall and proceed onto the bus parked on the street, in front of the building. As we left the building, we were surrounded by a very vocal and quite large group of women who were chanting and carrying placards saying, 'Save Our Sons'. My mates and I were quite bemused by this as we had never seen a demonstration before, let alone one comprising all women. We hopped on the bus and left the army representatives to disperse the group. We only assumed they were there for our benefit.

Next, it was off to Kingsford Smith Airport at Mascot (or perhaps Bankstown) and my second aeroplane ride. This time we were loaded onto an army Caribou aircraft and were flown to Singleton Army Camp. Most of us thought this was a bit of all right even though the Caribou is one of the least comfortable aircraft available to the army. We presumed that aircraft such as these were probably available to the army all the time, and we would spend a lot of time moving from one area to another in them. We quickly learnt that this was not to be so. Singleton, as it turned out, was an old Citizen Military Forces camp which had been modernised (rebuilt virtually) for the advent of National Service. Neither the kitchens nor the accommodation had been used until we arrived that afternoon on 2 February 1966.

We were off-loaded from the buses and immediately joined a processing line. We were documented, vaccinated, medically inspected, issued more clothing than any one person could ever possibly need in jungle green, and issued a bed space. By the time this was complete, it was 6 p.m., and we were told to stop everything and get down to the mess hall for the evening meal. Again, we formed a queue and waited to be served dinner. For the second time in one day, it was almost impossible to eat what was served up. I think I ended up with corn meat and spinach. Fortunately, the staff had to eat the same as us, and they were not to be fed until we had all been served. I think some of them only managed to get the spinach. The meals improved considerably from that point on.

The next day was a new revelation. We were roused at 6 a.m. and made to parade outside in our pyjamas (issued). The roll was called and then we repaired to our bed-spaces to tidy them up, dress, and prepare for breakfast. Breakfast held little temptation for most of us, so we just waited to see what the initial reports were like. One of our mates stuck his head out of the mess hall and yelled, 'It's okay!', and we were down there like a shot filling our bellies with toast, syrup, and hot tea.

When we returned, our allocated member of the Hitler Youth, Corporal Somebody, was already there looking immaculate in his starched green uniform and yelling for us to 'Stand by your beds!' I guess I got off to a good start. Living in boarding houses for the last four to five years had taught me to keep things tidy if I was to keep them separated from everyone else's possessions. Living with the Duncans had taught me to make a tidy bed. The corporal had just about destroyed everyone's living space when he came to mine. All of a sudden, I realised he was human. He stopped yelling for a moment and said, 'Not bad, you learn quickly.' He immediately assembled all the guys in our hut around my bed-space and showed me how to improve it whilst showing the others how he wanted it. I immediately gained (albeit somewhat superficial) kudos from my hut mates whilst buying myself a couple of days breathing space from the corporal. I must admit folding socks neatly is not exactly something mothers teach their children, particularly the male of the species.

We then spent the rest of the day learning how to wear our different orders of dress, how to 'bash' the famous slouch hat, were issued with rifles, and generally shown where everything was located including the parade ground and the training areas. It was then down to the barber for haircuts. Haircuts! I had just had a trim before I left Murwillumbah, surely they didn't mean me. 'Vickery—barber! On the double!' My only consolation was sitting in the barber's rooms watching him shearing the better-coiffured members of my intake. We were then told that after the evening meal we were free (no lessons), but we were not to consume alcohol for the first two weeks and there would be no leave for the first five weeks. It was a ten-week course. I began to review my earlier assessment that this place was tolerable.

The next morning convinced me that this was not the place for me. After roll call, breakfast, and hut inspection, we were introduced to our platoon sergeant. It seemed that he was trained to yell even louder than the corporal. Nothing could ever be done quickly enough, and already he was handing out extra parade ground punishments for those who summoned the temerity to answer back. I had to watch myself very carefully here as I had developed a total lack of tolerance and a quick temper. Parade ground drill occupied most of the second day—learning how to march and how to salute. God, it was boring. Next, we progressed onto weapon drill, and to ensure that we didn't lose concentration, the corporal kept re-introducing foot drill. Singleton, at this time of the year, has temperatures that regularly exceed 32 degrees Celsius, and the flies were as big as caterpillars.

After some days of this, we were advised that it was time for us to learn about weapons. So we marched out to the local training areas where it was dry, dusty, and hot and the flies were in abundance. The weapon training was good, but I still considered that there must be something I could do to avoid all of this. Bingo! On about day six, we were introduced to our officer. No one knew we even had one or what he did. He fronted up in his nice starched greens, with a peaked cap and a clipboard, and in a very modulated voice announced that an Officer Selection Board for the Officer Training Unit at Scheyville would be at the camp within a couple of days and asked if there was anyone interested in applying. I couldn't get my hand up quickly enough. Here was my salvation; anything had to be better than here. Hell, I hadn't had a bloody beer in almost a week, and I was bored out of my socks. I liked the way the officer didn't seem to do much, and he also didn't yell. I was particularly impressed with the way he never seemed to get his boots dirty. This was for me!

On about the eleventh or twelfth of February, I was called off parade to attend the selection board. I was told that I would be absent for most of the day. Already it was working. Initially, we were briefed on our futures if we were accepted into the Officer Training Unit and then interviewed individually. In all honesty, I can't remember how this went or what I said, but I do recall that I was telling so many lies that I had to be careful not to trip myself up.

The truth here would have totally destroyed my chances of getting out of this place. After the interviews, all candidates were grouped together, seated in a large circle facing each other, and were asked to discuss a number of topics. This was very nearly my downfall. Most of the other candidates were part way through university degrees or had deferred from university until after their National Service commitment. I, on the other hand, was an intellectual midget. The discussions got very philosophical, and I quickly realised that I was almost out of my depth. My street cunning, however, saved the day for me. I was quick to seize upon the fact that none of these pseudo academics could agree on anything, perhaps they didn't really know more than I did, perhaps they were all bullshitting like myself, perhaps there wasn't a written answer. I waited until they had all shown their best effort to impress, mentally summarised as much knowledge as one can gain from such a discussion, selected a path, and then, standing, proceeded to kick their opinions to pieces. This was my finest hour. This was not the same person who, five years before, could not string a sentence together. This was a command performance, and everyone was actually listening.

After lunch, we were taken out to an area where there was a whole range of apparatus set up and painted red and white. We were split into teams, allocated some bits and pieces such as a piece of rope and three lengths of timber. We were then shown a number of cement posts (in the ground) which represented the footings of a bridge and told that we had to work out how to get everyone in the group over the river, with the material provided, in a specified time. There were a series of these exercises, and they were carefully contrived to see who emerged as natural leaders. Again, the university students had seen these types of exercises before, and they all immediately jumped in and started shouting at us about what should be done. I sat back a bit and studied the problem for a few minutes. By the time I had worked out what I considered to be the solution, the others had already blundered ahead and were now realising that their solution was not going to work. I immediately reminded the group of the time constraint, grabbed two of them, and started applying my solution. Surprisingly, the remainder sat back and watched. As it turned out, the problems did not actually have solutions. My solution, although probably more practical, still would have left us stranded about ten foot short of the other side of the river. The fact was that I provided an alternate solution to that of the group and was confident enough to apply it. The same sort of results emerged from the other exercises, although some of the candidates were removed either because they were not contributing or were already considered to have passed that phase. This gave the marginal candidates a chance to prove their competence and leadership potential.

The selection board concluded, and we were returned to our lines. At that particular time, I did not know whether to feel elated or depressed. I had never experienced anything like this before, and I did not have a clue what the board was looking for. I had a feeling my lack of education would cost me the opportunity to attend OTU. Whilst I was waiting for the results to be notified, I observed the officer very closely.

I still could not work out what he did. He seemed to be treated with some disdain by his NCOs, and he seemed to give us lectures on matters which were less than interesting, e.g., how to read your paybook, how to budget, etc. A couple of days later, one of the NCOs advised me that he (the officer) was one of the graduates of the first Scheyville class, and this was his first posting. This made sense; Scheyville officers were still a novelty to NCOs at that time, and their ability had yet to be tested. Rank was always acknowledged, but respect, in the army, always had to be earned.

On the morning of 18 February 1966, I was advised, on parade, that I had been accepted to attend the Officer Training School. Along with the others who were selected, I spent the next couple of hours handing in almost everything that I had signed for fifteen days ago, cleared out my locker, bid a quick farewell to my friends, and boarded an army bus for Scheyville. The trip was a particularly slow one with another infamous 'cut lunch' provided.

We pulled into the front gates at Scheyville. It wasn't very compelling. Originally built in 1804, the area was designated as 'The Pitt Town Common' and was set aside as a common for local settlers. It became a labour settlement, a labour farm, a dreadnought farm, and in 1940, was set aside for 'Military Uses and Migrant Accommodation'. My uncle, Bill Huggins, in fact, stayed here as a migrant when he first came out to Australia in 1928 as a 'ten quid Pom'. He formed part of the dreadnought farm scheme which was to sponsor young English boys between the ages of 16 and 19 for the purpose of learning the basics of farm practices. These boys were then employed on properties throughout the state (my uncle was sent to the Southern Highlands of New South Wales). In 1965 the camp was utilised for military purposes as part of the Officer Training Unit for National Servicemen. Here we were!

If my memory ever fails me, this day will still prevail. The bus drove quickly through the camp and pulled up on the parade ground. There was quite a large group of senior NCOs and warrant officers to meet us. This looked like a nice formal greeting. The door to the bus opened, and I do not think that my feet hit the ground for more than a second at a time from that point on. A huge warrant officer by the name of Laurie Tilbrook bellowed into the bus, and we emptied it in record time with, in my case, my worldly possessions. He yelled some more instructions at us, and although loaded like pack camels, we were ordered to start jogging in step. This was called double-marching. WO2 Tilbrook ran with us as we were herded down to our accommodation. He had a list and allocated huts to individuals as we went along. Wouldn't you know it, my room was the second farthest from the parade ground, a fact that was to prove rather costly to me throughout the course. I entered my room, about the size of a small bathroom, dropped my gear, and not knowing what else to do, walked to the screen door. I looked across the pathway and saw everyone else doing exactly the same thing. We all shrugged at each other as if to say, 'What have I done!'

None of us was game to leave the room. We didn't have to wait long. For the rest of the day, we were doubled to the Quartermasters Store, to the library, to the armoury, and on a tour of the facilities. Nothing could have prepared me for this day. Everywhere we went, we were yelled at; on recall, this was one of the reasons I applied to leave Singleton. Eventually, we were told to clean up and double up for the evening meal. By this time, I was knackered and totally depressed. No one could keep up this pace. Just as we were preparing to go to the evening meal, our senior class finished instruction for the afternoon, and the whole thing started again. Even they were shouting at us. We were to stand to attention when speaking to them and be totally subservient at all times. This could not be happening!

Eventually, we got to the mess for the evening meal. What a pleasant surprise. It was old-worldly, quiet, serene, and the bar was open! I stood at the bar and swallowed a stubby whilst ordering another. Logically, this was not considered to be officer's behaviour, so I was immediately admonished by a senior cadet who was rather miffed that I held up the queue. I tugged my forelock and retreated to the anteroom where I started to meet a few of the other cadets. My senior cadet (they were referred to as 'fathers') entered the room and ordered me to get him a beer. 'Get it yourself, you lazy bastard,' I answered and watched him slowly sizzle. My group went quiet. I reflected on the wisdom of my approach. 'Say "please", and I will see what I can do,' I quickly retorted. Logically, I got the beer and averted a major disaster on my first night. This was a wise move as after dinner we were placed in the total care of the senior class who demonstrated what was required for room inspections and where everything had to be placed.

Reveille was at 6 a.m., only on this occasion we were required to stand outside the door of our rooms with our sheet over our shoulder to make sure that we weren't sleeping on the floor to avoid making our beds. We then cleaned and tidied until seven o'clock when we breakfasted, again at the mess hall. On return, our seniors were waiting for a room inspection. If they found something wrong, they arranged for us to do extra drills, which were held on the parade ground at 5.30 a.m. This was difficult for a few of us because we lived so far from the parade ground. I think it took us about three or four minutes to run from our rooms to the parade ground. If you were late, you received extra drills; it was a never-ending story. Inspection of our rooms was conducted by a member of staff during the day, when we were absent, and if anything was amiss, both you and your senior classman did extra drills. One particular member of the staff, a captain in artillery, was particularly sadistic. He seemed to gain particular pleasure in allocating extra drills as frequently as he could. His favourite trick was to don white gloves during a room inspection and wipe those gloves along all your ledges.

If the gloves got dirt on them, even the smallest speck, extra drills. He also always kept you late when he was running the extra drills, which was the task of the staff duty officer. On one occasion, it was raining, so he made us take our entrenching tools (folding shovels) out of our packs and clean a drain around the parade ground. He made sure we were running five or so minutes late, which meant that if we didn't run all the way to our rooms, we could not make breakfast; it also meant that we did not have time to clean our shovels. On our next parade at lunchtime, he inspected our shovels and charged us all with not cleaning them. Bastardisation at its best! He should feel quite privileged that I never saw him again after graduation as he was the only staff member that I really disliked, and I would have taken great delight in re-acquainting myself with him.

It did not take long for me to learn that surviving at this institution was a matter of organisation. Living so far from the parade ground made it a roundabout that was difficult to get off, but I decided that once I got off, I would get myself organised enough to stay off it. This happened after about five weeks, but to do it, I had to sacrifice most of my first weekend's leave. Instead of heading into Sydney where I knew no one, I spent the Saturday night at the local RSL and spent most of the Sunday getting all my gear and my room right up to scratch. I then found that, within limits, it was pretty easy to keep it that way and only got caught out when I got careless or complacent.

The course was tough, but the cadets were good blokes albeit very competitive, and the instructors were first class. I was finally mature enough to have a thirst for knowledge, although the fifteen-hour days were making it difficult for me to absorb everything that I was being taught. I often referred to my notes which were clearly written if taken during the day lectures but receded into scrawl or a line down the page where I had fallen asleep in some of the night lectures. Dare I say it, but I was actually beginning to believe that I could graduate even though the pass rate for the previous two classes was only about fifty per cent.

Again, I found myself mixed in with some pretty smart students. Many of them knew each other from various universities and were not too keen, initially, to allow outsiders to penetrate their circle. I assumed this to be because the mixture of physical and academic activities would prove too much for me. They were very nearly right. I assessed myself as not being too bright, but I knew that mentally I was very tough and the harsh physical program that Scheyville demanded meant that I was able to display many sporting skills that I had acquired in Murwillumbah but had never been fit enough to excel at. I also loved being out in the field and had no problem surviving without the assistance of the other students. These attributes gave me the edge in all but the academic endeavours.

They also allowed me to break down the barriers and become accepted for performance rather than background. This was the strength of the Officer Training Unit.

Sport was compulsory and viewed very closely by the staff. We were made to rotate in all sports but were allowed to select our main sport and play it most of the time. I selected rugby and was astounded when just before our first game, we had to walk up the field in extended line and remove any rocks that were protruding. I had never played rugby union and was terrified that I would get severely penalised for my lack of understanding of the laws of the game and therefore not gain any credibility from the staff or other students. I had played fullback and centre at rugby league, but when asked what position I played, I stated 'Number 8' as I knew I could tackle and run with the ball and therefore should stay out of the area that I least understood, rucks and mauls.

The course was going well; I wasn't exactly a star but was managing to pass the exams, understand the military ethos, stay off the parade ground (for extra drills), and excel at fieldwork. Sport was a great equaliser, and I found that the added fitness the course offered and the array of sports that we were required to play opened up new levels of credibility. Rugby was my chosen sport, but I had played a lot of soccer up until I came into the military, so I had a few games of that and did well. I also tried Australian rules and, with a bit of coaching, found that I could position myself fairly well to have a lot of involvement. Kicking in Australian rules, however, is an art that takes a while to master, and I can't say I achieved that in the short stay I had at Scheyville—it certainly made me realise the skill that is evident in many of the great Australian rules players, and as a result, I learnt how to appreciate the game a lot more.

I think that my father and my stepmother visited me twice whilst I was at Scheyville. They towed a caravan at that time and called in on their way between fruit-picking seasons. My father and I were not particularly close, but it was good to see him especially as he was an excellent cook. I recall him calling in late one Saturday morning when we were preparing to move down to the rugby field for our afternoon competition match. I had the task of arranging to get the team's jerseys down to the field, which was about 600 metres away—I knew this would be a struggle. All of a sudden, my father turned up and said that he was allowed to park his car, a very big 1958 Ford V8 (which had previously belonged to Doctor Barry Jones of Pick A Box and Australian Labor Party fame), just outside the gate. This was fortuitous in more ways than one; firstly, I was able to transport the jerseys, and secondly, after a fairly torrid game (directing staff were always on the sideline assessing leadership qualities, attitude, sporting abilities, etc.), I had a means of transporting them all back to the lines again. I played very well that day thinking that I had finally attracted a spectator, however, I was wrong. Even though my father had watched some of the match, he had left part way through the game and returned just before the end. He was very proud of the comments that were passed to him about my game.

Immediately after the game, I regained possession of all the jerseys and took them up to the car—my father insisted on packing them in the back seat and quite mysteriously unloaded them back at the lines and carried them down to my room. As soon as they were put on my bed, I heard the clinking of bottles, and my father very boldly produced six long-neck bottles of Reschs Pilsener. I almost had apoplexy as drinking outside of the mess was totally and absolutely taboo. What the hell! I quickly rounded up the cadets in the rooms closest to me and invited them in for a drink. They thought my father was a great bloke and asked if he had the other half dozen in the boot of his car. Unfortunately, this was not the case, but we were quite satisfied because we did not wish to smell of alcohol when we fronted the duty officer for our weekend leave pass. Nonetheless, it was a good finish to an afternoon, and it was really good to see my father again. I signed out for the weekend and went and stayed with my father and his wife, Hazel, in the caravan. We didn't really do much during the weekend except drink and eat, but it was good to exchange experiences and catch up on some common identities. It was nice to think that I still had family.

Brian (centre) with fellow officer cadets Gary Bryant
and Ian Arnison on weekend leave

We were getting near the end of the course, and for some weeks I had been complaining of a sore wrist that was a legacy of a football game we played against the School of Infantry. I had been to the camp doctor about it hoping that it was something simple such as a strain or something as the penalties for being unable to continue on the course were quite devastating—you either repeated the last three months with the following class or you marched out as a private soldier. The doctor dismissed me as 'just another whingeing cadet', prescribed aspirin, and advised me not to come back unless I had something wrong with me. Fair enough, perhaps I was just 'swinging the lead', however, I found that I couldn't do push-ups at the gym and had trouble with rifle drill—the push-ups I could cover by working a bit harder with my other arm, but the drill was becoming a real problem. Being extremely tall, I was normally the 'right marker' on the drill square and therefore was a fairly obvious target to the drill instructors who were in a very powerful position—every time I dropped my rifle, they would make me do twenty push-ups. Bloody hell, this was getting difficult, and I could see no resolution.

Four weeks after first being advised that I was a 'malingerer', we played another rugby match against a visiting team; in fact, it may have been the School of Infantry again. I was feeling pretty sore after the game and decided even though it was a Saturday, I would not go into town for a beer but would have a couple of beers in the mess and have an early night. At four o'clock in the morning, I woke up screaming in pain and could not stop the continual throbbing that was emanating from my left wrist. The cadet in the adjoining room came running in and, within half an hour, had me half dressed and up to the Regimental Aid Post. The corporal in charge immediately sent me into Windsor Hospital to have the wrist X-rayed. By this time, the wrist was extremely swollen and the limited out-of-hours hospital staff found the X-ray very difficult to read but suspected a broken scaphoid bone in my thumb. It was also not possible to plaster it whilst it was so swollen. I was returned to Scheyville, but the decision had been made to send me to the Second Military District Hospital at Ingleburn. I was received there as though I had the plague—early on a Sunday morning, a staff cadet (who were considered to be lower than a private soldier in those days), nothing more than a broken thumb and needed to be admitted. One of the sisters even commented sarcastically that 'it's always the big ones that feel the pain the most'. I didn't really feel up to telling her that I had played two games of soccer, a game of Australian rules, and three games of rugby with it strapped up only with a stretch bandage for the past four weeks, not to mention the two hundred push-ups I had done for dropping my rifle.

The duty doctor examined the X-rays and ordered that I be admitted and have the arm elevated for two days, and then they would consider plastering it and returning me to Scheyville. This was great, we were coming up to the final weeks of the course. We had three exams coming up within a week and then our final field exercise—anyone who failed a written exam or did not complete the field exercise was certain to be 'back-squadded' to the next class. I was about to miss two days of study and would have a plaster on for the field exercise—this appeared an unappealing challenge. I had left Scheyville with only a few clothes and my shaving kit, no study books. The interesting thing about this visit, although it wasn't obvious to me at the time, was that I secured a lifelong friendship with one of the other patients, observed a badly wounded Vietnam veteran die from gunshot wounds, watched a romance flourish between a nurse and a patient, and later married the nurse who probably treated me with the most disdain.

Two days passed, the swelling went down, and the doctor put a plaster cast on the hand, wrist, and lower arm. I assumed that I would be discharged, but I had had a sore throat for a few days, and with continual hospital observations, I had been diagnosed with a severe throat infection and could not be discharged until it was cleared, so onto a course of antibiotics and await the outcome. Whatever the reason, the damn thing wouldn't clear up, so I just waited, growing more impatient and disturbed every day. After a week, I knew that things were getting serious and my future as a commissioned officer was in extreme doubt. I had also not received any contact from Scheyville, including books for study.

On my tenth day of incarceration, the duty officer from Scheyville turned up and advised that within an hour I would be discharged and returned to Scheyville. In the afternoon, I would sit for two examinations and a third after dinner. At 3 a.m. I would then be picked up by Land Rover and driven to the exercise area in the Singleton training area to join my classmates on their final field exercise. This was crazy, no revision, no study, no hope. All the forecast arrangements were performed with military precision.

I arrived at Scheyville at 12.30 p.m.; I was immediately sent to the mess for a quick meal and told to be in the examination room by 1 p.m. This I did, and at 1.30 p.m., I was served with a three-hour paper on minor tactics. This was not a subject that I had seen on paper; I was used to it being a practical subject taught in the field. Apparently, the subject had been brought inside during the week and a half that I was in the hospital—not too tough though, so I thought I might have scraped through it. At 4.30 p.m., I was told to grab a cup of coffee and be back ready for an English exam at 5 p.m. This I duly did, and I thought I may have passed it okay. At 7.30 p.m. I was allowed a quick shower and an evening meal (no alcohol) and sat down for my final exam at 8.30 p.m.—can't remember the subject, it was something extremely important though esoteric called Logic or something similar. Whatever it was, I had not had any instruction in the subject, obviously a subject broached in the past ten days. Rather than waste the time sitting in the exam room with no idea about any of the questions, I handed in my paper and headed for the cot. I had to be up at 2 a.m. to start packing. Boy, what a deflating day. I could only feel that I spent the whole day contributing to my own demise.

Sure enough, the Land Rover was ready to roll at the gate at 3 a.m., the only problem was that an officer was also going up to the exercise, therefore, I had to sit in the back for the next four hours. I think it was the most uncomfortable trip I have ever experienced particularly when we got off the bitumen road and into the exercise area. My employment now became problematic. I wasn't able to carry a weapon or put up a hutchie because of my hand being in plaster, therefore, any level of tactical deployment was impossible. The staff, however, had a couple of tents which were out of observation by the cadets, so I was kept at this location with another 'wounded' cadet to keep this area tidy—we were briefed daily and advised what the exercise was trying to achieve. Occasionally, we were allowed to wander down to the cadet's position, when they were static, and talk to them about the exercise—this was very civil from my point of view and aggravating to my fellow cadets who had blood running down their arms and blisters all over their hands from digging a defence position with inadequate tools in very hard terrain. I, of course, played this to the hilt and 'ragged' them like a staff member pretending that I was superior and didn't need to get dirty and then headed back to the administration area to sleep under a tent. Belying this, however, was my fear that if I could not do any of the work, I could not possibly be fully assessed and therefore graduate.

Life, however, takes many forms, and in a couple of days, things changed considerably, fortunately for the better. In between each of the phases of war, cadets were given a fresh meal, and the activities were declared 'non-tactical'. A complete day was allocated to a TEWT (Tactical Exercise Without Troops) whereby cadets would be taken to a piece of ground and issued with a theoretical tactical scenario and provided with a problem. The cadets would have to walk about the ground and physically establish how they would fight the battle and where they would place their troops—this allowed the staff to assess how well cadets had assimilated classroom instruction and how well they could apply it to ground. As it turned out, this was a very important part of the course and carried a lot of points towards success or otherwise for cadets on the final field exercise. This was why I was brought to Singleton. My future depended on how well I was able to apply theory to ground. Fortunately, I fancied my chances on these types of exercises and thought how civilised they were compared to having to dig holes, lay barbed wire, and eat hard rations. This alternating system continued throughout the ten days of the exercise, and I remained a slave to the staff during the physical phases and was put under very serious analysis during the TEWT phases. I was more than happy that at least I was given a fair chance to graduate even though the provision of some study books during my ten days in hospital would have enhanced my chances.

The exercise finished and the cadets were made to march twenty-five kilometres of the trip home. It was interesting that some sections chose to jog it; I think probably to get it over and done with. I travelled back in a truck much to the mockery of my fellow cadets—they already thought I had had it too easy for the past two weeks. I did, however, have to pay a penalty—anyone who did not do the march lost their right to weekend leave which, of course, included me. The bar would also remain closed. A pretty miserable weekend was spent by about five of us watching television or reading with no study to do, no room inspections to look forward to, and no chance to get a beer.

Within days of returning to Scheyville, the results of the exams were posted and so was the field exercise. I had failed two of the three exams (failure of one only was allowable), however, I came third in the field exercise, and I knew this carried a lot of weight with the warrant officer and sergeant instructors. I began to sweat as I cast my eyes down the page to see if I would graduate. I think from memory the abbreviations were 'reposting to class 2/66' or 'march out to . . . unit'—if there was nothing beside your name, you would graduate. There was nothing beside 'B. J. Vickery Officer Cadet'—I couldn't believe it, I somehow had survived this testing time.

I do have a theory, however, which I think needs to be expressed. Being a national serviceman, I had no idea about the hierarchy that existed within the military, neither did I care. I sought to complete my National Service obligation and return to the post office. I did notice on a couple of occasions that visiting senior officers would ask me how my father was going—I thought this to be courteous chatter and paid little attention to it. I was not aware that the CMF member for the Military Board was Judge Advocate N. A. Vickery—he was a major general and, by all accounts, a popular one. My father's name was Norman Axford Vickery or N. A. Vickery who was a cherry picker/sorter or cook for SPC Canneries in Shepparton, Vic. My father was an itinerant worker, and therefore, I had no fixed address for him, so I just put his address as Tweed Heads, NSW, in my AAB83 or Official Record of Service. It wasn't until some years later when a more ambitious friend and fellow officer said to a mutual friend over a beer, 'Now take old Vickers here, his father is a general, and you wouldn't know it.' All of a sudden, the penny dropped; anyone who had heard the name Vickery and had any suspicions that I was the general's offspring had immediately looked up my records and saw that my father's name was N. A. Vickery and made the assumption that the general was my father. Interesting that I failed two exams and still passed the OTU course. Just saying.

Graduation was another exercise in futility for me. I knew no one in Sydney, so I had no one to invite to the graduation parade and did not have any female friendships to draw on for a partner at the graduation ball. I also had no one to take photographs for me. My arm had just come out of plaster, and I was immediately ordered back on the parade ground to prepare and rehearse for the graduation parade. We only had a few days, and I knew that I had lost some physical condition during the period of my rehabilitation. Again, due to my height, I was made right-hand marker. During the course of the rehearsals, we had a 'full dress' rehearsal whereby we had official guests, a reviewing officer, and all wore dress blues, which we would wear for the graduation, that being our winter dress. We were called into the 'Present Arms' position several times but for quite a lengthy time when we were being reviewed—this required the weapon (an SLR) to be brought around to the front of the body and held upright by both hands with one foot at an angle behind the other. We seemed to hold the position, which I always found quite uncomfortable, for a lengthy period of time while the senior officer inspected and spoke to many of the cadets.

I could feel my right hand and arm going to sleep—still the inspection went on. Eventually, the order was given for the rifle to be returned to the shoulder position—'Shoulder Arms'—I commenced to follow the order, felt nothing in my right hand, and watched my life pass before me as the rifle, completely out of control and in slow motion, head for the bitumen of the parade ground. Fortunately, the bayonet which was affixed, hit the ground and the rifle bounced back to a position where I could grab it and salvage something from the exercise by immediately regaining the stance of the other cadets—not quick enough unfortunately for the RSM to miss it.

The following day, the RSM got us all on parade and asked everyone but me to 'take one pace step back—Officer Cadet Vickery, you are not to step on *my* parade ground ever again. You will be the flag orderly for the graduation parade—I sincerely hope your parents are not looking forward to seeing you march'. Fortunately, I was saved that indignity and performed the duties of flag orderly with great care, and it was with enormous pride that I went forward and received my service commission even though the huge crowd was perplexed when I came from behind the commandant (flag station) rather than from the parade ground. Even the RSM grinned.

One of my fellow cadets arranged for a young lady to accompany me to the ball that evening, so this chapter in my life was complete—an experience well worth the undertaking. The unseen bonus in this experience was the friends that I had made at Scheyville were to become friends for life.

Brian dressed in greens as a second lieutenant in 1RAR

CHAPTER FOUR

LEARNING THE TRADE

MY FIRST POSTING after graduation was to the First Battalion, the Royal Australian Regiment, which had just returned from its first tour of South Vietnam—they were, in fact, the first infantry unit to do this. My request for corps selection was infantry, infantry, infantry, so I guess you could say that I had gotten my wish. I was advised that I would take up this posting immediately after returning home for some well-earned leave. I returned to Murwillumbah and tidied up some loose ends knowing that I would not be returning for some time—when I left to return to Holsworthy, I took with me my trusted FC Holden, and it contained pretty much everything I owned, total value probably $300.

Military life at the First Battalion was so much more relaxed than my time at Scheyville, although my baptism wasn't quite as heralded as I would like it to have been. Two National Service officers had graduated into the battalion three months earlier but none to D Company, so as I marched from the company commander's office to my small box-like office, all the soldiers, many of them very experienced, hung out of the windows of the building that I had to walk past to get a glimpse of this new 'phenomenon'—I likened it at the time to a walk down 'death row' and wondered what the future would hold for me with these guys. My sergeant was a 'tough as teak' corporal by the name of Wayne Aitkenhead or more commonly referred to as the 'Angry Ant'. He, too, was perplexed by my nature and was full of questions about how well trained I was.

I bumbled around in my office for a while, on that first day, not knowing what to do when there was nothing to do—no records, no files, no planning charts. Wayne saved the day by bouncing in to my office and announcing, 'I think it is time you spoke to the troops, sir.'

'Good idea, Corporal, but what the hell do I say to them?' I think he had been secretly thinking about this because he rattled off a number of things which made perfect sense and suggested I order a weapons inspection. This turned out to be ideal advice, and even though I buggered a couple of things up which ruffled the feathers of a couple of the NCOs, my size and aggressive nature soon won the day particularly when they found out I played rugby—both Corporal Townes and Corporal Aitkenhead from my platoon played in the battalion side.

National Servicemen were starting to reinforce the battalion which had received little priority for additional soldiers, being that it had returned from a year of active service and was unlikely to be returned to an active zone for some time. Barry Bryant was one such 'nasho' who was a quiet soul but big, strong, and also a very good rugby league player. Barry played first grade for the Mighty Magpies Western Suburbs—he was posted to our company and, of course, put straight into the battalion rugby side. Doug Walters, the Australian cricketer, was another national serviceman, and he was allocated to my platoon—to my mind, this was a great waste as he was on top of his game at the time and needed to be anywhere but in an infantry battalion. Bob Fulton, the Australian five eighth, was posted to School of Artillery at Manly where he could continue to train and play with the Manly Warringah Rugby League Club, but Walters was not given any dispensation at all other than the assurance that he would play in the battalion cricket team.

Walters and Bryant both got me into big trouble, unwittingly, because of my belief in their cause. Barry was put on kitchen duty by the CSM, 'the Grey Ghost', for some minor misdemeanour and came to see me because the weekend's match was Match of the Round and he had been selected to play in it which was worth a lot of money compared to a private soldier's salary. I asked to see the company commander and put the case to him. He was sympathetic, but when he called the CSM in, he displayed an intense dislike for Bryant and refused, under any circumstances, to sanction any changes. I went back to Barry and advised him of the result. He was distraught and advised me that he would simply go AWOL. I counselled against this but told him to play the game (afternoon game) and then return to the kitchen after the game was over and hope that no one would notice—what a bloody gamble, what was I thinking. I have always been a student of consequence, so actually, I did know what the result would be if this backfired.

Murphy's law suggests that if anything can go wrong, it will. My girlfriend lived at Penshurst very close to Jubilee Oval, the home of the St George (Dragons) Rugby League team. They were not playing until the Sunday, so for the first time in many years, we dropped into the Kogarah RSL for a drink. The game of the round was Western Suburbs versus East Sydney, and it was being played on this huge screen—my heart stopped beating, and I thought, 'I hope no one else is watching.' Barry had had a quiet game and had hardly rated a mention, so I bought another beer and sat down to watch the rest of the game. Wests had introduced a new play which was a simple double cross over with both players 'dummying' to receive the ball, but the ball going to a third player who drove straight through the centre to crash over for a celebrated try. The player to score was Barry 'Bloody' Bryant who won the match for Wests and was chaired off the bloody field in amazing clarity before the television cameras. I ate my glass.

Worse, however, was yet to come. As we were leaving the RSL, up walked the CSM (Kogarah RSL was his home club). He tapped me on the shoulder and said, 'Sir, Monday will be interesting!' I muttered something that sounded incredibly like 'Fuck off' under my breath and proceeded to have a thoroughly miserable weekend. I did recall, however, when the CSM spoke to me, he was undeniably drunk.

Monday became an anti-climax. My weekend of worrying about consequence fell a bit flat when the CSM fronted myself and Bryant up to the officer in command (OC) and reported merely that he had heard that Bryant had quit the kitchen on Saturday afternoon and not returned until 6 p.m. and that he should be given a further weekend's penalty. The OC, with a slight grin, agreed and asked Bryant and the CSM (who was extremely satisfied with the result) to leave but for me to remain. The OC advised me that CSM had not seen the game, but he (the OC) had. He advised me I had disobeyed a lawful command (I think military regulations said you could still be shot for this). I refused to beg but had no defence except shrug my shoulders and cop it on the chin ('Shoot straight, you bastards'). Fortunately, the OC was, in real life, a kind man who handed me a strong lecture on misplaced loyalties and told me to shine up my Sam Browne as I would need it in the coming weeks. He awarded me four weekends of extra duty officer and a lifetime of misery if I were to contemplate doing something as stupid again if I chose to follow down this path. Good advice; pity I wasn't smart enough.

You would have thought that I would have learned something from that experience, but I continued to see Bobby Fulton being treated like royalty, Kevin Sheedy being given the keys to military heaven, and Harry

Neesham being flown back to Perth every weekend for football league games. There was still no justice for Doug Walters. I attempted to get him posted to Victoria Barracks as a 'barracks wallah' so at least he could get over to the nets of an afternoon and keep his hand in. Unfortunately, I received no sympathy from anyone. I decided that the only way I could nobly be of assistance to Australia was to make him my 'batman' so that I could arrange for early release for him each day to head into Victoria Barracks from Holsworthy and get time in the nets. This action was, of course, the subject of much ridicule and the butt of many jokes; however, it was starting to work, but once again the 'Grey Ghost' emerged. I suspect in an act of sheer bastardy, he put Walters in the kitchen for the Saturday as a penalty for not attending dismissal parades of an afternoon after work. I had made him my batman so that he didn't have to attend dismissal parades.

Again, I approached the OC, this time with Wayne Aitkenhead who I knew had great favour with the OC and might help swing my case. We were going great until the CSM was called in. He had been listening through a hole in the wall. He stuttered and stammered and refused to budge an inch. Quite sadly the OC again sided with him and told us all to 'Get out—except you, Vickery! Do not cross me on this one young man or you will not survive as an officer.' I genuflected, saluted, and left his office a very troubled young man. Walters also had a selection match for the NSW State side on this coming Saturday.

I spoke at length to Doug Walters, who had already stamped himself as the world's greatest gentleman prankster and could make light of the most bizarre circumstances. I also asked Aitkenhead to help me work out a plan; he was very sympathetic, but the Grey Ghost was a hard man to buck. I didn't wish to put Aitkenhead in an impossible position as he had proven to be a very professional NCO (in fact, we ended up lifelong friends), so I asked if we could find a substitute for Walters on the Saturday, would he overlook it when he checked the extra duties in the kitchen? Yep, he was up for that but no further. So it was settled, my future in the army was again on the line, but I was happy that justice might at last prevail.

I was still doing my extra duty officers on the Saturday afternoon in question and asked Walters to just let me know when he had completed his game and was back in the kitchen (keeping in mind it was about a forty-minute drive from the North Sydney oval where the game was to take place). Doug, at that time, owned a lime-green mini minor, which was good for all the scooting around Sydney that he was required to do. It did lack a little repair, however, and it had a big hole in the muffler. Needless to say, the green mini could be heard from a long way off. I was a little apprehensive when, by 6 p.m., I hadn't heard from Walters, so I wandered down to the other ranks (ORs) car park to see if his vehicle was parked in its usual spot. It wasn't, but almost on cue, I heard the sound of the holed muffler from Walter's mini minor turning into the front gate before returning to the car park. I was very relieved and, as such, returned to my office to continue my duties. The remainder of the weekend went very quietly.

On Monday morning, Doug Walters came to see me and asked if I knew what had happened. I told him my version of events, and I was happy the way it had worked out. Walters then advised me that he had seen me walk off as he parked his car, but no sooner had he alighted and headed for the kitchen than a somewhat inebriated Grey Ghost had materialised out of nowhere and advised him that he was nabbed. The CSM had apparently checked the kitchen, found Walters to be absent, and spent the afternoon in the sergeant's and warrant officer's mess and walked down to the car park at about 6 p.m. All of a sudden, I began to sweat. I was standing beneath the Sword of Damocles. Life can be kind, however, I received no summons to the OC's office, and Walters picked up the next Sunday as another extra duty which somehow seemed to suit everyone. Peace was at last restored and my ulcer suppressed. I also think that Aitkenhead went to bat (sorry, bad pun) for Walters during the considerations.

Walters had the craftiest little mind that I had ever encountered; it never seemed to stop working. The OC had decided we would do a company route march out along Heathcote Road which was a busy road but acceptable for route marching if the basic safety standards were applied. This was a bit of a test for me, controlling about thirty blokes, walking in section groups on opposite sides of the road and staggered for safety reasons. I lost a bit of control early by trying to demonstrate my leadership ability by marching with each of the groups and chatting to them as we marched. When I ended up with the rear section, I noticed the forward section speed up, and I had to work pretty hard to try to catch them.

As I rounded a corner, I saw two of the section flag down a truck and jump on board—so much for my leadership ability, however, there were two volunteers for the next kitchen duties we were allocated. I learned from this that I would be better off warning the sections to watch me for commands and I would march with the middle section. This I did and the lead man was Doug Walters. I marched for about forty minutes having a good chat to him about his attitude to the army, etc., when all of a sudden, he said, 'Skip, see these white posts along the road, how far do you think it is between them?' These were, I think, survey pegs indicating where the road was about to be widened. I answered by saying something like sixty metres, and he followed up by saying, 'I'll bet you a case of beer that I can guess closer to the distance between pegs than you can.' Being an inveterate punter (although he wouldn't have known that at the time), I said, 'You're on.' We agreed that we would pace out the next three pegs and then average the distance. My guess was sixty-five metres, his was sixty-eight. Sure enough, and within minutes, I realised that I had been rolled—the bugger had been averaging this distance out for the last two miles, and of course, the distance was sixty-eight metres exactly, Walters having known that before he made the bet. Second lesson in leadership: do your research.

I was a bit miffed at having lost two soldiers to a passing truck and a math contest with Doug Walters. However, the day wasn't over, and I was determined to recover some lost pride. It was a hot day, and we were marching on bitumen so at the ten-kilometre peg, we were told to turn around and head back for camp. We got back to camp and were nearing our lines when Walters asked if I wanted a chance to win back the case of beer—now logically, I was a bit wary, but I asked what he had in mind. He said that the telegraph poles in camp were about thirty metres apart, and he challenged me to a sprint between the last two. Now I knew that he was used to running the length of a cricket pitch (twenty-two yards), and I fancied myself as a sprinter, so thinking that I would trail him most of the way, I could probably overtake him over the last ten metres. The deal was that we would drop our packs as we got to the first pole, and then it was first one over the line. Sounded fair enough except that Doug was so used to reacting quickly that he had his pack off and was sprinting before we got to the line and really got the jump on me. I cursed and got after him, and my theory was almost right as I was very close to him by the time we got over the line, but he had stolen the march, and with about fifty cheering soldiers all on his side, a protest would simply have been in poor taste. Third lesson in leadership: never give a sucker an even break. Doug Walters was grinning like he had won the Ashes. I am pleased to say this was all good-natured stuff, and I think eventually I gained as much kudos from the soldiers as he did.

On exercises, soldiers spend a lot of time waiting for things to happen. This was no different in my platoon, and during this waiting period, someone would always find a packet of cards. Euchre or 500 were the two games of choice, and I noticed Doug seemed to favour euchre. I was a moderate player but noticed few could match the memory of Doug Walters. He had the ability to remember every card that had previously come out of the pack and could store that information for when it suited him. I was clever enough never to take him on at cards; however, I was able to harness that incredible memory for my own purposes at a later time.

We were on exercise in the Shoalwater Bay Training Area acting as the enemy for Second Battalion RAR who were doing their final assessment exercise for their tour of Vietnam. We had stayed overnight in an area and were told to move to another location about ten kilometres away. We did this arriving after lunch when I was advised that we were missing our large radio (foldable) antenna. I realised that we had last used it at the previous location, so although it had been dismantled, it probably hadn't been packed. I felt that the signaller might have been responsible, but because he had been carrying the radio all day, it would be a bit brutal to send him back for it. I handed the platoon over to the platoon sergeant and grabbed Walters (because I knew he was fit) and said we were going to make best possible speed to the overnight location, search for the antenna, and then return hopefully before it goes dark.

The area we were in was medium foliage with lots of streams and paperbarks, but no noticeable features to rely on for direction, so it was going to be all by compass bearing. We took off and made good time to the previous night's location. The antenna was about where it should have been and was folded ready to be put in a pack but obviously overlooked. We had already walked over twenty kilometres that day and still had ten kilometres to go. The fact I hadn't processed was that we were down in a valley, and although it was only about 4 p.m., we were losing the sun. We started to return realising the urgency of the situation as the shadows got longer and streams which we expected to recognise easily on the way back were becoming just dark areas.

This is where the wonderful memory of Doug Walters came to the fore. We would come to a creek line and I would say something like, 'Bearing takes us up that bank and along the western side of the creek'. Walters would reply by saying, 'No, I distinctly remember that white paper bark leaning into the creek, we should take the eastern side!' This happened the whole way back with Walters having some hidden information at every difficult or confused junction we came to, and although it was a much slower trip back, we arrived right on the mark with a combination of compass bearing and dead reckoning—remarkable result, remarkable recall.

We continued having little adventures during this exercise until we were at the highest point in our area (a large hill) and a radio message advised, 'Bradman required for external activities, send to our location now!' So obviously there was an important cricket match that Doug had to attend and again he was going to have to foot it out, so he packed up and off he went. I later heard from someone who met with him after he came down the hill that he had a fair bit of anxiety dodging brown snakes all the way down. I don't think I saw him again after that. When I returned from the exercise, he was away on some other cricketing task, and I was posted to the School of Infantry, so I had moved before he returned.

Fortunately, I, along with the rest of Australia, was able to follow his progress once he was released from the army. I found both Doug and Barry Bryant to be wonderful characters and felt privileged that conscription had given me the opportunity to have met them and spent a little bit of time in their company.

It is interesting to note that in a book published in 2015 simply called *The Nashos*, Doug Walters couldn't remember who his platoon commander was only that he was very tall and asked to be called 'Skip'—it was subsequently stated by the author that this was later determined to be Tim Fischer (Two-Minute Tim of National Party fame) who I doubt was in the battalion at that time as he graduated at least three months after I did and, when he arrived in the battalion, was allocated to Transport Platoon and remained there until after I left. Adage has it that everyone is entitled to their 'fifteen minutes of fame', but it would seem that time (fading memories) had robbed me of mine.

It was during this time (and prior to the exercise at Shoal Water Bay) that the officers from 1RAR were invited over to drinks (probably a party really) at the Nursing Sisters Mess at Ingleburn. There were not enough chairs, and as the evening wore on, I knelt down on my knees to speak to one of the sisters who had secured one of the lounge chairs. A fellow subaltern walked past me and knocked me off balance, and to halt further carnage from this awkward position, I put my left hand out to break my fall, realising too late that this was the hand that had caused me all the pain at Scheyville. I landed on my hand and gave out a little yelp of pain involuntarily. The sister I was speaking to immediately identified me as the pathetic cadet who had been admitted to Second Military Hospital with a broken wrist. I immediately recognised her as the Witch of the West who gave me such a hard time in hospital that I wanted to strangle her with a bedsheet. I couldn't believe that I hadn't recognised her immediately and she was of a similar disposition. Didn't seem to matter really, I asked her out the next week, and we were married a bit over a year later. Funny how life works.

As my time in 1RAR advanced, I got to know the soldiers really well, particularly those who had served in South Vietnam. My interest was high, and their stories were 'boys own adventure' even though they became more exaggerated as time wore on; alcohol enhanced this process even further, but I was hooked. I had already started to think that I might make the army a career, and I realised that if I did so, a tour of Vietnam was an essential ingredient. I needed to think about how I could make this happen.

I approached the CO and advised him that I would like a transfer to the School of Infantry at Ingleburn and be placed in the Reinforcement Wing. The CO asked me to reconsider as he had just received news that the battalion would be going to Malaysia within the next twelve months and I should stay on and go with them. I questioned him as to whether the battalion would be returning to South Vietnam, and he could not confirm that it would occur. I reinforced my wish to be transferred to the School of Infantry, and the CO reluctantly accepted it and said that he would make it happen. He did and I was transferred within two weeks. I was sad to leave the First Battalion as it had shown me a lot of friendship, a lot of good officers and soldiers, a lot of good leadership, and the true meaning of the word 'comradery'. My grounding as a young officer had commenced, and I was thoroughly enjoying the experience.

⚶

CHAPTER FIVE

THE SCHOOL OF INFANTRY

T**HE SCHOOL OF** Infantry was the corps school for all who entered infantry. All recruits who were allocated to infantry had to pass through the school where they were taught the finer points of their trade before being forwarded to their units. National Service had placed a tremendous demand on this system with so many soldiers being required to reinforce battalions going to or currently being in the war in South Vietnam. Battalions began conducting their own training companies so they could get the soldiers direct from recruit training and train them in the 'ways of their battalion' right from scratch. This system proved to be very effective and took a lot of pressure off the School of Infantry who then were able to train soldiers specifically as reinforcements for battalions currently serving in South Vietnam.

The school also ran specialist courses for the corps such as Assault Pioneer Courses, Mortar Courses, Signal Courses, etc., and provided specialist instructors for courses from all infantry units in these specialised subjects. It was a wonderful and exciting place to be for a young subaltern.

For me, surprisingly, it was not overwhelming; many of the soldiers who had toured South Vietnam with 1RAR were here as corporal or, in some cases, sergeant instructors, and they were waiting for me. This just amplified the experience for me, the role providing tremendous meaning to the job; we were training soldiers for war, and I had the greatest group of instructors to do it with.

Wayne Aitkenhead was appointed my platoon sergeant and 'Blue' Mulby one of my five instructors. 'Blue' was ex-SASR (Special Air Services Regiment) and also assisted with the SAS selection courses when they were conducted at the school. Jim Koeford was my administration sergeant (he was an ex–Korean veteran), seemingly of little humour, but his administration was always right on the mark. Paul Slattery, ex-2RAR, and Jim Whatling were both corporal instructors with a great sense of purpose and a genuine sense of humour.

It was during my first six months at the centre that Carole and I had decided to get married (November 1967). Our wedding was a wonderful affair, however, not without its problems. The weeks leading up to the wedding were very demanding ones for me with a series of exercises being conducted at Shoalwater Bay, meaning that I had to organise my side of the wedding in a very limited time frame. This was going okay until one of the unions decided they were going on strike and would not deliver beer from the breweries to the hotels. Now to my mind, a wedding without beer could only be declared a disaster, so a huge pall began to form over this pending event. Carole's father, Laurie, found out that some bottled beer was making its way to the hotels but only in limited quantities and competition for it was fierce. I was still on exercise in Central Queensland and starting to panic, however, Laurie and Carole's brother, Phil, dedicated themselves to getting enough bottles of beer to allow the wedding toasts to be made.

To their eternal credit, Laurie and Phil drove all over Sydney buying one case of beer (long necks) at a time, sometimes at exorbitant prices, just to make sure we could provide the beverages that every wedding deserved. My additional effort when I finally got back from the exercises assisted in providing the most assorted range of bottled beer ever experienced at a wedding. However, we managed to scramble together enough beer and some wine to meet the needs of a thoroughly enjoyable wedding. So good, in fact, that Carole and I were loath to leave the party, however, we had to drive to Parramatta (which was some distance away) where we were staying overnight before heading up the coast on our honeymoon.

Our honeymoon was a relaxing one, returning briefly to my hometown of Murwillumbah and working our way back down the coast to Sydney. I didn't realise until I got to Murwillumbah that my licence had been cancelled for a couple of drink-driving offences I had accumulated. I hadn't changed my address on my licence, so the infringement notices kept coming to Murwillumbah police station where they sat awaiting a forwarding address. Logically, I had no other way of getting back to Sydney, so I drove very carefully from that point on. Carole and I stayed at a resort just North of Coffs Harbour (Emerald Beach, I think) and had a thoroughly enjoyable, relaxing holiday. We both returned to work at Ingleburn as Carole was still working as a registered nurse at Second Military Hospital, and I was working across the road at the school.

The workload at the school (or the centre as it was then called) was seemingly endless—non-stop roads of recruits reporting for courses. I must admit the system for dealing with the recruits was wonderful but not much time was available between one course marching out and another marching in. Each morning, we inspected the food lines for hygiene at 6 a.m., and most weeks, we worked at least three nights, sometimes more seldom finishing before 10 p.m. We had night stalks, night navigation, night lectures, night attacks, night ambushes, night patrolling, not to mention we still had to do our share of school duties such as duty officer, duty sergeant, guard commander, etc., which of course also extended into weekends. It was an intensely busy time, but there is no better way to measure the calibre of the Australian soldier than to put him under pressure, and these guys seldom failed, although being Australian, whenever alcohol became involved, the event always seemed to end in a fight. I did tire of going to march-out parties only to find I had to referee a fight, put someone in jail, or call an ambulance. I do recall the staff mocking me at one stage because my favourite saying was, 'Corporal Slattery, march this man to the cell', but it generally cooled the party down.

We did have an exceptionally interesting experience whilst I was at the school. Simon Townsend (who later ran the very successful show *Simon Townsend's Wonder World*) became the first publicised conscientious objector to the Vietnam War, and as such, he refused to fulfil his National Service obligation. He served a period in Long Bay Gaol, and then he was interned at Holsworthy prior to his court martial, which had been scheduled to be held at the School of Infantry at Ingleburn. This caused great concern because of the possible disruption to this extremely busy training institution. Somehow politics prevailed and the date was set, etc. Then the whole charade began. The court-martial room was swept for hidden microphones and military police were placed on the front gate. The interesting thing for me was that I was appointed as the duty officer and was supposed to supervise all of this including the care and keeping of the prisoner on the night before the court martial. Fortunately, none of it mattered too much; it drew so much attention that the RSM (I think it was 'Gunner' Stephens) took charge and handled it magnificently. The prisoner arrived escorted by military police, Gunner showed them the cell, the prisoner was positioned in the cell, and the door was locked. Gunner handed me the key, said, 'See you in the morning, sir', and left. Logically, I quickly handed the key over to the guard commander.

Sure enough, the next morning, the RSM was there bright and early, again the spooks were in place sweeping the court-martial room and the press galleries were being organised. I think even the military police were replaced with federal police. Ideally, I would have liked to have stayed around to watch proceedings, but I had a busy job of instruction to do and left it all in the hands of the RSM. Not even a photograph with Simon Townsend—it would be wrong of me not to admit that I really did not care for his objection, so I was totally unsympathetic to his cause. I really don't know what happened to him, his history is not, seemingly, for public record. I think he was found guilty, jailed for a month or so, and then dishonourably discharged, but I can't guarantee my memory to be fully accurate. Nonetheless, an interesting episode which I suppose has some place in history. I know Simon went on to be spectacularly successful with his 'Wonder World' series which seemed to run forever. Simon passed away in 2016.

Work at the school was tough, and a lot of responsibility was placed on the shoulders of the platoon commanders and the staff who supported them. Although weekly conferences were held with the wing commander (Battle Wing), we were pretty much left up to our own devices with the task of training, assessing, and graduating the young soldiers who formed our platoons, many of whom were regular soldiers and would go on to have distinguished careers. We, therefore, set our own standards and 'got on with the job', which meant that we constantly attended lessons, rewrote scripts, argued concepts, relocated venues, and did almost all the instruction with a staff of about five officers/NCOs per platoon. This put a lot of pressure on all of us. So much so that it almost brought me undone on at least one occasion.

We took the platoon out on a night navigation march to put into practice the theory of map reading and navigation. After unloading from the trucks, we split into three groups, gave an initial brief, and advised the soldiers which leg of the march they were required to navigate, appointed the leader, and then set off on the march. At about midnight, I stopped the march, advised the staff that we were getting very close to a cliff and I didn't wish to proceed any further that night. It was pitch black, and we were exactly where we were supposed to be. I wanted to pitch camp for the night and then demonstrate to the soldiers how close they were to the cliff face and how they had not pointed that out to staff before they started on the march (a lesson in correctly reading the topography off the map). I advised the staff I would go forward about ten metres, check our location, and they should get the soldiers to put up their tents and catch some sleep. The staff got on with their job. I walked forward about five metres and immediately hurtled down the face of the cliff which was only about ten metres high at this point. However, I fell badly, twisted my ankle, and was in extreme pain. I looked up the cliff face and saw no one. I could barely walk, and I felt the ankle swelling. The cliff face was steep, and I couldn't climb it, so I took a quick look at my map and began walking north to find a way up. This took me some time as I was travelling slowly, and there was no paths up the face. Eventually, I found enough vegetation to allow me to pull myself up the face, and about 1 a.m., I arrived back at the camp. I assumed the staff would be looking for me, but I checked and both they and the soldiers were all sound asleep. No one had even noticed that I was missing.

The next morning, the staff could see that I was a bit battered and asked 'what happened'. It seemed funny at the time, but I informed them that I was barely able to walk and would have to somehow make my way back to the road (about ten kilometres) and try to hitch a ride back to camp. They would have to stay on and finish the navigation exercise. This they did and I staggered back the way we had come. I walked about five kilometres and came across a dirt track at the same time as our sergeant administration Jim Koeford drove down it to provide water for the platoon.

I was saved although very worried what they might find when I took my boot off. We returned to camp, and I visited the doctor who advised me that I had a very sprained ankle, put me on crutches, and gave me a chit for ten days' complete bed rest. I took this back to my OC who tore it up and advised me that we didn't have any 'reserves' for an athletics meeting we were having the next day (Saturday) and I was required as a judge. Sympathy, supposedly, was not in the dictionary for officers!

It was during this period at the school that I made lifelong friendships probably because of the shared adversity generated by the demanding nature of the courses. Everyone worked hard, but even those less inclined towards over-achievement were swept along by sheer need to get everyone trained for a role they might soon play in an operational theatre, namely Vietnam. It was during this time that I also received a phone call from the postmaster general's department reminding me that my National Service obligation was almost at an end and they wished to interview me to outline some plans they had for my future in the postal service. I was given a couple of weeks to answer and knew that it was decision time. Even though the postal service was offering me a very promising future in senior management, I had become extremely used to working outdoors and shaping the future of young men's lives. I knew also that if I decided to stay in the army, I would, for the sake of my future personal and professional credibility, need to do a tour of Vietnam and preferably as a platoon commander. This may have swayed a lesser man, but I enjoyed the life, I enjoyed the stories, and I was looking forward to the adventure, so despite being recently married, I decided that the military was for me. Now I had to work out how to make it all happen.

There were plenty of officers and NCOs willing to offer advice and help me develop as a young officer. There were characters whose faces will remain with me forever, and there were names that were legendary amongst the warrior class. These were the people who made the military attractive—the stories about many of them were almost set in folklore many due to acts of bravery not recorded. Names like Barry Petersen (the Tiger Man of CIA and some say *Apocalypse Now* fame), Michael Barrett (the Bear), 'Snow' Wright and 'Blue' Mulby (SASR), 'Knuck' Arnison (later to become the governor of Queensland), Bob Convery, Robbie Raper (of the famous footballing Raper family), Wayne 'The Angry Ant' Aitkenhead (later an RSM), Jim Koeford, RSM 'Gunner' Stephens, 'Tassie' Wass, John McAloney, Reg Pollard (later to become colonel commandant of the corps of infantry), and many, many more. I can still almost remember a story about each and every one of them.

Working long, hard hours meant that every now and again it was good to catch up with fellow platoon commanders and 'blow off a little steam'. This was normally done at the officer's mess on Friday afternoons at 'happy hour'. These were always pleasant affairs, and most of the officers managed to organise their week to attend. A similar activity was held in the warrant officers and sergeants mess. Most weeks we would get about forty officers attending, and there were some very good, very experienced, and very hardworking men amongst them. I was starting to see my place in the pecking order would be determined by how I compared to these young warriors.

Mess activities were generally made attractive by the provision of loads of 'smallie eats', lashings of fairly low-priced beer, and the fact that breathalyser laws hadn't yet been introduced. It was at one of these events that I hatched my plan. The senior officer in the mess was not the commander or the commanding officer but the president of the Mess Committee who was generally the senior major in the unit.

At this time, the senior major was Gordon Nichol who was, indeed, very senior. In fact, I think Gordon was the senior major in the corps at that time. Gordon enjoyed a drink and was very pleasant company although a little pompous. I had been to visit him a couple of times in his office with my request to transfer to an infantry battalion. The answer had always been, 'No, you are serving a very useful role here and doing it well. You will be considered for transfer when you have completed your posting here' (I still had one year to go). This was not good at all, so at a subsequent 'happy hour', I decided to test Gordon's sense of humour, and whilst speaking to him, I grabbed a pair of scissors from over the bar and cut his tie off. An amazing hush came over the mess, Gordon was turning purple, and whilst he was spluttering at this impudent attempt to belittle him, I said, 'Now will you listen to me, I want a transfer to an infantry battalion.' No words were spoken, the PMC slammed down his beer and stormed out of the mess—not quite the result I had been looking for.

The next day, I was summoned to Gordon's office and advised, without humour, that I was being transferred to Ninth Battalion, the Royal Australian Regiment in South Australia, and I was to be out of the unit within ten days. I suspect that I was sacked. I also suspected that I would have been made a third lieutenant if such a rank existed. However, I had achieved my aim although the air was fairly thick around the headquarters for the next week, so I steered clear of any need to visit it for any reason. The next phase of my military career had started.

CHAPTER SIX

NINTH BATTALION, THE ROYAL AUSTRALIAN REGIMENT

MOVING TO SOUTH Australia on such short notice was a little more difficult than it might first seem. Carole and I were living in a married quarter at Ingleburn at the time, and we had to pack up (not that we had many possessions), move her back to Penshurst to live with her parents, and I had to dispatch all of my military possessions to Woodside, S. A., as there was no married accommodation for us immediately available in South Australia. We had also just been advised that Carole was pregnant.

In addition, I had been informed in a letter from the adjutant of 9RAR that the battalion had been warned out for Vietnam, and little leave would be forthcoming before we sailed for Asia in the following November (in five months' time). I therefore saw little need to take the car, so I had to arrange my journey by train which was not a comfortable journey in the middle of July.

Farewelling Carole on Central Station in Sydney in the middle of winter at 9 p.m. and not knowing when I would see her again was a sad scene that along with several others in the next couple of years would live with me forever.

I was entitled to a sleeper, which I was grateful for, but the trip, nonetheless, had a stopover for the afternoon in Melbourne. This proved to be quite fortuitous. I knew no one either on the train or in Melbourne, so I decided I would take a train out to the races at Caulfield. Somehow, after a couple of small wasted bets, I had one decent bet on a 16/1 winner and was able to catch the train for Adelaide feeling pretty smug with myself and sat in the dining car drinking beer, on my own, for as long as they would serve me. My mind returned to the night before I joined the army when I lost every penny I owned.

9RAR was the baby battalion of the regiment. It had been formed in Keswick Barracks, Adelaide, on 13 November 1967 and was warned out for service in Vietnam commencing in November 1968. It was afforded a commanding officer LTCOL A. L. (Alby) Morrison, MBE, a regimental quartermaster sergeant, an adjutant, a quartermaster, four majors, two warrant officers, and seven other ranks and told to be ready to go to war within a year—a daunting task for any CO. Fortunately, 4RAR had recently returned from Malaya and many of its senior NCOs were also allocated to 9RAR. This provided the necessary experience that 9RAR needed to construct an efficient combat force. 9RAR were allocated Woodside Barracks in the foothills just past the well-renowned Oakbank Race Course.

I joined 9RAR when they were in the field on Cultana Range. I was given time to dump my belongings in a room at the officer's mess at Woodside, grab a meal, get a 'Welcome to 9RAR, get your gear ready, you are going out in the bush for two weeks' speech from the adjutant Terry

Gee and was dispatched on the next available vehicle that was heading West to Cultana.

Cultana, as it turned out, was a soulless, featureless, cold, bleak wasteland which served as a live firing range and a training area for units stationed in South Australia. My first thoughts were confused as I was of the belief that we were training for tropical warfare in South-East Asia. However, a quick brief by the CO quickly reminded me that it was the end of July, and we were heading to war in November. His words of advice were simply, 'Get on with it or get on your bike, we don't have time for doubters'. In fairness, I think they were the harshest words I ever heard him speak. Almost magically, a runner appeared from nowhere to guide me to my new platoon which was First Platoon, A Company, a platoon I stayed with until we returned from Vietnam in December 1969. Logically, I agreed with the suggestion that we changed the platoon name to A1.

At this time, I had been a commissioned officer and a platoon commander for two years, so by military standards, I had a fair bit of experience particularly as I had served with 1RAR who had just completed a tour of Vietnam and the School of Infantry which was our premier infantry teaching establishment. However, I was still a National Service officer, having extended my national service rather than signing on for a regular commission. National service officers were quite a new concept to most soldiers and, therefore, were to be treated with some suspicion particularly those who had a few years of service behind them.

This fact had preceded me to the Ninth Battalion. First Platoon, A Company was getting a National Service officer as their new leader! How could they possibly survive? Some of the platoon, I think, would like to have seen me fail first up, some would like to have seen me as a wimp who really didn't fit the leadership role, some were just ambivalent—what surprised them most was that I was six foot four tall, extremely fit, and didn't really give a toss about what they had heard or assumed. I had landed right in the middle of an exercise and immediately took control of the platoon from the sergeant, carried out a series of actions that I thought appropriate (although not tactically all that correct as I recall), regrouped the platoon, and said, 'I will get to meet you when we settle down for the night.' Seemed to work, I paid each soldier a visit after dark, and we got on just fine. I knew the platoon sergeant and I were never going to like each other, but he was experienced and intelligent, so I knew we could work together, and we did. Surprisingly, most of these soldiers remained with First Platoon until we got to Vietnam, and many changes there only came about through necessity (injury/illness, etc.) or the opportunity for soldiers to get off the front line and a bit further away from where the bullets were fired—fairly sensible reaction really! It is also interesting to note that I was the only National Service officer who left Australia with the battalion, and we (9RAR) were the only battalion to achieve that statistic for the remainder of the war.

I stumbled through the remainder of the exercise in the cold and wet of Cultana. Each day the troops got more miserable, and I quickly realised the need to push a bit harder to get these soldiers hardened and prepared for a very dangerous experience that would extend beyond a couple of weeks. We were all getting on fine, however, and it was getting easier to learn the strengths and weaknesses—some of the soldiers were better than others, and some of the NCOs were better than others, but overall, we had a good team, and I had time to change any of their bad habits before we left the country. The exercise eventually finished, the CO seemed happy with the result, and we headed back to Woodside for a couple of days' rest and maintenance.

This was where I first got to meet my fellow officers of the battalion as the exercise was very insular, in that we worked principally in platoon groups within a company framework, and I didn't really get to see any of the other officers. After I finished down in the platoon lines, I headed up to the officer's mess and looked for a room. Rod Curtis was the first I was to meet, and he said that the room next to him was vacant, so 'bunk in there'—this I did, and that was the start of a great experience and a great friendship.

I wandered into the shower block, and there was a fair-sized group of officers, all without rank, trying to scrape two weeks of grime off their bodies. I met about five blokes who seemed in great spirits and were readying themselves for a drink. I had no idea what positions they held within the battalion, but they readily accepted me without hesitation and told me not to be long getting to the bar. I didn't have long to wait as I was without my wife and was living along a wooden veranda attached to the mess. I was about to be measured for character; it would be interesting to find out how I stood up alongside some of the wildest men I had ever known.

I entered the mess and was surprised to see there were already about twenty officers in front of me; they all had a drink and were seemingly trying to obliterate the memory of the cold, miserable two weeks we had spent out on the range. I immediately recognised Mick Bell who I had shared a mess with at Holsworthy back when I was in 1RAR. I knew his drinking standards were high (he offered to kick my door down the night before my wedding if I didn't go into Kings Cross with him), his sense of humour was strong, and his friendship unswerving. We greeted each other like long-lost brothers. I knew this would be a big night. Mick quickly introduced me to all including the PMC, and my first night in the 9RAR mess was underway.

Within an hour, the mess started to fill up as the married officers had gone home (married quarters), showered, changed, and brought their wives back to the mess. I had the opportunity to meet all the officers and most of the wives on the first night. What a cheerful, fun-loving group of people. The only thing that seemed to slow a few of them down was the fact that we had been in the field on hard rations for two weeks. Logically some were starting to get stomach cramps from having consumed the specially formulated survival meals for two weeks which depended on limited levels of water, so dehydration was having an effect. Slowing down the pace a bit and drinking the odd glass of water seemed to solve this problem—well at least until the next morning.

We all woke up feeling a bit 'doughy', showered, breakfasted, and got down to work. After exercises, there is always a lot of cleaning up to do, and we were only four months off leaving for Vietnam which meant that all medical and administrative arrangements still had to be made (needles/ wills/full dentals/ next-of-kin arrangements, etc.), so we laid out all our weapons and equipment and started cleaning and preparing for the next exercise. In the meantime, soldiers were called to dental appointments, interviews with the Company 2IC, or sent to the RAP to have their next series of injections (some of which made them ill for several days).

As a Defence requirement, all units going to Vietnam had to undergo collective training at the Jungle Training Centre (now the Land Warfare Centre); individuals (reinforcements, etc.) had to do a three-week Battle Efficiency Training Course. Fortunately, the battalion had undergone this training before the end of July, therefore, we had only two final exercises to do, one at Leigh Creek in the Flinders Ranges and one at Shoalwater Bay, which was our final exercise. Leigh Creek almost relieved us of our last resolve—it was colder even than Cultana, and sleep at night wearing only tropical clothing (with a few adaptions) was nearly impossible. The ground was hard and seemingly composed (mainly) of flint.

The first part of the exercise was, however, interesting, in that in order to improve our map-reading skills for Vietnam (mainly flat and low lying with lots of bamboo), the CO had all the contour lines removed from our maps, leaving only creek lines and our personal navigation skills. This would not have been a problem had we known the given start point, but unfortunately for our company, it confused the RAAF also, and we were placed about 1,500 metres from where we're supposed to be, however, everyone accepted that it was correct.

It was, of course, very difficult to check exactly where we were without any features from which to do a resection. So we bumped around for a couple of days until I informed the OC that if we were using real artillery, we would have shot ourselves up by now and we needed to readjust our orientation and navigational thinking because we had been dropped in the wrong spot. My obstinance was very hard for the OC to accept as he prided himself on his navigation and the RAAF couldn't have been wrong, and after all, I was only a second lieutenant. He refused to accept my view, so I nodded and got on with my job, eventually gaining some satisfaction in hearing a radio conversation where the battery commander (artillery) advised the OC that he thought he was in the wrong location to the coordinates he was sending in for fire support requests (fortunately and for safety reasons, the Battalion Headquarters group had maps marked with full relief). Not sure I ever received an apology for that one, but I sure felt good.

The final exercise at Shoalwater Bay was a Defence requirement for all battalions going to Vietnam and was designed to allow us to function as a battalion and test all the skills we would need to carry out our role in Asia. 7RAR (recently returned from Vietnam) was allocated as our enemy force and tried to replicate as many situations for us as realistically as possible. This was a good exercise, and our battalion did very well. Time was running out, however, and those of us who had not joined the battalion until after 1 July still had not completed our compulsory time at the Jungle Training Centre. I began to worry as we only had four weeks left after the exercise before we departed for Vietnam. We were all entitled to seven days' pre-embarkation leave, and my wife was in Sydney, so doing the math, it left very little time for us to still get our leave. I decided to speak to the adjutant about it in the field. He got back to me within a couple of days and advised that there were ten of us still to do the course, and Canungra had agreed to reduce the course to ten days for us. I was very relieved.

At the end of the exercise, the battalion packed up and headed home and the nine unqualified soldiers and myself headed for Canungra. On arrival, we were treated the same as cooks, signallers, bean counters, and reinforcements in general (many had done no preparatory training for Vietnam that was why this course was introduced). We were not treated as fully trained individual soldiers who had learnt all their skills in the field and were just here for ten days to qualify under government legislation. I immediately asked for a parade to the course commander who was a very understanding artillery officer but advised me that he had no advice that we were only there for ten days. We were to do the full course of three weeks. If this were to transpire, there would not be enough time for the soldiers or myself to complete our pre-embarkation leave. I hadn't seen my wife for two months at this stage. To depart without seeing her would have been unacceptable to me and similarly to some of the soldiers who were with me as most were married or had permanent girlfriends. (I feared a revolution, well certainly a revolt.)

It was time for me to stand up and be counted. I immediately demanded a 'parade' to the chief instructor who at this time was a no-nonsense, uncompromising, but totally professional lieutenant colonel by the name of Ron Grey who later went on to become a major general. I was not looking forward to this confrontation because I knew that if I didn't have all my ducks in a row, I would be shredded on more than one level. I now had to wait to be summonsed.

You wouldn't believe it, but I had just finished completing the Confidence Course which comprised a series of tough obstacles including a couple of mud ponds (one was called the bear pit for good reason) when the word came down that I was to 'parade' to the CI in one hour. Panic set in severely as I realised that during my jump from the twenty-foot tower into the river, I had lost one of my epaulettes off my shoulder. I was already dripping wet but had time to change my shirt on the way past the tents to the CI's office. The problem was that I had come to Canungra directly from Shoalwater Bay and only had limited clothing being in the field for the past six or seven weeks. I asked the young officer running the course if he had a solution, otherwise my career would end in exactly forty-six minutes' time. To his eternal credit, he slipped off one of his epaulettes and encouraged me to put it on. The only problem with this generous 'Aussie' solution was that he was an artillery officer, and they were the only corps (to my recollection) that had RAA embroidered under their rank badges. I decided to accept the offer imagining that I could turn slightly ajar when speaking with the CI and perhaps, just perhaps, he mightn't notice.

How puerile was my thought process? I raced up the hill, changed my shirt, put on my one sagging, waterlogged epaulette and the nicely ironed one which read RAA. I was about to face a long, slow death of a thousand cuts which I doubted that Batman would have recovered from. Water was still seeping out of my boots as I stood outside the CI's office, and the marrow was slowly seeping from my bones.

'The chief instructor will see you now, sir,' announced the wing sergeant major running his eye up and down my extremely unkempt appearance. I hadn't got one pace into the colonel's office when this powerful voice roared at me, ' Vickery, what are you doing wearing an RAA badge of rank!' Somehow I had enough composure to remember to salute and then started jabbering. It was a long story, I was tired, life was a shit brick, and I was beginning not to care. I could no longer remember the short version, however, I mentioned what a professional Ron Grey was and suddenly he showed it. He summed me up in about thirty seconds, rang my CO in Adelaide, hung up, and then said, 'No one knows about this ten-day course you were supposed to do including your CO, but I have checked on the behaviour and professionalism of your soldiers since you have been here—my staff are impressed with your troops and rate you personally to be of the highest quality. We have arranged for you to leave here at 10 a.m. tomorrow. Please wish your troops the best of luck from me for their tour of Vietnam. Now get out of here so I can get the floor mopped.' There was a God. I later went to work for Ron Grey when he was general officer commanding Field Force Command. He continually reminded me of how pathetic I looked standing in front of his desk straight from the bear pit. He also never forgave me for wearing RAA rank badges.

With our final training completed, all that was left to do was to finalise our administration and take our seven-day pre-embarkation leave which we had all earned. Getting to the war from here should have been easy. For some reason, I never seemed to do the easy things. Whilst at Canungra, I had become acquainted with a mature, likeable RAEME corporal (who was by chance a motor mechanic), Don Nottage. During some chats, he advised me that he and another member of the battalion were going to drive to Sydney for their pre-em leave and were looking for a third party to join them and share the driving and the cost. They estimated that it would take less than eighteen hours each way. This was a good opportunity for me as I had been sending all my money (which wasn't much) to Carole and an airfare seemed almost beyond reach. I agreed, and at about 2.30 on the Friday afternoon we were all released, we were off.

We had been travelling about an hour and a half, and I started to feel a stiffness in my right elbow. Curiously I examined it and found it was very swollen and very red. I didn't think it would pose a problem and promptly ignored it. The other two guys had agreed to drive first, so I was in the back seat, and gradually, we drove towards the closing light of day. We were just about to change drivers, dusk had fallen, and farmhouse lights were becoming apparent when Don, the owner of the car, advised that we were losing power and there were other signs that the car was in trouble. We immediately stopped and the two mechanics lifted the bonnet and started checking water and oil levels. Meanwhile, I noticed that my arm (at the elbow) was becoming increasingly sore. Logically, I got out of the car and tried to show my highest level of interest, knowing very little of what might help with this encroaching problem. All of a sudden, Jim said, 'We've blown a head gasket or a valve and will need to repair it to proceed.' We all agreed that many farms would have some facilities, and we might be able to get someone to bring out some parts from a local town (I suspect Murray Bridge might have been the closest, but my memory is a bit hazy about that night). We saw a farmhouse on our left and drove towards it, turning off the highway at a very slow speed.

We walked up to the doorway and saw that the family was just about to sit down to dinner. We explained our situation and asked if the farmer (a warm, solid-looking young guy about 35 years old) had anything that could help us. Without hesitation, he advised that he had a full workshop 'out in the shed' and we could pull the motor out and have a look at it, but first he needed to eat his dinner. He then asked if we had eaten, and of course, we answered in the negative as we were just going to grab a pie or something at a roadside stop when we refuelled. The farmer invited us in, introduced his whole family, and then asked us to join them for dinner. We were somewhat hesitant as we hadn't seen our families for about six weeks or so and we wanted to 'get on with it'. However, this was a generous gesture and we had run out of options, so we agreed and sat down to a typically friendly, most enjoyable country meal—all this time my elbow was getting sorer and much more stiff.

After dinner, we repaired to his shed, and there was a workshop capable of building the *Ark Royal*. He had everything. Logically, we expected that he would show us where everything was and then retire. Not so, he asked us to position the car and got ready for a long night of work. The two mechanics and the farmer got into it. I was bloody useless, firstly, because of a lack of knowledge, but secondly, because I could no longer move my right arm. I sat in a chair and tried to stay awake whilst these three wonderful blokes toiled away to get the car back on the road. The farmer's wife assisted by bringing out hot drinks and sandwiches throughout the night. Meanwhile, I just felt more and more useless.

About 4 a.m., I was jolted awake by joyous cheering as the machine was kicked back into life, and Don drove out the doors to give it a test run. All three of them were exhausted, but the drivers knew that they were right because I was rested and could drive from here and they could doze—wrong! I had to 'fess up about my arm and tell them that I couldn't drive. They were devastated, and I could hear them say under their breath, 'Bloody officers!' We thanked the farmer, told him we were off on the HMAS *Sydney* as soon as we came back, so probably wouldn't get a chance to drop by and again thank him before we left. He was happy for what he had achieved, shook our hands and wished us luck, and waved as we drove out the gate about 6 a.m. I sat in the front passenger seat to keep an eye on the driver whilst the other passenger grabbed some shut-eye. What a night, what a massive effort by those three guys. Logically, we had to drive at a much slower rate because of the new short motor, but at least we were travelling in the right direction.

The remainder of the trip was steady but uneventful, and we reached Sydney without too much fuss. Needless to say, the five remaining days were spent getting affairs in order and preparing to be absent for twelve to thirteen months. This was a big step, and neither Carole's parents nor Carole was looking forward to the experience. The last day was very quiet with everyone trying to contain their personal thoughts and be brave about personal outlooks. I imagined it was going to be a very thoughtful and somewhat emotionally difficult trip back to Adelaide. No one had quite prepared me for this part of the journey.

The next morning, the boys turned up on time, and I said my farewells. A very sad moment that I knew the other two young men must have gone through just a couple of hours before. A hug, a kiss, a wave, and then into the car, dwelling for a moment would not have made it easier. All of a sudden, we were heading up the street, swollen with emotion but on our way to war. I now understood how difficult the next twelve months would be.

We had a good drive back with the two blokes recounting to me how they had spent their time and how they had found it to be exactly the same black spot that I had encountered. Any tension between us was dissolved when I explained that I had been to the doctor and he had diagnosed bursitis in my elbow and provided a magic potion which had encouraged the swelling to go down, reduced the redness, and thus allowed me to take my turn behind the wheel. By the time we reached Adelaide, we were well acquainted and were telling stories as though we were in the 'boozer'. It is interesting that I only ever bumped into either of them once or twice again over the next twelve months. I am really disappointed that I can't recount the name of the second mechanic as they were two first-class soldiers to whom I owe an enormous debt of gratitude.

CHAPTER SEVEN

OFF TO WAR

WITHIN A WEEK, we were assembling on the dock in Adelaide Harbour, families were saying their final farewells, and we were being asked to board the Vung Tau Ferry, the HMAS *Sydney*. What a proud moment it was as we, members of the Ninth Battalion, the Royal Australian Regiment (the youngest Australian battalion ever to go to war), along with the ship's company, lined the dock side of the flight deck and said our last farewell to Adelaide. At that point, in a battalion that was comprised of 60 per cent national servicemen, I was the only National Service officer in the battalion—a fact that no one actually discovered until I was asked to sign on for a five-year short service commission by the commanding officer during our tour.

Our only port of call between Adelaide and Vung Tau was Perth. I think this was occasioned by a number of our members actually coming from Perth and some arrangements had been made to pick them up there along the way. I suspect that some logistical aspects must also have been involved or a naval requirement as we pulled into Perth for about six hours.

To get leave, you had to quote a substantial reason, so a group of us advised that we had close relatives in Perth and we would like to visit them. This seemed to work, and we immediately grabbed a taxi for the Ocean Beach Hotel and spent five hours enjoying their hospitality. I don't think the CO was too happy to see us in a pretty happy state when we returned. After that, it was out to sea, turn right, and head for the South China Sea. This was beginning to feel like the adventure that I had imagined.

The trip aboard HMAS *Sydney* was a tremendous experience. It took me a little while to realise what an intense dislike sailors (matlochs) held for soldiers (pongos). Initially we were treated like intruders on the ship by all the sailors (not the officers, I should point out); however, the program on the ship soon smoothed these ripples, and we simply became highly competitive without angst. A surprising number of activities were available to us, including daily PT with WO2 Bob Fulton as our senior PTI. Our friendship through rugby meant that he had found someone to give his two monster-sized cans of VB (tubes) to each day (Bob didn't drink at all in those days whereas I couldn't believe Australia produced anywhere near enough to satisfy my thirst). Fortunately, we were only allowed two tubes each per day (the equivalent of four cans), although I had the added advantage of Bob's allocation.

We were given weapons lessons, unarmed combat lessons, cultural lessons, and were treated to live shooting at balloons off the back of the ship. The day's activity, however, always ended in a very aggressive game of volleyball with company teams playing navy teams and then the 'no-holds-barred' battalion versus ship's company game. This was played in the main hold, and as we were in tropical waters, it was bloody hot. These were fantastic games with more than a few minor injuries, but the navy was very practised at volleyball and gave us a bit of a towelling. It did give us a good excuse to have a drink with the sailors, and the distrust and loathing that appeared early in our trip soon disappeared.

A transfer of equipment and personnel between the HMAS *Sydney* and a destroyer who came alongside provided interesting viewing for our soldiers who had not witnessed this first-hand previously. Well executed by the navy displaying an amazing array of skills and professionalism. Crossing the equator provided some sort of a necessary diversion for the sailors who set up and dressed up especially for the occasion. The soldiers were supposed to provide 'cannon fodder' for the sailors who were out to ridicule the soldiers under the guise of this 'quaint' custom. The soldiers, however, weren't having any of it, so the high jinks dissipated into a fairly tame ceremony which we participated in and King Neptune presided over. It was a far better result than the gigantic brawl that was simmering, just waiting for an incident to trigger it.

The Sunda Straits acquainted us with the tropics. Dhows (Indonesian boats) started to emerge on the water obviously chasing fish and the shores of the myriad of islands all were adorned with coconut palms. Small sandy beaches existed everywhere. This was clearly a new phase in my life.

If we sailed into Vung Tau harbour thinking that we were the valued new saviours who were to be protected and saluted as we dismounted, we were sadly mistaken. Our ship was surrounded by a multitude of small boats offering their wares of fruit and vegetables, beads, and trinkets. The Third Battalion was off-loading from trucks and couldn't wait to replace us on the ship, and there was noticeably no air cover. The Third Battalion had no sympathy for us carrying hand-made cards that said, 'No one has 364 days and a wakey left in country'. We took this in good faith and wished them a safe journey. They responded by saying that they had been anxiously following our journey by the trail of balloons. As we moved to and loaded onto the waiting trucks, we were handed two magazines of live ammunition, one of which we placed directly on the weapons we carried. We were now in a war zone.

CHAPTER EIGHT

OUR TOUR BEGINS

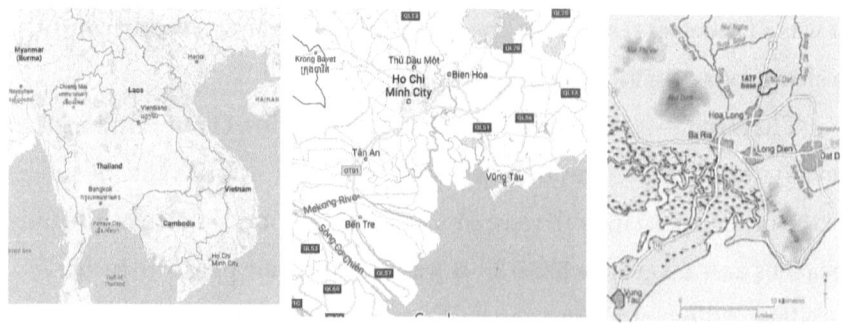

*Maps of Vietnam – l=(L) the country (c) Saigon
to Vung Tau and (R) Task Force Area*

THE TRIP FROM the harbour to Nui Dat was a sobering one. The distance was about twenty-five kilometres, and we knew that the road had been attacked many times by hostile VC. We were escorted by only a couple of APCs, and most of our vehicles did not have centre seating. It was also noticeable that the whole country smelled differently, and as we travelled along at 40 km per hour, we took our first chance to view the make-up of our adopted country. The people were certainly different, buildings were either stone/brick or tin (made up of tin sheeting used to make Coca-Cola cans), drains were uncovered, bridges were vulnerable, and the local ARVN (Army of the Republic of Vietnam) seemed distracted and uninterested. It was difficult trying to take all of this in and was certainly different from what had been envisioned. Every second person we passed wore black pyjamas and conical hats which we had learned were the dress of the local Viet Cong. This was all very different to what I was expecting. How was I going to live up to the promises I had made to many of the mothers, wives, girlfriends, et al., on the dock when I told them, 'I'll bring your boy home safely'? Sort of made me feel like John Wayne, and I think, at the time, I actually believed it.

We travelled on, pretty much in silence, until we reached Nui Dat where we were met by members of the rear detachment of 3RAR who gave us a quick briefing and then showed us to our lines. Members of our advance party were waiting in our lines and had already allocated tents to sections which made the whole matter of 'settling in' a lot easier. Logically, there was not a lot of time to lose as now that we were in location, it was our responsibility for defending the perimeter so equipment had to be adjusted, weapons allocated, ammunition issued, and certainly in my case, I wanted all my soldiers to know every inch of the perimeter and what was outside it. This included knowing what the main threat was, where the wire was and in what condition it was in, knowing if our perimeter was mined, and knowing where the claymores were located. I also wanted to know the state of our defences, e.g., the location of weapon pits, the effectiveness of the main bunker, and the protection offered if the claymores were fired. All this and we hadn't test-fired our weapons.

By the time we got a complete take on all of this, we began to realise we were in the tropics and just how bloody hot it was—and this was the dry season (Vietnamese winter). We were covered in sweat to the extent that we realised all our tropical green clothing had turned black, which would make identifying the Viet Cong just that much harder. During this busy 'first day', the OC called his officers in for a briefing to allow him to allocate his priorities. I saw this as a waste of time and begrudgingly attended to be informed of the program for the next and subsequent days of that week. It was filled with a bit of everything and would not allow me much time for supervising the work effort around my platoon area.

Fortunately, the Australian Army trains its sergeants well, and mine was no exception. Warren Featherby would be in his element getting the place into order, particularly without me being around to distract him or impose my rather definite views on how things should be done. Keep in mind I was a bit unique myself in that as a National Service officer, I had served out my initial obligation to the military of two years of service and had extended a further two years. I had also spent one of those years with the First Battalion RAR (who had done a tour of Vietnam) and another seven months with the School of Infantry, so for a second lieutenant, I was more experienced than most of the other platoon commanders. I had also worked with some very good and experienced junior and senior NCOs who taught me a lot about my job.

When I returned to the lines, I realised that showers had to be organised for the soldiers as they had worked tirelessly in 40-degree heat on their first day and needed to freshen up. We were also getting close to last light, so the evening 'stand-to' would prevent any work being done for at least an hour. Warren had all pickets and rosters arranged, and work on our defensive position was proceeding at a very good rate.

The showers and toilets were rudimentary affairs with a constant fire being needed to heat a forty-four-gallon drum of water for the showers which was continually filled through a hole cut in the top by replacing the amount of water you took out for your shower bucket (you took four gallons out, you put four gallons in and convection kept all the water hot). Everyone showered together, that is, four or five at a time depending on the number of shower buckets. The toilet block was similar, no privileges for rank, a five- or six-seater where you covered your spoil with lime when finished. Every day the battalion hygiene person (commonly nicknamed 'the blowfly') would visit, cover the waste in kerosene or gasoline, and quickly throw in a match. This process was, of course, too tempting for the Australian sense of humour and the number of times additional fuel was put in the pit by impish soldiers just before the blowfly visited was too numerous to count, thus, ensuring the 'blowfly' got an enormous fright when the small burn-off action was replaced by an enormous 'carump' as the fuel exploded. Another favourite trick was to smuggle in a smoke grenade when all the seats were full, pull the pin of the grenade, throw it in, and then jump up and shut the lid of your seat. Logically, soldiers would go everywhere or end up with a big red, yellow, blue, or green butt. It never ceased to provide amusement, and in fairness, whereas myself and the sergeant gave stern warnings about it, we never actually took any action—too funny.

Typical tent for two people in Nui Dat

It was the general feeling that soldiers took at least two weeks to acclimatise to the intense heat and the constant sweating that accompanied all manual tasks. It was policy therefore that with the exception of morning and night clearing patrols (foot patrols which would ensure that the Viet

Cong had not penetrated or damaged any of our defences during the previous night), we would spend the first week attending briefings, the second week doing local patrolling in 'safe' areas, and by the third week, we would be sufficiently acclimatised to attempt fully operational duties.

Bloody hell, I have never attended so many briefings in my life. We had briefings on the local enemy groupings (intelligence), our attitude towards locals, the penalties for shooting local animals (e.g., buffalo), a new simplified means of calling in artillery (fire mission), calling in gunship and tactical air support, calling in aero medical support (CASEVAC), the state of roads, the state of bridges, the lack of water, the peace talks in Paris, the likely targets for TET (Vietnamese New Year), rations to be carried, the beer ration, concerts, standard of camouflage, and so it went on. Sitting in the briefing room in 40-degree heat six or seven hours a day, without air conditioning, made concentration levels very suspect, so how much of it we retained, I am not sure. Officers were also informed that when we were in Nui Dat, the battalion CP (command post) also had to be manned twenty-four hours a day. I finished the week unsure if we actually had time to do everything that had been outlined, although I guessed many of these things would become second nature and many would be done concurrently.

By the second week, we were reminding ourselves that already we had been separated from our families (in my case for six weeks) for almost a month. The OC decided that we would do some training outside the wire (in the allocated safe areas) to get our procedures and timings right and to get any of our new members familiar with how each of our subgroups worked. We combined this with some shooting on the range, and we fired off some claymores to ensure that all claymores in our defensive position were fresh and operative. At the end of the week, we considered ourselves 'ready for action'.

The OC issued orders for a company ambush to be set up in the 'safe area', and we prepared ourselves for a five- or six-kilometre hike ending with a company ambush of three platoons and a company headquarters along a disused track. The whole company went through the process of preparing itself for an operation. Weapons and equipment were checked, rations were packed, and weapons were test-fired—all systems seemed to be in order. We were ready to spend our first night outside the wire. Surprisingly, we felt that the heat was having less effect on us now than when we arrived, so the 'two-week acclimatisation' period seemed to have worked.

At the given time, we stepped through the wire with a strength of about eighty all ranks and headed for our destination. It was getting close to night fall, so we moved fairly well until we were close to our ambush site where the platoon commanders went forward to be allocated their positions within the ambush. When done, the section commanders were also called forward, and all positions were finalised and arcs of fire identified. My platoon was allocated rear and flank protection, so I had no role in the ambush other than to ensure that we didn't get rolled up from a flank nor attacked from behind. All soldiers were placed in position (including sentries), claymores were set up for firing, and then darkness enveloped us all. The OC called (by radio), 'Stand to', and everyone got into their position and laid behind their weapons, and we listened to make sure that no one had followed us nor discovered us on the way into the position. We were unfamiliar with the sounds of night in Vietnam, and as such, everyone was straining to identify every single sound. After thirty minutes, the OC signalled all clear and ordered us to complete the preparation of the site. Immediately, soldiers began to dig their 'shell scrapes' to allow them some protection in case of attack.

In my case, I was keen to ensure that all arcs of fire were identified by night and each soldier knew where every other soldier was located. We also laid communications cord to the sentries so that they could follow that back to the main position if they sighted or heard any enemy activity. By the time I got back to my position, an hour had passed, and all digging had stopped. The OC ordered us to go into night routine, which meant that as we had placed our soldiers in twos, one was to sleep while the other stayed awake. I was the only one who hadn't dug a pit. Silently, I withdrew my shovel, and as quietly as I possibly could, I began digging my shell scrape. Almost immediately, the OC was on the radio asking who was still digging and insisted that he desist. I didn't claim ownership but quietly acknowledged the OC's order and stopped digging. My only protection in the case of any attack was now a four-inch under-developed rubber tree. Well, it shouldn't matter, we were in a 'safe area', and I had the whole company around me.

The night went well until at about 4 a.m. when forty Viet Cong wandered into our ambush site. By any standard, this was a large party to enter a company ambush site, and we salivated at the prospect of a good result on our first night outside the wire. There is good reason that Task Force Headquarters designated these 'safe areas' to new battalions, and we were just about to completely justify their decision.

Firstly, our claymores were fired but fell over and were therefore ineffective because we had not fully appreciated the hardness of the soil and therefore had not planted them deep enough. Secondly, our machine guns fired a couple of rounds and then stopped. Our nervous gunners had not ensured the linkages were straight when rounds were fed in or foreign matter (twigs/leaves) had got into the breech during the approach march, and thirdly, because we were required to tape (wrap a layer of electrical tape around the safety levers on our M26 grenades), our ambush party threw them at the enemy with the tape still on but the pins out (there is more to this story which I will relate a little later on), which meant that they couldn't be detonated unless the tape moved. Now the enemy did not enjoy this position they found themselves in, and because we had been so ineffective, they were able to return fire into our position before they fled. I remain certain to this day that the only person that they saw in that Australian perimeter was me. They fired enough rounds at my tree for me to think that I was the groundsman at a rifle range during a free-range shoot. I was trying to dig my shell scrape with my eyelids. Fortunately, this little interlude lasted only for a short duration (about thirty to forty minutes), but it got all our hearts pumping, and whereas we hadn't caused anything more than a few blood trails, none of our company had been injured or killed. Artillery was called in to cut off possible escape routes, but I doubt we even scared the enemy; they were long gone.

The story, however, didn't conclude there as the OC asked me to get together a clearing patrol to search the killing area (target area of the ambush) for any dead or wounded. I was expecting this and had already warned out Corporal 'Rock Hudson'. What worried me most was not finding any enemy but finding the unexploded grenades, with their pins out, and the safety lever held in position by a meagre piece of electrical tape. By the time we got in position to commence the search, it was close to 5.30 a.m., and it was about 30 degrees Celsius. The OC had advised me that there were still three grenades unaccounted for and we should be very wary of them. In this heat, in the longish grass in the killing ground, the tape was beginning to melt. Our search revealed one thong made from a car tyre and some blood leading off into the jungle. We found two of the grenades and rendered them safe, however, the third grenade avoided detection, and Rock walked over it and was about ten metres past it when it exploded. Rock was hit in the shoulder and went down. We formed a quick perimeter (only had about ten of us) whilst I had a look at him. Luckily for all of us, the strength of the grass had absorbed most of the impact, and he took a piece of shrapnel in the shoulder which bruised him badly but didn't break the skin. It was time to quit this 'safe area'.

Oddly enough, the OC seemed fairly happy with the exercise mainly because our routine for getting in and out of the ambush worked perfectly well, our procedures seemed well timed, and layout and noise levels were extremely good (although we had done a lot of work on these matters before leaving Australia). Logically, we had to do a lot of work on citing of claymores, problems with M60 links, and allowing enough time for coordinators such as the rear defence platoon commander to complete his task and still be able to 'dig in'. We began working on these weaknesses immediately, however, we still had a thousand other tasks to complete before we were ready for battalion-sized operations. This became an extremely busy part of our tour.

Into our third week and mail started to arrive, but so did a warning order that we would be going out on two operations almost immediately. The first was a cordon and search operation of a village thought to be harbouring local Viet Cong and the second was a reconnaissance-in-force mission in the Hat Dich area about twenty kilometres north of the base at Nui Dat. The name of the village to be searched was kept secret for security purposes (An Nhut), although approach routes and detailed maps of the village were issued so that planning in detail could commence. Our battalion had done a lot of work on village search in Australia, so the routines were easy to accommodate.

The battalion left Nui Dat on the afternoon of 11 December 1968 on its first attempt at war (9RAR was the youngest battalion ever to go to war in the history of the Australian Army). Each of the companies moved to lay up positions about 3,000 metres from our cordon position. About 11 p.m., we 'saddled up' and commenced the move to our final position which we occupied by about 2 a.m. It was gratifying not to be able to hear anything from the other companies. Our aim was to provide a perimeter around the village of An Nhut and, at first light, provide a helicopter (manned by intelligence and psychological operations troops) to circle over the village and advise the villagers of what was happening. They were to be told to take one day's rations and move via certain paths to a holding area where they would be interviewed and categorised and eventually allowed to return to their village or their gardens where many of them worked.

This was a simple plan; we had moved in well, and my company was preparing to commence a full search of our allocated areas immediately after the helicopter had completed its task. It was fairly dark as first light was still a couple of hours away. Several of my soldiers including my sergeant advised that their packs (weighing about twenty-five kilos) were moving along the ground. Quickly it was discovered that we were surrounded by huge rats who, smelling the sweat on our packs and the food inside, decided to attack us. All of a sudden, about ten of my soldiers had their entrenching tools out and were counter-attacking the rats, but in doing so, made a hell of noise as they belted every rat they could see—so much for perimeter security. Eventually, the rats withdrew, and we had the night to ourselves again. Again, we were peaceful when all of a sudden a .50-calibre machine gun opened up and we could see the tracer rounds following the path of the road that ran beside the village. Shit, this was supposed to be a simple operation. We were advised by radio that the local ARVN post had decided to fire a burst of fire down the road to make sure any local peasants weren't sneaking out to start work in their fields before the curfew lifted at first light.

Peace again, but not for long; three Viet Cong had heard some of the troops moving into position and decided to escape from the village. Unfortunately, they bumped into the cordon and opened up on them. A brief firefight ensued, but the troops held their positions and the VC moved back into the village. This was quite an amazing scene as all weapons carried a tracer round every fifth round in their magazines so that during night firing, you could keep track of where your rounds were going particularly if you were firing high. As a result, we, who were about

100 metres away, saw the pitch-black sky light up with tracer rounds going in both directions. This was getting scary! Then as quickly as it started, the sound of silence.

Just before first light, we could hear the villagers starting to wake up. Dogs were barking, men were coughing, fires were being lit. We also heard the sound we've had already become familiar with, the sound of a UH-1B Huey helicopter. Right on time, it began to circle the village, and the loudspeaker commenced the briefing in Vietnamese. Time and time again, you heard the same message repeated in the sing-song Vietnamese voice of the translator. It was not well received by the villagers, and many attempted to scarper out the back door, but we had all those gaps covered, and we herded the villagers back to comply with the loudspeaker demands. The armoured vehicles (APCs) moved into position, and we were ordered to commence the search. We had clear, although hand-drawn maps of the village, ensuring that we stuck to certain boundaries to avoid friendly clashes.

We began the search. Now this was tiring work, and we had been up all night—by 10 a.m., it was 40 degrees. We were carrying full packs and only took them off to search inside huts or toilets (revolting, unhygienic pits) which were a renowned hiding place for Viet Cong to hide weapons. The men were getting exhausted, so at noon, I called a halt and we had some lunch (ration coffee and a biscuit), and the men needed water resupply which my sergeant already had under control. We had only completed half our area, and the OC was getting anxious that we were falling behind.

With some reluctance, I got to my feet knowing that I was going to have to crack the whip during the hotter part of the day. Again, we recommenced searching. The afternoon was long and tedious, and a war photographer who had been with us all night decided he needed to find some more action, so he left us, I suspect, to find a cooler place. This was really becoming a test of endurance. However, as soldiers do, we stuck it out, and about four o'clock, I allocated the last couple of houses to be searched. One was clear, but one of my soldiers approached me and advised that there were still villagers in the last hut, and they would not leave. I demanded that he get them out, but he said he had tried, and they wouldn't leave. Against the strong protestations of my sergeant, I stormed into the hut and saw a small group (probably three) people standing in a corner. My section commander Colonel 'Blue' Hammond advised me they wouldn't leave, and he only had one area left to search but it was a suspicious one and wouldn't take too long to search. He advised they should stay until he completed the search. I agreed and turned and left the hut—you guessed it, before I was out the door, a shot was fired, and I heard the word 'contact' shouted. I slid the 'safety' off my weapon and called for a report. The civilian people inside started screaming. My sergeant was yelling for me to take cover. I was calling for a report and then the OC turned up and wanted to know what was going on. I told Warren to brief the OC whilst I found out what had happened.

I stepped back into the hut. Corporal Hammond was trying to get himself under control, and there was a dead VC with an AK47 lying on the ground. He had been hiding behind a bamboo screen. Corporal Hammond covered the screen with his rifle and had a soldier pull the screen away. Crouched behind the screen with the AK47 between his knees was the VC. Corporal Hammond fired one shot from about four feet away and was deadly accurate. I immediately stepped outside and asked the OC to get an interpreter, a policeman, and someone from intelligence. This was done with great alacrity, and we handed the matter over. My men were shattered, but I wanted them to see what we were up against and explain the way Corporal Hammond had handled it, which in my opinion was very professional.

Unfortunately, at this time, more and more people were flooding into our area. We brought the body outside for the relatives to claim, and I advised the OC, First Platoon had done enough for one day. The interesting thing here is the war photographer was the only journalist who knew me and the platoon, so he was able to get the basic details from the headquarters, add some additional details that he had gleaned from his night with us, and lodge an article with the *Sydney Morning Herald* within hours. It was in the next day's edition of which I still hold a copy.

A helicopter slick waiting to unload load troops (UH1Bs)

The next operation was active for 9RAR, but without any noticeable results. We were deployed from the day after our venture into An Nhut (11 December 1968) until Christmas Eve, 24 December 1968. We gained valuable experience in patrolling and searching camps and attacking bunkers systems, but most of them were recently vacated or the enemy chose to withdraw rather than defending any position. We discovered that this was because they were a local provincial battalion (Chau Duc Company) and were low on men and resources.

Our company returned (somewhat unexpectedly) for Christmas Eve and a few days over Christmas. Delta Company was not so lucky; the province chief had asked for a special operation to be carried out around the Rung Sat area which contained fields of mangroves and mosquitoes but contained the waterways which allowed the VC to transport food, personnel, equipment, and supplies unhampered throughout the province. So for the seven days of Christmas, Delta Company patrolled this enormous sewerage-laden bog hole. It was some time before we caught up with members of Delta Company to hear what a dreadful time they had of it. It was a swamp, and it was tidal. Every day was a chore, and every night was a trial. Mosquitoes the size of attack aircraft and tides so high the soldiers had to tie themselves to trees at night to ensure they didn't drown. I don't think we lost anyone to the Rung Sat, and although Delta Company had stories to tell their grandchildren, I think it was an experience they would rather not have had. There were many contacts with the enemy but not to the extent expected.

We moved on to Operation 'Goodwood' on New Year's Day 1969 for an operation that was both intense and long. 'Goodwood' was conducted in a known haven for the local VC, which was north of the task force area in the Hat Dich. 9RAR were deployed by air (9 Squadron RAAF) and, along with the other companies, commenced their patrolling tasks immediately. There was an immediate feel amongst the patrolling troops and myself that this was a 'hot' area. We had done a lot of work with helicopters both in Australia and since arriving 'in country'. It seemed very grandiose travelling into a war in a helicopter. You had a great view sitting up above the earth and feeling as if nothing could touch or hurt you. Looking back, you could see the rest of the company calmly taking in the countryside and probably feeling the same way I did.

The biggest problem travelling on helicopters, however, was the fact that you actually left Nui Dat in a fairly clean condition having probably showered the afternoon before the operation and probably donned a clean set of greens, which stayed with you for the duration. When you hit the landing zone, however, you had to remove your 'giggle' hat because it posed a major threat to the rotors which did not stop when the choppers landed, and as such, the dirt and grass and shit that the blades threw up from the landing zone went right through your hair, up your shirtsleeves, down your collar, and into every available crevice imaginable. Hence the first day of your operation was spent patrolling with leaves and sticks and dirt working its way down in behind your pack and under your webbing—most uncomfortable and most times occasioned a need for a halt about an hour away from the landing zone to allow everyone to take off their webbing and rid themselves of the additional debris. The second biggest problem of travelling with helicopters was that you were never sure who might be waiting for your arrival. However, it was more of a fear than a regular occurrence, but soldiers always breathed a sigh of relief when they reached the safety of the treeline.

Our company was given the task of searching a very long ridgeline with my platoon being allocated the eastern (right-hand) end of it about 1,000 m away from the rest of the company. Early in the morning of our first day, we found clear signs of enemy movement and quickly located a fairly large bunker system which we commenced to search. Surprisingly the system seemed empty although there were small signs of recent, casual use. We had an engineer splinter team with us and asked them if they had enough explosives to do any damage to the system. They just chuckled and said that this was a major system and this was going to require a lot of explosives or CE crystals to neutralise. This was a job for a bigger group of engineers. They advised me that they would report it, and it would be given a priority for demolition.

I had just finished speaking with our engineer team and moved up to our forward gunner (who was standing) and asked him what was up. He was very still and appeared to be listening to a noise he had heard. All of a sudden, a burst of automatic fire opened up and went straight between his legs, penetrating his loose green trousers. He immediately returned fire and a brief firefight erupted. I felt it could get complicated, so I ordered artillery to attempt to cut off any retreat. It was here that it got very complicated. The forward observation officer (FOO) in at company headquarters advised that because of the location of the guns, the ridgeline we were on, and the target on the far side of the ridgeline, the guns would have a low level of elevation to achieve the target. This might be a problem because the ridgeline was quite high, and it had fairly high trees on it, so there was a chance the rounds might clip the tops of the trees and detonate. Now I am in the middle of a firefight while I am having this discussion, so running a bit short of patience. I advised the FOO to fire the guns and I would get my troops into the bunkers as they travelled overhead. The gunners were good, and within seconds, I heard the battery fire and ordered the men into the bunkers which, of course, they were a bit reluctant to do because the bunkers had not yet all been cleared. I could hear the rounds in the air and just screamed out to get in the fucking bunkers. Sure enough, the advice was good; one of the rounds struck a tree right in the middle of our position and detonated. A quick check revealed we were all right, no bad guys in the bunkers either, so I ordered three rounds' fire for effect. After these rounds, I ordered 'check fire' and told the gunners to stand down whilst we finished clearing the bunker system.

At this point, we were feeling fairly pleased that the enemy had decided to withdraw rather than fight for the remainder of the system. However, as I started to plan our next move, the radio came alive advising that Third Platoon was in heavy contact and my platoon should start moving back closer to company headquarters in case we were needed to do an attack. We quickly packed up, loaded on our packs, and started to move at the best pace to company's location back along the ridgeline. We had gone about 400 m and were making good time, the OC was continually haranguing us to get there quickly, when my scout stopped and called me forward. He had detected several trip wires running across our path.

Shit! I called the engineers forward, and they neutralised them for me, but the OC was still haranguing me for not moving fast enough. We slowly moved forward, and there was the mother of all weapons caches containing AK47 Kalashnikovs, ammunition of all types, grenades, etc. I could not leave this here for the enemy that we had contacted to come back and remove. The OC was still yelling on the radio. The platoon commander of the Third Platoon had been hit, and we were needed to extract him. I had a quick chat with the splinter team and asked how long it would take to wrap all their detonating cord around the cache and set a long fuse so that we could get on our way. The OC was threatening my survival if I didn't get there soon. The splinter team advised 'ten minutes' if I provided full protection while they worked. I threw caution to the wind, deployed the platoon, and the engineers got to work. While they worked, I got the lead section to be in position to be ready to sprint the minute the engineers gave the word. In about fifteen minutes (when I was about to be promoted to third lieutenant), the engineers came out absolutely covered in sweat and advised that we had about four minutes and then they would come back and check the damage. Bullshit. I called in my two sections, got the lead section to start jogging, and we took off. Talk about cutting it close, my rear section just cleared the immediate area as the explosion went up. We jogged after the lead section, and I was able to tell the OC that we would arrive soon. Engineers love to see the results of their work; I advised them we would return at a later time and check it out. We never did.

On arrival, the OC tried to admonish me for not following orders, but when he saw that we were saturated with sweat, one gunner had his trousers almost shot off, and the engineers looked heartily satisfied, he just decided to dismiss me and get on with the battle. Second Platoon, in my absence, had arrived and were attacking with Third Platoon providing covering fire. The enemy was in bunkers, and the commander of the

Third Platoon was still isolated, in between, having been shot somewhere in the foot.

My task was to take a group of soldiers and retrieve Adrian Craig. I grabbed a couple of soldiers, spoke to the soldiers providing covering fire, and told them to stop until I got back, and we worked our way forward until we reached Adrian. He was hurting a bit, but with the help of his platoon sergeant Fred Crawford, we got him back to where the CSM and the Company 2IC were preparing a site for evacuation. My platoon then joined the Second Platoon in the attack (with bayonets fixed as the enemy was very well entrenched).

Second Platoon had lost a man in the attack, and I think a couple got wounded. This battle went on for over two hours, and we had already been in a previous attack that morning (and blew up an enemy cache), so we were fairly glad when we reached the edge of the bunker system, just as night was falling. Second Platoon was almost finished their assault and was starting to reorganise and count the cost. Helicopters were starting to arrive to evacuate the dead and wounded and provide water and ammunition resupply. I think from memory the splinter team was taken out also wishing to report their efforts and arrange a major demolition.

In war, respite is sometimes hard to come by. It took some hours to complete the evacuations. Everyone was pretty tired and spiritless having lost a wonderful young man from our company. We still weren't sure where the enemy were; we had pushed them out of the bunker system, but as we saw earlier in the day, this ridgeline was a haven for the enemy, and we would have to search the complete system and then pursue the withdrawing enemy. Through the night, we were advised that we would attack the system, and my platoon would follow up any signs of the fleeing enemy. We were to be accompanied by some tanks from the armoured squadron. This was a relief, but it was pretty tough country for tanks, although they were superb at smashing bunkers. We were up at 4 a.m., and final preparations were made for the arrival of the tanks. We had also withdrawn about 300 m so we could soften up the position with artillery before we assaulted. We managed to complete the assault without event, and the remainder of the company and the tanks went about searching and destroying the bunker system.

My platoon commenced the follow-up of the withdrawing enemy, and it wasn't long before we found newly dug graves which we were obliged to uncover to ensure they weren't just hidden weapons caches. We found a lot of human remains, and though it was difficult to ascertain exactly how many bodies were buried, we assessed it be about eight. The remainder of the enemy group we attacked seemed to have disappeared in thin air. We continued the follow-up for the rest of the day and then went back to our original task of search and clear.

9RAR soldiers returning to Nui Dat from operations

Unfortunately, this wasn't the only major situation we had during Goodwood. One of the other platoons came upon a very fresh track which seemed to be well used. The OC decided we would use this track as our axis and we would patrol, platoon width on either side of it. In the scrub that we were in, this allowed us to cover about forty to fifty metres either side of the track. My platoon was last in the order of march, and we were searching to the southern side of the track. It also meant that we were about 250 metres from the lead platoon. The radio crackled, and I was advised that the lead scout of the lead platoon had sighted an enemy; the lead platoon was deploying to the northern side of the track and the enemy would be engaged. We were told to close up to the company as quickly as possible.

Almost simultaneously, word came in from my flank section that they had found signs of fresh digging and were investigating. I allowed a few minutes for them to confirm or negate the fact that we had uncovered another bunker system. Soldiers don't like to be hurried when they are exploring the possibility of a bunker system. However, life was never meant to be fair, and firing started from the platoon at point.

Apparently, as the platoon assembled to do an assault from the north, another enemy group had come (quite coincidently) up behind them, saw them about to attack, and jumped them. Logically, at this point, I wasn't able to follow what was happening up front as my flanking section had confirmed fresh digging (without finding bunkers) and the OC was literally yelling for me to close up and querying why I had not already done so.

I decided to take another risk with my career and made my platoon leap-frog forward, which was very demanding and, of course, much slower than running forward as demanded of me by the OC. I was taking no risk with being rolled up from my right flank.

We caught up with Coy HQ, and as expected, I was suitably berated, however, my assessment was that the company had only sighted one sentry and they had two platoons of soldiers, so I didn't think they were in danger of being overrun. Sadly, the company had lost another soldier during this assault, so morale immediately dropped down a level. The forward observer was adjusting artillery in the hope of cutting off the retreat of the enemy group who had attacked the Second Platoon, and the CSM was calling for CASEVAC to evacuate our casualties. Light was fading fast, and helicopters were arriving with water and some items of resupply.

I approached the OC and briefed him very clearly about why we were late and strongly advised that we move from that location and return the next day to check out the fresh diggings which were too important to be ignored. The OC reasoned that it was now well after dark and any movement might be at our peril. He called the three platoon commanders in and advised that we were to coordinate the perimeter, put our claymores out, and be ready to send out clearing patrols of section strength. I reinforced the fact that we had found fresh diggings and that the platoon facing that location should be aware. I assessed that they would have been about 150 m from the existing perimeter. Claymores were positioned and clearing patrols were sent out. It was very dark, so for clearing patrols to maintain contact with the perimeter, they could only extend out about thirty metres.

Evacuation and resupply had finished at this time, although we were very short of water. Six litres a day did not last more than that, and there were no creeks or streams in our area. The additional water provided by the resupply would have to last us through the next day. As usual, we were up early, and the order went out for clearing patrols. I was hoping that the Second Platoon would find some evidence of a bunker system that would allow me to convince the OC that we should at least clear that area. He was open to this suggestion; I just had to get our morning routine out of the way, and I would ask if we could do a sweep through the area on our way to our next RV.

The clearing patrols returned—Second Platoon having cleared out to about 100 metres without incident. We posted sentries and cleaned our weapons, shaved, breakfasted (coffee and a biscuit), and commenced to withdraw our claymores. Warren, my sergeant, returned from speaking to John Cock, the platoon sergeant from the Second Platoon; they were good mates, and John was quite close to us filling in a waste pit at the back of the Second Platoon position. I said to Warren that I thought the Second Platoon party that was taking in their claymores was making a lot of noise. They were laughing and talking and yet were seventy-five metres from our position. We were higher on the terrain than they were, so obviously the noise carried fairly well, but I was conscious of the signs we had seen the day before

I told Warren to get all of our soldiers to 'get down' in their positions— that is, I wanted them at ground level. Almost on queue an RPG came hurtling through the undergrowth and took out John Cock (five metres from where we were situated) and withering fire (AK and machine gun) swept our position. All of this attention came from about 150 m out in the direction of the diggings we had found the day before. My position was almost devoid of living growth, all the bushes in our area had been cut off just above ground level. My intuition had saved a number of lives, quite possibly my own although the claymore party from Second Platoon, along with the platoon sergeant paid a heavy price with three soldiers being wounded and John Cock killed.

Again, we needed to arrange casualty evacuation, and we needed to ensure that we would not be attacked again from the enemy position. I was tasked to provide a protection party for the CSM who would arrange the evacuation. The Second Platoon needed to reorganise and secure their perimeter, and the Third Platoon was tasked to provide a covering force close in to what we expected was a bunker system but were told not to get sucked into a battle we were not prepared for at this time.

Already it was getting hot, and the additional activity was taking its toll. Morale was really starting to sag. Third Platoon reported that there was no activity around the system, and it was their opinion, without a full search of the system, that the enemy had fired and fled. The OC called me in and advised me that we were the only platoon that was intact, and he was going to quit the area and we were to lead them out. We were to head for an area that the OC hoped contained water where we could regroup, refresh, and re-establish ourselves as a company in light of the tragic events of the past two days. I briefed my corporals, and off we went hoping that we wouldn't run into another live bunker system in the short term. Our fortune held except that there was no water in the creek line that we targeted, so we had to search for a suitable LZ and arrange a water drop. The CSM did this efficiently, as always, and we were able to pursue our mission.

Within the space of a couple of days, A Coy was given two days; rest and refit back at Nui Dat and were given orders for the next operation. Little rest for the wicked.

Our next operation was 'Federal', which started out with some promise but ended up as a tough slog with few results. The first day provided a lot of excitement for me personally and almost the end of a promising tour. We were inserted on a large fire trail. Fire trails were paths ploughed by the Americans, 100 metres across, accomplished by huge machinery called Roman ploughs, which were massive bulldozers with blades of commensurate size capable of felling a 200-foot-high tree. Fire trails were designed to allow spotter planes to identify where enemy groups were crossing so that ambushes could be accurately laid, and if the enemy groups were caught crossing (caught in the open), they could be annihilated by armed helicopters, planes, or artillery or a combination of all three.

Our task was to lay a company ambush along a promising piece of fire trail that could be seen extending for miles. Our company was dropped by APCs, and we were spread along about 500 m of the trail. I can tell you that travelling by APCs beats the hell out of walking, but they also provide difficulties. First of all, they are subject to mines, so roads are avoided where possible unless they have local traffic on them or clearances are given by 'road runner' vehicular patrols which temporarily cleared the roads for mines by travelling over them. Travelling in the back of APCs, though protected from light attack, was still vulnerable and, therefore, always made the troops who were 'down in the well' nervous.

Travelling across country was generally rough, and there were a lot of hard, sharp edges in the back of an APC, so 'are we there yet?' was a common cry. Finally, the most common and most painful was the large green ants who built their accommodation in the leaves of overhanging branches of seemingly every type of tree that existed wherever we were going. Mainly, it was the APC crew commanders who put their arms up to pass off a branch who found that they were, in fact, shaking a nest full of ants all over their upper body. As a consequence, ants ran everywhere including down the neck openings of their tank suits or up the sleeves. The infantry commander (whatever rank) standing in the well also got the cast-offs as well as anyone else who was standing at that time. These ants were brutal, they were angry, and they were vengeful, and many a tank commander was seen to throw off his helmet and start discarding his clothing without regard for his or anyone else's personal safety.

This simple event could hold up any level of progress for up to twenty minutes as all clothing was searched for the last remaining remnants of the colony which felt rewarded for having its home upset. Fortunately, I don't recall bumping any enemy during these short distractions.

When we deployed my platoon was right flank, but I also saw that a secondary fire trail snaked away to my right about 300 metres on my flank. This left me very exposed on the right flank, so before I positioned my men fully, it was important that I ventured out and had a look at what was there. I briefed my platoon sergeant who was livid that I was going out without a radio and with only one other soldier. I provided a couple of instructions that were to happen if shots rang out. I warned the sentries that we were going out and they were not to shoot at anything until we came back in.

I chose 'Milo' as the soldier to accompany me as he was my batman and I thought probably the most available whilst we were preparing a strong ambush position. We got out about 150 metres and came across a pile of logs that had been positioned there by the Rome ploughs when the fire trail was cut. I asked Milo to climb up the logs and tell me what he could see. Milo climbed up slowly but almost tumbled back down to the ground. He was a bad shade of white. I asked him, what was the problem? He indicated that there were enemy on the other side of the logs and we should return to the platoon.

I ordered him to cover me and proceeded to climb up the pile of logs. Sure enough, sitting on the other side, on a stump, was an enemy soldier, with a rifle, facing away from us. He was obviously a sentry, and I was left in a quandary. The area that he was covering was the fire trail that we were ambushing. If I knocked him over, I might alert whoever he was providing sentry for and give away the advantage we currently held by the enemy obviously not knowing we were present. On the other hand, if I let him survive and the enemy came from a different direction, I could get rolled up from my right flank. Fortunately, this decision was made for me when a second sentry appeared on foot and, I thought, stared right at me. I immediately realised I was in serious trouble. I thought I had apoplexy, slid down the pile of wood, collected Milo, and headed for the nearest cover. I pushed Milo to the ground and told him where to watch. He still couldn't speak; he was absolutely petrified from his experience thus far. After generating no reaction from the sentries, I decided we hadn't been spotted, so we headed back towards the platoon location.

After reporting my sightings to the OC, I reflected on my decision to return to the sanctity of the platoon location rather than starting a firefight that I might not have been able to finish particularly with Milo showing his reluctance to win the war. It was the right decision. I, at least, knew what the terrain was like outside our position and also knew that I had to protect the exposed flank, so I set my ambush position accordingly. We had a pile of compacted earth on the right of our position, so I decided to use that as a machine gun position to give us some height. The logs in the mound also provided a modicum of protection for the gun from that right flank. Our main killing group I burrowed under a large clump of bamboo which certainly gave them cover from view and allowed them the ever-important advantage of surprise. Darkness had begun to fall but our position was almost ready, so we settled into night routine.

During the night, one of my section commanders reported some movement from our right flank, and he felt that our position was being re-conned for a possible attack. I ordered him to stay calm and not be spooked by the fact that we knew the enemy was in the area. I arranged for some random 'light' flares to be fired by our artillery battery without making it seem that we were in an ambush in that location. There were small amounts of movement throughout the night, but nothing eventuated, so we settled down waiting for the new day. I sent a section out at first light to both the area where I had been previously and to the area where movements had been detected, but there were no signs of the enemy anywhere. We finished preparing our ambush position and settled into the long and tedious task of waiting.

Late in the afternoon, I was actively checking out my position, ensuring arcs of fire were satisfactory, and generally talking to the soldiers when the gun from the second section opened up and the word 'contact' was called. The section commander advised me that several NVA soldiers had cautiously approached the fire trail and commenced to cross it. The gun had opened up, and one of the enemy soldiers was seen to be lying dead on the trail. The others had gone to ground amongst the undergrowth, and we could not determine if any others had been hit. We had also only taken a couple of bursts of return fire.

I advised the OC and called in some artillery into the locations where I thought any backup from the enemy might come from. Cautiously, we waited until the artillery had completed the fire missions we ordered, then I sent out a patrol to check the dead soldier and see if we had been more successful. The patrol returned, advised that we only had the one enemy soldier killed, however, we must have 'scared them' a bit because there were quite a few blood trails, but heading into the late afternoon, it was not a good time to follow them up. We searched the dead soldier, removed some photos and personal letters from him, and buried him as humanely as we could within our perimeter. All information was sent to our headquarters who had it flown to Task Force Headquarters.

The helicopter, however, also delivered mail which was the first time in three days we had been in the ambush situation. There was a telegram for me; it said simply (coded), 'Daughter born 3/2/69 – both well Love Carole'. This was outstanding news, and all I wanted to do was tell everyone, however, by the time I got this, it was 4 February 1969; we were in ambush, and all I had to celebrate with was sterilised water. As it turned out, Carole was quite disheartened by the fact that she had not heard back from me, but I did not have the means to do anything but attempted to send a reply of a coded message, which probably looked something like 'bbg ccl ttok tmno jjhj klpp bbgq'—not exactly expressing my true feelings.

Quite logically, we all spent a nervous night expecting that the soldiers were scouts for a major force following up. Every sound was magnified by our own imagination, and every report suggested that we were being surrounded. During the night, one of the other platoons opened up with machine-gun fire and we all stood to. My sentries said they had thought they saw some movement, but it was very slow and deliberate, and they could not determine if they were enemy soldiers or shadows. I called for artillery flares to light up the area to our front to see if any movement was discernible. Nothing was seen. The next day, the OC decided that we had shown our hand and had not attracted any attention, so he sent out a final patrol, and we moved on to continue our mission.

Vietnam provided an enormous array of adventures, most of which were totally unexpected; some were quite horrific, and some were quite remarkable. The country had a wide variety of vegetations from wonderful four-hundred-year-old trees housed within primary jungle which provided shade, cover, and protection from observation from greater than ten metres away. Other areas were almost endless paddy fields, some of which were in great condition and were being worked by local farmers, and some were uncared for and unkempt probably because of the mines placed indiscriminately around the fields or because the young men had been 'black birded' to join the local Viet Cong network primarily as a labour force.

These open areas were merciless as they were open to the sunlight and, of course, to observation and ambush, so Australians avoided crossing these areas whenever possible. The other major area was bamboo, and Vietnam was full of it. It was a strong, stringy bamboo that stood about fifteen feet tall and was like a matted wall. To traverse it meant setting a bearing and picking your way through the low entrances between the clumps which meant being bent over to get under the matted branches for hours at a time. I was six feet four inches (193 centimetres) tall at this time in my life, I carried my ammunition and my water on my belt and the rest of my survival equipment on my back—most soldiers did the same. Being doubled over with this excessive weight was agonising both on my quadriceps which took all the weight from my belt and my back which, of course, wore the weight from my pack. Bamboo was just plain hard work, and logically being short in stature, it copped the heat, and being matted, it held the heat so people got testy travelling through bamboo as it was slow going, painful, and you couldn't follow a set bearing because your path was dictated by the gaps in the bamboo.

The company was moving into another area, and to get there, we had to traverse an enormous field of bamboo. After travelling for about 1,000 metres, it was necessary for me to stop the patrol and check my map for any sign that would confirm an exact location. To do this, and as standard practice, I would sink down on my knees, place my rifle against my knee, withdraw the map from inside my shirt, and try to plot our position against the compass bearing we were roughly following. On this occasion, I called my section commanders in and asked their opinions for a map reference. They varied greatly to my own. This was not unusual in bamboo, but eventually, we would have to all agree.

We continued on our path and stopped again after another 1,000 metres. I called for the section commanders and got down on my knees; I started to withdraw my map when immediately in front of me I heard yelling and saw many of the men moving (with great speed). In an instant, I saw this huge boar charging at me head down and baring its enormous tusks. I knew that I was finished if it kept on that path. The only thing I could think of to do, in the time life afforded me, was to take my rifle and plant it immediately in front of me in the hope that this may take some of the 'sting' out of his charge and perhaps (?) stop his tusks from tearing me apart. All of this had taken about twenty seconds, and I was terrified. I could not believe anything could look so fearsome up so close. All of a sudden, the boar turned at 90 degrees at full speed and disappeared into the bamboo. This was worse than any encounter I had had with the enemy thus far. For a few moments, there was total silence and then a few nervous laughs, and then everyone was almost disappointed that we didn't have pork on the menu for lunch. I got to my feet, pretended that it was a regular event, and told the patrol to continue along the same bearing. This was a hair-raising experience that I certainly hadn't expected. It also tested the strength of my heart.

Later that same afternoon, we were still in bamboo, and I was still concerned about our exact location (location was always critical when you had to call in artillery), but we pursued the same course of action as we had during the morning. At one of our stops, I called in the section commanders, and because of the heat and the bamboo, they were a little slower getting to me. I had an uneasy feeling that we were being watched. I slowly turned and looked over my right shoulder, and just one clump of bamboo away was this magnificent tiger slowly walking parallel to the way we were going. He seemed to be struggling a lot less than we were. The marvellous thing about the tiger was that he blended in perfectly with the bamboo and shadows and was very difficult to see. This was one of the most worthwhile sights on my trip so far. I mentioned to the section commanders that he was present so there should be no sudden movements and no shooting unless he attacked. They later told me that only about three people could actually see him although he followed us for about half an hour and then just faded off into the distance. A memorable, in fact, unforgettable experience.

We stayed in the bamboo for the rest of the day getting close to the perimeter of it by late in the afternoon. The OC called for platoon commanders and the artillery FO and asked us for a location. No one could agree where we were, but the FO was most certain and offered to call in a couple of targets for the night, and we were able to shoot back bearings from the fall of shot and establish our exact location. We weren't too far out, but when we were patrolling, we used to calculate distance by equating 120–130 paces to 100 metres in primary jungle. In bamboo, it turned out that we needed about 150 paces per 100 metres for closer accuracy.

We redeployed from that area of operations (AO Wondai) to AO Arunda which was northward of our current location to provide a defensive position and patrol base to prevent enemy incursion into the US Air Force Base at Bien Hoa and the Logistics Base at Long Binh during the TET Offensive. The 1968 TET Offensive had provided a massive push by the NVA to gain domination in the south, and huge battles were fought out everywhere. 3RAR had fought one of these battles at Baria (which is now the province capital and is located just south of Nui Dat).

We were very apprehensive about our location as unlike the jungle environment of the Hat Dich, this area was open paddy and grassland with very little cover and only copses of trees for sanctuary. Our major defensive position, however, was on a fairly prominent hill which allowed us to see all the rockets and mortar fire evident every night around the US positions, which were performing much the same role as we were. We spent a fair bit of time preparing our defensive position on the hill and the ground was hard and the sun was hot. Bloody hell, this was hard work.

I was counting the blisters on my hands when the OC contacted me and advised that I was to take a patrol out about 1,000 metres and set up a half-platoon ambush. This was just what we needed, an all-nighter after digging in the sun most of the day. What was more, the OC advised that we were to prevent a suspected regiment of VC/NVA from advancing down a fairly wide road right in the middle of our ambush zone. I chuckled ironically as I rounded up twelve of the platoon and told them that we were going to write history as we executed a linear ambush with twelve men facing a regiment of about four hundred enemy. This was stuff that the Spartans would have loved. What was probably worse was that the area between our defensive position and the ambush site was almost bare-assed with only a couple of small copses of trees and a local village evident. I decided that we wouldn't leave until just before last night, and we would 'lay up' in one of the copses and move into the final position in the dark.

All was going well. We had reached the furthest copse (which also housed a large pile of alluvial rocks), and because the village was close by, I wasn't going to be seen moving until dark in case someone correctly assessed what direction we were headed. We were having our final sip of tea and smoking the last draw of our cigarette, I stood up to tell the men to 'saddle up' when all hell broke loose. A huge volume of fire was pumped into our location; fortunately, the men were mostly on the ground and the rocks were between us and the village. I was wounded along the side of the face but didn't realise it until later when I felt a stinging sensation on my cheek as the sweat ran down from my forehead. I advised the OC that I thought we were being attacked from the village and asked permission to return fire. No! No! No! Again, we took fire from the village. My men were getting a bit pissed about this. 'Withdraw and complete your mission!' were my instructions, and the men were starting to give me some stick over the blood on my cheek which they couldn't really see but saw the medic giving it a bit of a wipe.

To the untrained, it would seem a simple task to move a couple of hundred metres in the dark, but when you are carrying full ammunition, rations, and water and the ground has bunds and holes and rocks, the task takes on a much more difficult weight. I wasn't looking forward to carrying someone out with a broken leg. I quickly planned another route to our ambush location, and we worked our way into position and settled in for the night. I was also right in thinking that it was going to be a hard task to keep the men awake. They were exhausted, and the threat of four hundred bad guys bearing down on us wasn't enough incentive to fight the pull of dehydration and fatigue.

I spent the night trying to provide at least a basic modicum of alertness. At 5 a.m. I decided that TET 1969 was a fizzer and moved the guys out, taking a slightly longer route back to the defensive position rather than venture near the village. I waited about 200 m outside the defensive perimeter until after first light and linked up with the clearing patrol so that we weren't shot up by our own company entering the perimeter. I looked at our guys who were really sleep deprived, were filthy from digging the defensive position, and it was just starting to get hot. I thought, God, I hope we don't get attacked now.

I threw off my pack and headed up to Coy HQ looking for an explanation as to why we had been shot at. Apparently, the OC had taken a party down to the village at first light and was advised that the local militia had that day (yesterday) received a new shipment of M16s and had decided to 'test-fire' them into the copse. I have always believed that there is no cure for 'stupid'. We could have lost a couple of men, including myself, had we been one minute ahead of time. These stupid bastards knew we were in the area but still reckoned they had the right to shoot their weapons in any direction they chose. Chapter closed, somehow we survived.

The whole TET offensive was much more contained than in 1968, and from our point of, view it didn't really get off the ground although some of the US ground forces had some testing times. We moved into other areas of operations during Operation Federal, but it was a fairly steady, taxing time where we patrolled for days on end without any sign of the enemy. I think my platoon only had one or two more contacts during the operation, although there was one incident which we were only able to laugh about after it was over. My platoon had contact with one enemy soldier, and the forward section was getting control of that, and I decided to move another section up close to them but on their left flank just in case any more enemy revealed themselves.

I called the section forward and heard a *pthunk*, which was the sound of a 40-mm grenade launcher being fired just behind me. I immediately hit the ground, but nothing happened, including the grenade not exploding. I looked around and two soldiers were standing very still and I shook my head silently asking 'What happened?' The soldier with the 40-mm grenade launcher was stock-still with a frozen look about him and then started jabbering (natural under these circumstances). He advised me that his section commander ordered him to get the grenade launcher ready for firing (loaded). He did this, but a vine had snagged the trigger, and the soldier's forward movement caused the weapon to fire. The launcher fires a 40 mm grenade which rotates in the air to arm itself but takes about fifteen metres to do this. The soldier wasn't aiming it, so it flew off directly forward right into the backpack of the soldier in front and lodged there. The other soldier, frozen solid, was standing with a fired, live grenade lodged in his pack which was, of course, on his back. The only question was did the grenade go far enough to arm itself. This was more of a dilemma than may have seemed because I still had my forward section trying to secure an enemy soldier who was firing at them and may have some friends close by.

Needless to say, the OC was somewhere behind us asking what was the hold-up. We cautiously removed the pack from the soldier, gently guided it onto the ground, and then went about removing the grenade. We had dug a pit beside the pack (quickly), rolled the pack over using a toggle rope and some limited cover which freed the grenade, and landed it in the pit. I then got my signaller to arrange for one of the follow-up platoons to detonate it whilst I went forward to find out what was happening. As it turned out, the enemy soldier had been wounded and fled, and the forward section followed the blood trail for a while but then returned to our position. Now we could actually laugh; after all, the whole event could have ended up as a very bloody disaster.

We redeployed from Operation Federal on 2 April, having been out on operations almost continually since 17 February. Operation Overland was to have some grave consequences for A Company and my platoon in particular. Immediately Ninth Battalion moved into AO Goulburn, all companies advised of enemy activity. Within a couple of days, the Second Platoon had a sentry group attacked, and we lost another one of our soldiers with Cres Fackender being wounded. B, C, and D companies were all involved in various actions with the enemy. My platoon had run into a group of enemy, but they were travelling away from us, and we were unable to manoeuvre them into a battle. They moved off like a fleeting group of phantoms.

The next day, however, almost with precise execution my platoon walked into a well-concealed bunker system and we were caught. The intense fire stopped us cold, and two of my soldiers, Pte Lou Hyland and Pte Trevor Black, were wounded, Black severely. Blackie was well forward, and we had to get him out. Colin 'Blue' Hammond was acting platoon sergeant at the time, and I immediately dispatched him back to his section to assist them in fighting through the bunker system. The company medic, Cpl Peter Snell, came forward, and I sent him forward with a warning that he would be very exposed, so stay close to the earth.

Blue requested that he fire M72s (light rockets) into the bunkers. I agreed immediately and saw him preparing to fire one of them. M72s have a BBDA (Back Blast Danger Area), so I casually looked to make sure no one was behind him. Bugger me if the OC hadn't come forward for a look and to get first-hand knowledge of the battle. I screamed out for Blue not to fire and at the same time begged the OC to move back and let us get control of the battle. The OC was miffed but understood and moved back out of sight. I simply told him that I had nothing further to tell him. He must have been satisfied as himself, Corporal Hammond, and the medic Corporal Snell, and Private Arthur all got bravery awards from the action. Corporal Snell was magnificent during this action and took great personal risks to rescue and resuscitate Trevor Black. He was ably assisted by Barry Arthur (a stretcher bearer) who, together with Peter Snell, got Trevor out of the position for evacuation.

This battle lasted for several hours, and we were fast running out of ammunition. I had no platoon sergeant (evacuated with suspected malaria—a hangover from his time in Malaysia), so I got caught up getting sections to redistribute. I also called for Third Platoon who were not involved to send forward their ammo. After about twenty minutes, I repeated my request, and an anxious Cpl 'Grub' McGrath came up on the radio advising that he and a party were bringing it forward and walked right into another section of the bunker system and ended up in a firefight which they had to win to get me the extra ammunition I needed. I fired a burst of rounds into a tree to give Grub a heading, and he acknowledged and located my position without further distraction.

It was about this time that the medic Peter Snell and Barry Arthur moved through my position carrying Blackie on a makeshift stretcher. Blackie did not look good and, in fact, died aboard the helicopter on the way to hospital. Pte Barry Arthur was also awarded an MID for this action. It was late afternoon by the time we had captured the first line of bunkers, and because all three platoons had been involved with the enemy that day, we were short of ammunition and, I think, water.

The CSM Bruce Sutherland had busily been arranging medical evacuations, and the Company 2IC Dave Presgrave had been arranging a first line (full battle entitlement) of ammunition so that we could advance the next day. This posed a problem as first line provided a whole lot of stuff we didn't need, including two extra grenades per man, weapon cleaning materials, additional claymore mines (none used), etc., which meant that anything we couldn't carry, we had to destroy or at least burn. This took a lot of time, and we still had a bunker system to clear. The OC decided that we would withdraw from the bunker system, resupply, and reorganise, call in artillery and an airstrike, and assault the system in the morning. This we did, thus, causing a huge explosion when we blew up the ammunition that we could not carry.

I particularly remember the night before the assault as we had been informed that Blackie hadn't made it, and like Second Platoon the day before, a huge pall came over the platoon. Blackie's father was a Rat of Tobruk and had taken part in the Battle of El Alamein. Blackie himself was dux of his school at Bowen in Queensland and a rugby champion and gifted athlete. He was well accepted within the platoon and soldiered as if he was born to it. Another wonderful young man lost.

The forward observation officer and the OC spent the night preparing the position for the assault. Gunships had been called in to assist our withdrawal, but they had exhausted their ammunition just as last light was falling. However, the FO kept the artillery firing onto selected targets throughout the night and an airstrike was put in place.

Airstrikes are not immediate, in fact, they can be drawn-out events, albeit extremely reassuring. When the spotter plane arrives, he will demand that you throw smoke to identify the extremities of your position and your forward line of troops so that friendly casualties are avoided. This normally takes a while particularly if the spotter is not happy that you are far enough away from the strike zone, so a bit of jockeying normally takes place. The assault aircraft will then do a pass and drop a couple of bombs and then wait for an assessment, generally done by the spotter. Adjustments sometimes have to be made, and the aircraft comes in for the second run. Sometimes a third if they have the ammunition but strike aircraft don't like to land with bombs still attached (for fairly logical reasons), so even if a direct strike does occur, there is still a delay whilst the aircraft use the rest of their munitions. This is very powerful stuff, and even from 600 metres away, the impact is felt as the bombs detonate. Ground troops then follow in behind, however, you have the extra ground to cover to get back into the bunker system, but you do it quickly as this is time for the enemy to re-occupy the bunkers and provide a reception.

Fortunately, this didn't occur on this occasion; we found the system to be empty with the enemy having withdrawn again. Clearing the bunkers for booby traps and any remaining wounded or dead is slow, demanding work, and it took some hours before we were re-organised and ready to recommence patrolling. This we did with little contact other than locating caches of food and ammunition until we were advised that we would redeploy into another part of the province.

Brian (right) links up with Coy HQ and speaks to OC Maj Warwick Smith

We patrolled all through 'Operation Overlander', and whereas the rest of the battalion was kept active by small contacts, A Company was kept busy with the locating of several major caches containing large quantities of clothing along with significant quantities of ammunition and weapons. My platoon was almost caught out in one incident, however, where the enemy approached my ambush position from an unexpected direction late in the afternoon. A firefight ensued, and dark was quickly closing in. The enemy were well armed and seemingly happy to be engaged. I couldn't afford to get caught in an arm wrestle in the dark, so I closed ranks, worked out an exit strategy, and moved out of the area looking for a suitable night harbour and hoping that we hadn't been followed up. Fortunately, the night was uneventful. I patrolled back over the area where we were engaged and found signs of the battle, some vacated thongs, and one dead enemy. The remainder had departed.

After about five fairly unproductive days, the battalion commander (perhaps prompted by intelligence or brigade direction) decided it was time to redeploy to a completely new area with the operation being called 'Surfside'.

The new area of operations was quite a change from where we had operated previously. This area was south-east of Nui Dat rather than north where we had spent most of our time to date. The area was vastly different in that there was little primary jungle, most of the area was a secondary forest, paddy fields, swamps, and sand dunes. None of the vegetation was above thirty feet tall, although it was tall enough to provide cover for Viet Cong movement and shade for our operations. These more open spaces did allow us to work a little further apart, and my initial deployment was 1,000 m from the rest of the company.

One of the platoons in Delta Company was attacked shortly after deploying and suffered seven wounded. I think this was also the first chance our company got to work with the tanks, although none were allocated to my platoon. Delta Company also had a surprise visit within the first couple of days. They sighted several enemy and were just about to open fire when a European, wearing Australian clothes and a bush hat, appeared with the enemy. He was also wearing black pearl-handled .45-calibre pistols. Members of Delta Company were so surprised that they opened fire sporadically and the enemy group disappeared. Delta Company reported the incident and was advised that allegedly a Russian advisor was working with the local Viet Cong although his presence wasn't expected in the area and the wearing of Australian uniform was unprecedented. Vietnam held many surprises.

'Surfside' was also the first time that 9RAR had been placed under the additional stress of facing mines. Before our arrival, the Task Force had decided to lay a barrier minefield from the Horseshoe (although south of the Task Force Area, it was permanently occupied by members of our Charlie Company and some ARVN soldiers) to the coast, filling it with M16 (US) mines and patrolling it using local South Vietnamese (ARVN) troops. The purpose of the minefield was to prevent the Viet Cong from transiting the areas known as the Long and Light Greens and hopefully reduce their food supply from the locals, most of whom worked the rice paddies.

The minefield was about 11 kilometres in length, and Australian engineers laid approximately 20,000 M16 'Jumping Jack' mines. The local villagers hated the presence of the Task Force and, in particular, the minefield. The theory behind any minefield is that it has to be observed and patrolled. The barrier minefield in Vietnam was initially patrolled by Australian and ARVN troops, but the demand for troops to be tied up patrolling an 11 kilometre minefield twenty-four hours a day was too great for the Task Force infantry battalions, so the task was handed over to the local force militia.

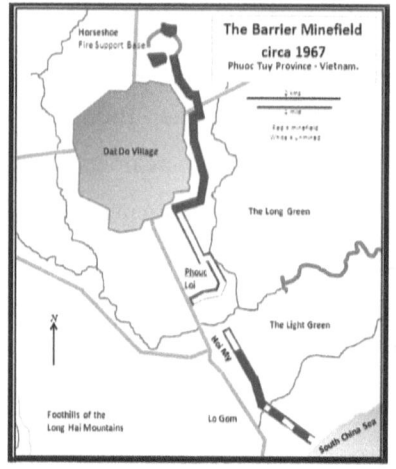

(L) Location of the Barrier Minefield south of Nui Dat;
(R) M16 Mine with anti-lift device attached

Local troops work well when they are supervised and commanded by a stronger force, but as soon as the Australians moved on to other missions, the theory of observation and control reduced enormously. The ARVN troops became lazy and negligent and did not wish to patrol at night; the consequence being the local Viet Cong gathered the local villagers and commenced learning how to lift the mines from the minefield for use against the allied forces. Many were lost, but quickly they learned when they could enter the minefield (due to lack of patrols) and how to place a safety pin in the device to prevent the mine being detonated and then 'lift' it for their own use.

The engineers had placed anti-lift devices under about half the mines to provide a fear factor and prevent the mines being lifted. Again it took many lives, but eventually, the local enemy work parties learnt how to maintain the pressure on the plate until two safety pins had rendered the mine safe. Again they were lifted for use against the allied forces which, of course, encompassed locals working their fields, etc.

Our sojourn into this area was accompanied by members of two cavalry regiment who were much more able to assist with patrolling in the more open, semi-tropical vegetation. Sand dunes, however, caused a fair bit of channelling when patrolling close to the coastline, so the cavalry vehicles were very susceptible to losing tracks to mines which were planted principally to kill or maim infantry foot soldiers on the obvious routes. Fortunately, these seldom caused major injuries to the cavalry or to the occupants of their M114 vehicles (although some back injuries), but once a track was blown off by a mine, the area had to be cleared around the vehicle (normally by engineers or pioneers prodding the sand with bayonets) large enough for the cavalry to repair or replace their tracks. It also meant that infantry had to be deployed to provide protection for the team that worked on the replacement as they were very vulnerable to sniper or small-arms fire.

I recall on one occasion the OC advised that we could take an APC and (ten soldiers at a time) let them have a swim. The first group loaded up travelled 200 m, ran over a mine, deployed, repaired the track, loaded, drove another 200 m drove over another mine. An hour had gone and they hadn't got to the beach, so they decided it wasn't worth it and returned to the patrol base. Going to the beach was not quite like it is in Australia. When we did finally make it, we positioned the APC with twin .30-calibre machine guns facing the hinterland. Half of the remaining troops would then strip off (except for their hat and their boots) and take up position with weapons facing the sand dunes. The other half would go for a swim. After half an hour, we would change over. Despite the water of the South China Sea being about 30 degrees Celsius, the feeling of being in saltwater was euphoric. Six months of fatigue seemed to drain from our bodies. It was worth all the effort to get there.

Although there was some activity throughout the battalion area, A Company continued to patrol but found very little of interest with the exception of a couple of caches.

I was also notified that I was going on R&R back to Australia on 4 May.

R&R for a single man meant getting out of the theatre of war, getting drunk, getting laid, getting drunk, getting laid, and perhaps having a sauna in Hong Kong or Thailand somewhere. R&R for a married man was a little more sombre, and getting drunk probably didn't even enter the equation. In my case, I hadn't seen Carole for about seven months, and I had a daughter who was 10 weeks old who I had never laid eyes on. I really did not know what to think other than it would be great to see them all.

The system was very supportive. When we landed (I think about 9 p.m.), we were quickly processed, and I could see Carole standing at the front of all the waiting wives/parents/friends, et al. I started to make a beeline for her when an armoured corps officer stepped in front of me and asked if I was from 9RAR. Suspiciously I answered yes, and he politely advised me that he was Peter Cosgrove's father and he just wanted to know if Peter was on this flight. I told him that I was a good friend of Peter's and had seen him recently, and although he was in good health, he was still in Viet Nam. He thanked me and retired (I later got to know him and his wife, Ellen, very well).

I quickly noticed that Carole's parents were on either side of her, rushed up to her, and kissed her. I started paying my respects to Carole's parents, Laurie and Doreen, and Carole asked me what I thought of our daughter. The basinet was at Carole's feet, and I had almost tripped over it whilst expressing my delight to be home. I looked down, and there was the most beautiful child I could imagine—tiny, innocent, asleep, and ours. I could almost not take in everything that was happening. How could four days be enough? Sadly, that thought occupied my mind for the next four days.

We quickly loaded into our car, quit the airport, and headed out to Penshurst where Carole's parents lived, and of course, we all had so much to tell that we chatted incessantly for about an hour and then decided to call 'lights out'. Carole told me that the family had arranged for us to stay out at a motel at Church Point on the northern harbour near Pittwater and we would be leaving in the morning. This would give Carole and me time together and provide time also for me to get to know my daughter.

What a great decision this was. The place was serene, absolutely quiet, had its own restaurant and a beautiful grassed area that bordered the harbour. We spent the three days simply 'chilling', although I was still very gun shy, rolling out of bed every time a boat went down the harbour. However, the seclusion was wonderful, and Nicole (our daughter) really did know me by the time our three days were over.

Carole told me that Nicole was a bit of handful in that she seemed to be very stressed all of the time and therefore was an inconsistent sleeper, a fact that I became very well aware of during our stay. Carole's dad, Laurie, was very helpful trying to attend to the baby when it woke during the night. Eventually, Laurie and Doreen arranged for Carole to spend some respite time with Nicole in the Canterbury Respite Centre. Guilt began to consume me, and I couldn't see how I could just walk out on the family and return to the war zone. Inwardly, however, I knew that to contemplate doing anything else would be futile and would probably create problems for our future that we didn't need. We rolled up our blanket (which we used for sitting on the lawn with the baby in a perfect environment) and drove back to Penshurst reflective and silent. We spent the final night with Laurie and Doreen, and I prepared to step back into the void.

Whereas the trip home on the plane had been full of laughter and nervous conversation, the trip back to Viet Nam was quiet and reserved, with the exception of the US servicemen on board who had spent their R&R in Sydney (primarily at King's Cross), and they seemed to be most satisfied with their visit. Most Australians on the flight were young married men or farmers who needed to see how their farms were managing without them and how their families were surviving. This was not a fun trip.

In fact, I had to get my mind back on the job fairly quickly as my battalion had finished their maintenance and local patrolling of Nui Dat and had moved back into the Long Green (Operation Reynella) which was on the western side of the barrier minefield and was overlooked by the Long Hai Hills which was a known bastion of the Viet Cong (nicknamed 'The Sanctuary') and was protected by thousands of M16 mines stolen from the barrier minefield. This was going to be a test of leadership and good soldiering, and we would be lucky to come out of this operation without a lot of casualties.

I was to find in the ensuing weeks that the Long Green was probably our toughest assignment to date. The Americans had 'land cleared' the area around the Long Hais so that any activity could be easily spotted by aircraft patrolling by day and by ambushing at night. The land clearing had occurred about a year before we arrived in the area, and as such, the trees and shrubs had recommenced growing but were, in most cases, only about six foot high. This meant that they were seldom tall enough to provide any shade, were growing in almost pure sand, and if any other company had an incident within about 2,000 metres, the sound, the smoke, and the evacuations were all observable from our location. This was really bad for morale particularly if a stream of 'DUSTOFF' helicopters were seen flying into a location where you knew one of the other companies was patrolling.

Almost daily an incident would occur within our platoon which would stand the hairs up on the back of your neck and make you wonder when your turn would come. Two incidents quickly spring to mind; on one occasion, my platoon sergeant Warren Featherby (returned to the field after a re-occurrence of malaria acquired on a previous tour to Malaysia) came forward to me as we were patrolling along a sand track and advised me to halt. I did. He advised me that the soldier patrolling in front of him had stepped on an M16 mine and the prongs (having been sitting in the sand for some time) snapped off, leaving the mine in the ground and thus saving us a number of casualties. Logically, all the platoon had to be notified to exercise care, clear their areas, and we would detonate the mine (downwards), which we did successfully and then continued the patrol with much greater caution. The other incident was similar in that a soldier down near the back of the patrol stepped on an M16, and it flew up about 25 feet in the air and detonated harmlessly; again we continued the patrol with a much greater appreciation of the danger we faced every day. This type of incident was also reported from other companies, although not all were quite so lucky, and the casualties began to mount. Almost daily reports came in that 9RAR soldiers were injured by mines, in the village of Dat Do, a vehicle from the district office drove beside some 9RAR soldiers and detonated a cluster of mines wounding three soldiers, and an engineer vehicle in Dat Do also drove over two M16 mines from a cluster of four and wounded six of our pioneers.

The enemy were also becoming quite aggressive. Fire Support Patrol Base 'Thrust' was established to house our Battalion Headquarters, our communications, our direct support artillery battery, and our mortars. It was dug in, principally in sand, and was central enough to be able to provide direct fire support to all of the companies patrolling in the Long Green. On 6 June, the enemy fired thirty rounds of 82 mm mortar into the fire support base, killing one of our soldiers and wounding a further seven. Nowhere was safe.

On one occasion, my platoon was called into FSPB Thrust for a briefing, and we were offered a shower and a can of beer. The shower was outstanding, although I am sure the VC from the Long Hais watched our lily-white bodies dancing under the showers and wished they had some longer-ranging mortars. We were then issued with one can of hot beer (not cooled or even cold but hot), and worse still, it was Fourex; we were issued a fresh ration which in itself was like heaven after eating hard rations for the past two weeks, and then I was given orders and we marched for an hour or so to occupy an ambush position.

It was usual for us to ambush every night; there were a great many opportunities, and we had some success as did other companies. I recall on one night I had identified an ambush position late in the afternoon and set about carefully laying out my gun positions as I thought the area might be productive. Whilst this was occurring, the section commanders had identified the positions for other weapons and the soldiers had started digging in and preparing for the night. I was satisfied where the guns were placed and returned to HQ area in order to dig a shell scrape for myself. All of a sudden, the area went deathly quiet, and the signal came back that enemy had been spotted. I moved forward again to the gun positions just as they opened up on two or three enemy who had come into focus in the allotted 'killing' ground. The enemy fell to the ground, there was no return fire, and I could see the section commanders had taken control, so I returned to my HQ and awaited the results. The section commanders arranged a sweep of the killing zone and returned with two bodies which contained some documents, etc., which I decided I would return to battalion the next day. I signalled the platoon to start getting ready for night routine and 'stand to'. I still had to dig my pit.

The next minute, 60 mm mortars began to rain on my position. I dived for the first cover available which was the platoon sergeant's pit. He dived in the medic's pit, and the medic was left stranded and extremely disrespectful. We received about six to eight mortar rounds and a bit of sporadic small-arms fire, but no attack which I was most surprised about. We had poured a fair bit of ammunition into the adjacent woods, and I had called for artillery support into the area that I thought might provide a forming-up place for an attack. I can say with remarkable clarity that it was a frightening experience, but none more so than for the poor bloody medic who was left stranded by my action of not having dug a pit. Surprisingly no one was wounded. Not surprisingly, this situation became the source of many jokes for a long time. I think the platoon sergeant has never forgiven me, and the medic mentioned it every time we met until he passed away in the 1990s.

Weapon pits were very personal things, and many took great pride in their construction and made sure that the depth of the pit was sufficient to protect the occupant from direct fire or remnants or shrapnel from indirect weapon fire. Weapon pits were a necessary nuisance as most days when we patrolled, we had probably spent ten hours on our feet carrying heavy packs. By late afternoon, all we wanted were a brew and something to eat, however, almost every night we ambushed or set up a defensive perimeter so that a pit was needed. Whilst the pits were being dug, we still had to maintain defensive integrity, so sentries were posted well out from the position in case we attracted any attention. The sentries had to then return to the perimeter and dig their pits which were often right on last light, so their priority was to get a brew on before 'stand to' was called, so weapon pits became a low priority. The same time pressures applied to the platoon commander who, if doing his job, would coordinate the three machine guns and check on the integrity of the perimeter. Hence the sad tale of the medic who got isolated when the mortars started to fall. He eventually ended up on top of me in the platoon sergeant's pit. It took a while for me to restore faith in my medic.

After this incident, I was ordered to continue patrolling along the scrub line getting closer into the base of the Long Hais. This was getting pretty tense as we were heading in the same direction that our attackers had withdrawn along a couple of days back. I decided to halt in a very dense piece of scrub, post sentries, offer time for a smoke, and just listen to see if anything was happening around us. Within minutes, one of the sentries reported that he had seen three VC observing a land clearing team that was operating about 2,000 metres from us. One of the three VC was female.

After observing for about an hour, I decided that the three were outside a cave, which was formed by huge rocks part way up the mountain. I called the OC and suggested that if we had a spare 90 mm anti-tank operator in the area, we might be able to get a shot on the observers and bounce the HEAT missile into the cave. The distance was right. It was agreed this was a good idea. It took an hour for a small anti-tank party to make it to our location undetected. I briefed them, and they started to set up the 90 mm. I also got my two best machine gunners and positioned them to fire into the cave concurrently. We cleared the back blast danger area, and I gave the word to fire. We took the observers completely by surprise, but the distance probably saved them as the 90 mm HEAT round and the machine gun rounds wound their way to the mouth of the cave. The observers were seen to react quickly diving into the cave and probably escaping the lethal fire. We popped another couple of rounds of HEAT into the cave, but I guess the results will never be known. Time to clear our heads, get our minds back onto our task, and move on.

It is interesting to note that in the official history of 9RAR's tour of duty, the author saw it necessary to write in conclusion about Operation Reynella that 'mine incidents were a cause for great concern and sapped morale'. My platoon spent most of the remainder of Reynella protecting engineer land clearing teams who were brutally trying to destroy, uncover, or clear the remaining mines in the barrier minefield using both manual hand methods and the power and weight of D9 bulldozers. The engineers had little protection but seemed almost oblivious to the M16 mines exploding literally all around them.

Fire Support Base 'Thrust' was situated centrally within the area of operations for 'Reynella', and because of the low scrub and the elevated observation platform of the enemy in the Long Hais, 'Thrust' must have seemed like an easy target. So much so that on 5 June, it received twenty-nine incoming VC mortar rounds, all within its boundary resulting in seven WIA and one Australian killed. This was the first occasion that our FSPB had been attacked on operations. The 9RAR doctor was nowhere to be found when the casualties started to mount. However, he later told the story that he was on the toilet having his daily 'constitutional' when the mortar rounds commenced to land, Being used to the forward observation officers (161 Battery New Zealand Artillery) adjusting the direct fire (DF) locations for the companies each night, the doctor merely assumed that the DFs were 'extremely close tonight' until, of course, a mortar round landed right beside the hessian, tearing it down, thus alerting him to the extreme situation the FSPB was in.

Many things were occurring as 9RAR wound down their final weeks in the Long Green. 5RAR had a massive battle in Bin Ba, about fifty kilometres to our north in which they killed about thirty enemy soldiers and captured a dozen. Nui Dat was attacked with about ten to twelve ground fired rockets with no casualties being recorded, and Hoa Long, the displaced village situated outside the perimeter of Nui Dat, was attacked by approximately three companies of Viet Cong who failed to take the village. Intelligence sources provided mixed assumptions from these activities, but we were beginning to wonder if going back to Nui Dat was such a good idea.

Before we returned to Nui Dat, however, I received a radio call from the forward observation officer Captain Pat Murphy (161 NZ Battery) who travelled with the OC in company headquarters. He advised me that the OC was seriously ill, and I should come to CHQ immediately. The reason that I was contacted was because I was the senior person (Infantry) in the company at that time other than the OC; the FOO was a Kiwi, Tony Daniels was on R&R, Adrian Craig was out wounded, and

Phil Gould (Coy 2IC) was away on liaison duties at one of the outlying ARVN posts, leaving me the senior man.

I asked the Pat where the OC was, and he pointed to a tree about ten metres away. There was the OC, bent over and looking extremely ill. I spoke to him, and he told me he would be okay, but I was not to be deterred. I picked up the company radio and called for the CO. He was somewhat confused as to why I should call him, however, I explained that the OC was incapable of commanding his company and he should be removed from the field immediately. He agreed and accompanied his chopper to my location. I carried the OC over to the chopper and knew that something was seriously wrong with him. He clearly weighed less than seventy kilos (later diagnosed with leptospirosis). The CO handed the company over to me and promptly left.

This left me very feeling very vulnerable with only my FOO, my CSM, a sergeant, and two corporals running the three platoons. I really didn't want to walk into a bunker system in the next couple of days. However, 5RAR replaced us in the Long Green within a couple of days, and we headed back to the Dat where at least we didn't have to be quite so careful where we put our feet. Phil Gould had also been recalled to Nui Dat to take over the company. This was a great relief as Phil was a good officer and knew the company. He would later be replaced by Bill MacDonald, a very senior company commander, who was currently commanding D Coy.

Nearing the end of our time in the Dat, Phil Gould said, 'BVD [old nickname], I am going to visit the SAS mess tonight and wondered if you would like to come.' I replied by asking if we had permission because I knew the gates between units closed at 6 p.m. and didn't reopen until 6 a.m., so it was a long time 'not to be noticed as missing'.

Phil said, 'No, but nothing is happening at present, if your platoon sergeant covers for you, we will get back in time for breakfast and no one will know you were missing.'

'Okay, let's do this', and we did. Phil got a jeep from somewhere, and at about four o'clock in the afternoon, we set sail for 'SAS Hill', which was the home of the SASR Squadron located inside the perimeter of Nui Dat. Phil was an ex–SAS member and had quite a few mates who were currently on location. We arrived to find that perhaps we weren't the only ones invited that night. The mess was on fire with plenty of beverages to go around—what a great night. I also knew many of the officers present, and it was a great way to reunite and trade experiences. Unexpectedly it started to rain, and about midnight, two explosions were heard followed by the words 'stand to'. Now, this meant that not only were we in another unit without weapons, webbing, or helmets, but the OC of A Company would be asking where the hell was the platoon commander . The squadron commander of the SAS Squadron, fully rigged in combat gear, was asking what all these officers were doing in his weapon pits without weapons or helmets and, in most cases, very drunk.

I quickly worked out that my future had a few holes in it about now and was wondering how I was going to get out of this. I picked up the phone and somehow got through to my company, explained to my platoon sergeant where I was, and that I was okay. He advised me that the OC was already on the warpath for my soul and that I was to report to him as soon as I returned. It was a bit hard to fathom that this was the only time, the only night in our whole tour that Nui Dat was mortared by the enemy—the one night we had chosen to visit another unit. Logically, the steam had gone out of the party, so when we were stood down, we had another couple of beers and then crashed out in a bunker somewhere.

The return the next morning was hilarious (now). The OC was furious and ripped into the 2IC and then called for me. I was only a second lieutenant, and somehow the OC thought that I was behind all this, so he awarded me five nights of CP duty (duty officer in the command post), so for most of the rest of the time in camp, I was unable to have a drink and after working all day would do CP duty each night for a week. All this for two little mortar rounds that didn't land anywhere near us.

The next two months saw us out on two operations primarily north of Nui Dat ostensibly in the area of the Courtney Rubber Plantation. The wet season had also commenced, and daily we were deluged with torrential rain that sometimes went all night—not a pleasant time of year. There were many minor incidents with short duration contacts and some large caches found. C Company seemed to get the worst of it when a late-afternoon contact occurred when they chanced upon some enemy at a water point. A fierce battle ensued, and many members of the lead platoon were killed or wounded (Don Tait was savagely wounded and has carried the results of these wounds for his whole life). So intense was the fighting that one of the bodies couldn't be recovered until the next morning. Two military medals were awarded this day to Cpl Andy Ochiltree and Pte Greg Salmon for their courageous efforts in trying to gain control under withering fire. In battle, nothing surpasses pure bravery. C Company eventually got on top of this situation but not without substantial losses—the dreadful cost of war.

It was during the second of these operations that I almost met 'my waterloo'. Tony Daniels (2PL) had bumped into a large bunker system, and because there was no resistance, he pushed into it and cleared over half the system. This took over an hour. Company headquarters and my platoon pushed right up behind him and secured the area that we knew to have been cleared. Tony continued to work forward, however, it was late afternoon and the company commander had to make a decision about occupying the system (holding ground) or withdrawing from it and attack it again the next morning in case any bad guys decided to occupy it overnight.

It was not a very good piece of ground as it was on the side of a slope, the trees were tall, and it was a very big bunker system. I positioned my troops so we didn't get a 'little tap on the shoulder' from behind and was in the process of locking in the support section with my platoon to ensure there were no defensive gaps. I had placed my pack at the base of a very tall, thin tree. I am not by nature a superstitious man, but for the past three days, one sentence had been repeating itself in my head making me extremely anxious. That sentence was 'The skipper's been hit!' I couldn't make sense of it and had managed to disregard it particularly since we had been in this very active, very new, large bunker system.

I walked over to Cpl Dick Lancaster, the section commander of Support Section, and had just started to engage him in discussion over our machine gun placement when machine-gun fire opened up, and I saw an RPG (rocket-propelled grenade) arc through the air and hit the tree where I had placed my pack. Instantaneously, I saw it explode and a piece of shrapnel came searching in my direction, slamming into my head and knocking me off my feet. It somehow bounced off my temple and lodged in my shoulder. I immediately put my hand up to my face as it inflated like a balloon and I knew I was in trouble. Immediately Dick Lancaster shouted out, 'The skipper's been hit!' Dick immediately searched for any sign of life and then, as if relieved to find a pulse exclaimed, 'Thank fuck you were there, sir! Otherwise, it would have been me.'

However, both of us were on the ground, we were out in the open and, as it turned out, in an enemy fire lane which the enemy was using to ensure that I never got up again. It had also started to rain, very heavily. The medic Peter Snell got to me and managed to get a bandage on, but the rate of machine-gun fire was too heavy, and he retreated to some light cover but was unable to drag me with him (I was barely conscious at this time.). He did arrange for some close troops to throw their packs in front of my head, and I remember hearing the bullets actually thudding into one of them. My next worry was that there may be a claymore mine or spare ammunition carried in one of those packs which wouldn't provide a good conclusion.

The date was 26 July 1969. By now the rain was pouring down, and I could hear the sounds of Second Platoon still fighting their way through the occupied bunkers. The medic advised that I would be okay but would have to be evacuated, meanwhile someone had stuck a cigarette in my mouth. The CSM Bruce Sutherland went looking for a DUSTOFF location. I was still fairly exposed with tracer rounds zinging past me, but as yet, I really couldn't get interested enough to move. The wet season really was establishing its ownership of the weather, and I next remember water streaming down this small gully I was in and washing over the packs that were providing my cover, then came the mud. Suddenly, the shooting stopped, and I heard a transmission that suggested that Second Platoon had cleared the occupied bunkers and were occupying those that surrounded them.

Dark was closing in. The CSM reported back to the medic that he couldn't find a suitable area for the choppers to come in (if he could get one to come in this weather), so I would have to be taken out by jungle penetrator which was an anchor-like device which could be lowered about 200 feet, the tines folded out for the patient to sit on, and then a shoulder-style safety belt was positioned to stop the patient from falling out. It was a most uncomfortable arrangement, and patients who survived the trip always recommended it for low extractions only if the patient ever wanted to have children. The wind had come up so the trees were swaying, the rain was torrential, and the CSM was unsure that the DUSTOFF would come. Apparently, the US choppers had knocked back the invitation because night was falling and the weather was uncompromising. The CSM, however, was optimistic that the Australian chopper would make it if he could find us in these tropical conditions. The CSM later (after the war) wrote to me about some Christmas lights that he had put on a tree in his front yard and continually viewed whilst having a beer late in the afternoons. I quote:

From that position, there are two lights that stand out. They are red and green, and they pulse on and off. I have dubbed these lights 'the Vickery Lights'. The reason for this is that they remind me of a late afternoon in Viet Nam in 1969. It was when I stuffed a modified, empty peaches tin over a strobe light in my right hand, and wrapped my sweat rag over the base of the shebang. I then detected two Hueys by their navigation lights, and switched it on. My radio operator called out 'they have us'. We then evacuated our casualty (2Lt Brian Vickery) by 'penetrator' through the tallest trees in Viet Nam, during the heaviest downpour I have ever experienced followed by the most miserably, uncomfortable night (I have ever spent). Therefore, on a little hill in the Gold Coast hinterland, Brian, you are remembered during this festive season.

(L) Side winch on a DUSTOFF helicopter; (R) DUSTOFF with patient

The previous comment I made about low extractions was now a proven fact. I was extracted right on last light, sitting on what felt like a very narrow piece of pipe which cut into my bony ass (I only weighed twelve stone about eighty-five kilograms then), but the chopper had me on maximum length, and the downdraft from the rotors was swinging me in all directions, and I was very conscious of the fact that the rest of the company were still sitting in a partially occupied bunker system. From my elevated position, I could see a lot of bunkers, and I was becoming convinced they were all full of bad guys. The penetrator is not known for its speed, and I am sure the extraction took the best part of thirty minutes. The rain continued to tumble down, and the wind kept pushing me into the trees—not recorded as my favourite ever ride.

Eventually, the agony was over (although I felt like I was almost cut in half), and those wonderful members of the RAAF, particularly 9 Squadron, hauled me into the chopper, did a quick check of eyes and pulse, gave the pilot the thumbs-up, and we headed off into the black abyss. The flight was rough, but the crew were outstanding, and I couldn't help feeling guilty having left the company. As it turned out, I would have been a bit light on if I hadn't been evacuated because the RPG which knocked me over had hit the tree where my pack was placed and sent shrapnel all through it, making it and everything in it completely worthless including rations, maps, hutchie, water, eating utensils, spare radio battery, and some ammunition. I suspect I used up three of those lives they keep telling me about all in one afternoon.

The next part of this adventure was yet to come. I had heard that the Australian Military Hospital at Vung Tau was very professional in their handling of casualties particularly mass casualties. Their system was geared to a 'care' team being on standby regardless of the number of casualties because they represented different specialist areas of expertise. The night I came in was a Saturday night, and the surgeons and staff were having a party with a 'psychedelic' theme, so it came to me as quite a surprise that the head surgeon who examined me (on a gurney, on the airstrip) had a huge psychedelic eye painted on the top of his bald head (Doctor John McNaughton, I think). He saw my eyes open as I spotted the painting and quickly and good-naturedly explained the situation.

Now, this had to be the most professional display of triage I have ever seen. As the chopper landed, three people ran to the chopper with a gurney (having been advised by radio what was coming), two wardsmen loaded me on the gurney, and whilst wheeling me to the adjacent hospital, they immediately began to cut my clothes off and my boots whilst the doctor started examining my eyes, testing pulse, etc. By the time I got to the hospital, they had all the vital statistics, I was naked, and they were examining my wounds. Logically I was swollen in the face and bleeding in the shoulder plus the shrapnel from the RPG was still in my shoulder. The biggest concern, however, was that I was covered in mud, which smelt quite strongly, and they were concerned about infection.

The senior nurse said, 'Hello, Brian, long time no see, how long since you have had a shower and how do you feel?' My answer was direct as I was concerned that my jaw was actually broken, so I didn't feel much like talking. 'Hi, Jan [a friend of my wife from Second Military Hospital days], thirty days since a tub and I feel like I have been hit by a f#*%*# train.' The doctors then ordered X-rays which they did in about three minutes while I was still on the gurney and then they put me into this huge bathtub and told me to get clean. I think we got the mud off pretty easy, but the cam cream tended to stick a bit. Back onto the gurney, into theatre, face cut and stitched, shoulder cut and stitched, and then into the ward for a troubled night of sleep (every time I heard a foreign sound, I would be alert and quite anxious when I couldn't find my rifle).

Sadly, that wasn't the end of the section for me. Two days later, some members of 6RAR had stepped on a mine, and while they were being evacuated, the CO and the battalion doctor had gone into the mined zone and tripped another mine, causing more casualties. The hospital went into top gear and displayed a level of professionalism all of our troops would have been proud of. The sad but interesting result of a disturbed night of movement and voices around the ward was that the Fifth Battalion commanding officer Lieutenant Colonel David Butler and the battalion doctor were both placed adjacent to my bed, post-theatre.

The CO and I conversed frequently over the next couple of days before he was cleared to return to his battalion, but the doctor was in a bad way having copped the full extent of the mine blast. He had lost two limbs and an eye, and the staff were continually busy trying to save another limb and his sight. He was in plaster from toe to chest, and it was changed every day because it was continually saturated in blood. I could not believe that the doctor would live, but thanks to the wonderful work of the surgeons, he did and went on to serve a productive life although I did not get to see him again.

David Butler and I saw each other many times after Vietnam, and even after he was promoted to major general, he still always stopped and spoke with me when our paths crossed. General Butler was, in fact, the general who was invited to provide a motivational speech to the Many Warringah Rugby League Football Club prior to their playing a grand final. I think this was in the late 1970s when Bob Fulton was coach.

It was quickly established that my jaw wasn't broken and my wounds had been cleaned and stitched, and therefore all that was required was for me to be cleared of infection. My battalion was back in from operations and had been given a three-day pass (rest and convalescence) at Vung Tau. Logically the guys came in to see me and were really disappointed when they found out I only had a bunch of stitches in my face and shoulder. It still hurt to laugh, but they 'gave it to me' so much that I couldn't stop laughing. They reckoned that I had requested evacuation myself so that I didn't have to spend that particular night in the bush. They all agreed it was the worst night they had spent in Vietnam. The next day, I was released, issued new boots and greens, and looking like a new reo (reinforcement), I joined my company at the Peter Badcoe Club (R and C Centre) in Vung Tau and had a beer. They did not wish to hear what I had been doing; they all wanted to tell me what a shit night I missed out on.

As it turned out, this incident caused great distress for my wife. I think the type of stress that was generated was wonderfully portrayed in the movie *We Were Soldiers*. The yellow taxis turning up to the married quarters to deliver the telegrams advising that another soldier had been killed in Vietnam. In my case, it was a padre and a young captain turned up at the front door at Carole's parents' place to deliver the news that I had been wounded but was okay. Carole saw them at the front door and immediately assumed the worst and promptly collapsed before they had a chance to speak. Carole's mother calmed the situation, spoke to them both, and thanked them for the welcome news. The wife or partner of any serviceman or woman always dreads the unexpected knock at the door.

Our company senior NCOs and officers shared a mess tent back in Nui Dat which served as a bar by night and afforded us our own sanctuary which had many purposes and a place to go to when speaking to members of the other platoons about their experiences on the previous operation. It also provided some incredibly memorable moments, such as the night that Bill McDonald, the new company commander, brought out six beautiful silver inlay wine glasses which he had gone to great lengths to acquire. Apparently, he identified the set in Hong Kong on R&R, but because of the restrictions on the transportation of US currency, he was only allowed to purchase two of them (they were very expensive items), so he got his batman to purchase another two for him on his R&R and Phil Gould, the company 2IC, to purchase the final two. Bill was so overwhelmed by the ownership of this set that he brought them out into the mess to show us. Sadly we had been drinking heavily and Bill, after a couple of beers, decided to retire, completely forgetting to take the glasses with him. Phil Gould, who had a great sense of humour, said, as a joke, 'I will now see if these are real silver', and bit into the flat silver inlay which ran around the top of the glass. Sure enough, a clear impression of his bite mark was evident on the side of the glass. There were only about four of us in the mess, but all speaking came to an immediate halt. We were horrified and had a vivid image of what would happen when the OC found out. We finished our beers, turned the bite mark inwards on the tray so that it couldn't be immediately seen, and then hightailed it back to our lines.

About 0900 hours the next morning, I was summoned to the OC's tent and, along with the other three officers present, stated that I knew nothing of the incident and that the glasses looked fine when I retired. The OC dismissed the others with a warning but asked me to remain. He told me that he suspected I was behind this 'sick' joke and I should take two extra duty officer penalties 'just in case he was right'. Bugger me, why was I always the suspect? However, we have all remained good friends since, and I know Phil Gould, many years later, admitted to Bill that he had sample-tested the wine glass. Bill had, at no time, suspected Phil was the culprit because he was an extremely loyal and professional officer; the other three of us were all lieutenants, therefore, not yet to be trusted. The story is recounted any time we gather, and we are still able to laugh about it.

Next day, it was back to business and briefing for our next operation which was protection of an engineer land clearing team that was working adjacent to the Long Hai mountains and along the coast. This team was trying to clear the residue of mines remaining in the barrier minefield and known areas where the VC had replanted the mines. So on 15 August, we were back into the low, hot, scrubby wasteland of the Long and Light Greens. Our task was a fairly sedentary one, taking up good observation positions to be able to fire upon any enemy that might try to interfere with the land clearing team and similarly set up ambush positions along the myriad of tracks by night.

After about a week of this, I decided to send the platoon (in two groups) down to the ocean for a swim. The platoon sergeant loaded half the platoon into a couple of APCs and headed for the beach. They had not gone more than 200 m when the APC ran over an M16 mine and blew a track off.

Now, this situation, in itself, is a problem. Fifteen platoon members are on board, plus driver and crew commander. The track has to be removed and a new link inserted (spare link always carried by APCs), but because the track is mined, it now has to be cleared so the APC crew can work around the track gear and replace the link. A number of soldiers are unloaded and start clearing around the APC (they have to be careful not to stand on other mines that might be in the area). Fortunately, the area is sandy, so clearing can be done with bayonets but is still a slow process. Eventually, the area is cleared, and the APC crew go to work and replace the link. After about forty-five minutes, the job is complete, and the beach party is again on their way. Although the soldiers in the back of the APC have just about lost interest. When they return, it is obvious that they are invigorated even though the South China Sea is about 36 degrees, but the soldiers just loved feeling the sand through their toes and the saltwater on their bodies—certainly worth the effort.

I took the other half of the platoon down for their swim, used a couple as sentries, arranged for their replacement, told the guys to 'fill their boots', and took my signaller a little further up the beach. However, just before we headed back to our hide, I decided that we might be able to take back a few fresh fish to supplement our hard rations. The plan was that my signaller, Noel Hamblion, and I were to hide behind a sand dune while I threw two grenades into the sea. Noel, after the grenades had detonated, was to run into the water, swim out, and collect the stunned fish. Everything proceeded as planned, the grenades exploded, and Noel raced into the water and swam furiously, head down. All of a sudden, I heard a watery scream and saw Noel heading back to shore at unbelievable speed. Even though the grenade had stunned some catfish, it had also broken the back of a sea snake, which, at this point in time, was very upset. Luckily, with a broken back, the snake could only swim in circles, so Noel made it to shore without injury. Unfortunately, no one volunteered to pick up the stunned fish.

The overall exercise was a success and, at least, broke the monotony for a while. The feel of sand between your toes was euphoric. The operations continued with the engineers destroying a great number of mines and the APCs having to frequently change track links. Eventually, we were tasked to move to another location, and half the platoon was briefed to provide a vehicle checkpoint near Xuyen Moc. The platoon sergeant took the checkpoint, and I took the other half of the platoon to another location where we continued our duties by day and ambushed by night. No real action through to the end of the operation when we again moved back to Nui Dat. Other companies also found the opposition to be 'light'.

Essentially, this was the finish of my combat role in Vietnam. It was the end of September and we had one major operation to finish our tour. Our final operation was to be named 'Operation Jack' and was to be back in the active area of the Hat Dich. Briefings had commenced when the CO called me into his office and said, 'Brian, I want you to be the assistant adjutant in BHQ for the last operation.' I was devastated. I argued that I had spent eighteen months with the same platoon and deserved to be able to complete the last operation with them. The CO countered that I was the only officer in the battalion that had not had a break from operational duties during the tour and that the assistant adjutant, Jim Joycey, deserved an opportunity to command on the last operation. I was immediately appointed the A/Adjutant, handed over my platoon to my platoon sergeant John 'Snow' Vautin, and reported to the chief clerk in Battalion Headquarters.

Despite my total reluctance at being placed in this new job, I decided to do the best job I could and would listen in at the command post to follow my company and my platoon's fortunes. I also resolved to visit the companies on the resupply chopper whenever I could; hopefully, this would diffuse my angst at being left off the last operation. As it turned out, my first major job was a fair bastard.

On 25 October 1969, there was a federal election being contested between John Gorton (Liberal current incumbent) and Gough Whitlam (Labor and leader of the federal opposition). Apparently, some fair-minded person, in Australia, decided that everyone in Vietnam, of age, should be given the opportunity to vote should they wish to do so. Now this was a problem! My job was to notify all the companies of this monumental decision and advise them that I would visit them on the resupply chopper, provide details on *all* the candidates, provide absentee voting forms and envelopes, and then return at the next available opportunity (after the troops had time to digest the information and cast their vote) and pick up the sealed envelopes.

I had been given about three weeks to do this in amongst my other administrative duties. This was a horror show, however, and I somehow had to make it happen. Duly, I managed to get the first part of the task done by delivering the required documents to the companies in mailbags. Some wanted nothing to do with them and some wanted to get them filled in and returned on the spot. I had to refuse these requests and advise what policy was to be applied. In the middle of an operation, this didn't wash well with the OCs, but to their eternal credit, they complied. I could make this work!

A week later, I notified the companies that I would accompany their resupply on the next drop and pick up the votes. The night before I was to visit A Company, they were involved in a big contact with a large group of enemy in a company ambush. I rushed to the command post and followed the contact expecting to hear of a morale-lifting result with no casualties to our own troops. The battle continued to rage overnight with artillery fire and 'Spooky' called to assist, resulting in a dawn attack which found no enemy dead but heavy drag marks where apparently many enemy had been 'dragged' away in the traditional VC style. As a consequence, the company advised me that they needed ammunition resupply and no visitors. They did offer to backload the votes that had been collected. I thought I may have got a chance to visit them on the next resupply in three days' time, but in the meantime, they had contacted another large group of enemy, and whilst forming up to assault the enemy, a support helicopter which was evacuating a wounded soldier was shot down. Two other helicopters both received fire and were damaged. As happens in war, the complexion of the battle completely changed, and the crashed helicopter now had to be secured and the pilot rescued and evacuated (which was done very successfully and professionally). So much for my plan, although I had managed to secure at least one company's votes.

Visits to D and C companies were largely uneventful, and they handed me the mailbags with the votes. B Coy was another story. The CSM was arranging the resupply and distribution when I landed, and he advised me, in a very definite tone, that he would worry about the votes when he had finished distributing the resupply. I decided to visit Peter Cosgrove and sit with him until the CSM was ready for me to leave. Now, as I was a base 'walla' and was not operational, I only carried a 9-mm pistol which was more for convenience and show than anything else. I made my way down to Peter's HQ and he greeted me and offered me a brew (standard greeting when time permitted). He made the brew and we were chatting about nothing in particular when a mini-battle broke out about fifteen metres from where we were sitting and obviously involved Peter's soldiers. In his usual aggressive and courageous style, he said, 'See ya', grabbed his webbing and his weapon, and ran at full pace towards the firing. At this stage, the perimeter had become deathly quiet, everyone was still, and I was isolated. B Company was on alert, and I was unknown to all but a few of the soldiers because I was from another company. I also only carried a pistol. My instincts said, 'Brian, sit still until the pressure is off, then walk back to the helipad.' However, over and above everything else I could hear the pickup helicopter on its way in. With great trepidation, I slowly stood up and began to walk back along the track to company headquarters hoping not to hear a nervous safety catch being slid to 'fire'. The approach of the helicopter had the work party up on its feet and getting prepared for the backloading of rubbish and stores. The CSM also stepped forward and said in his inimitable style, 'This is the best I could do, sir', and handed me the B Company votes. I thanked him and the company commander and boarded the chopper. Bloody hell, this was harder than being a platoon commander.

I managed to round up votes from the scattered platoons from Support Company and Battalion Headquarters. I sorted the votes into a semblance of order, put them in a mailbag, sealed it, and sent it to the Task Force Electoral Officer and, to this date, have not heard a word about whether I got it right or they were even received. However, there was a small article in a newspaper I saw much later that said all electoral votes from Vietnam were deemed to be ineligible. What an incredible waste of effort.

The last operation drew to a close; the troops were really getting tired after a year of continual patrolling particularly in the tropical heat and with the final operation being an active one where many contacts with the enemy occurred. The battalion had done its job well despite being the youngest battalion ever to go to war for Australia, and many friends had been bonded for life even though many didn't know it at this time. The job now was to keep the Task Force area safe (TAOR patrols) and successfully hand over to the Eighth Battalion who were on their first tour.

The final month of our tour had begun. The final operation had been completed, and we were all back in Nui Dat preparing for our return to Australia at the end of the month. TAOR (tactical area of responsibility) patrols were still required as these were the battalion's front-line defence to protect Nui Dat from any form of attack or reconnaissance. These patrols were conducted all year round and would comprise all our 'left out of battle' personnel such as our cooks, storemen, and those recovering from wounds and infections, et al., waiting to return to the forward areas. During the final month, this patrolling was increased and, of course, was done by the platoons who would otherwise spend their days preparing for their return to Australia and orientating 8RAR towards the problems most likely to confront them during their tour.

TAOR patrols were very easy for troops that had been patrolling for about forty weeks and working together, however, this was not such a natural task for a group of 'misfits' who were put together for probably one task but not really familiar with the use of claymores, grenade throwers, flares, and a collection of weapons drawn for this purpose. These groups certainly had little training in minor tactics, ambush layout, night navigation, or weapons deployment, so many of these groups ventured out high in the hope that they would come across no enemy.

I do recall on one occasion when the patrol was sent out and commanded by our sergeant cook who was absolutely terrified of coming across any enemy activity, so he decided to set an ambush up in the middle of a paddy field so he would have reasonable fields of observation and be able to suitably control a firefight and yet have the protection of the bunds which ran around and through all paddy fields. Unfortunately, during the night, his untrained, somewhat undisciplined troops all went to sleep (including the sentries) and a group of enemy entered the perimeter (unwittingly) and unchallenged. The group of about six enemy soldiers was right in the middle of the ambush when one of the soldiers woke up, quickly assessed the situation, and logically, opened fire. Talk about an Irish ambush. Soldiers awoke and started firing; the enemy still not quite sure what they had walked into, commenced firing, and bedlam reigned supreme. More bullets were fired than at the Battle of Long Tan. The sergeant cook didn't feel confident enough to call in artillery and was relieved when the battalion duty officer suggested that perhaps a 'spooky' gunship might be of help and arranged for it to attend the position. Logically, it all got a bit untidy, however, everyone was relieved when, at first light, a troop of APCs arrived to search the area and return the troops to Nui Dat. Fortunately, a couple of enemy were found (DOA) and none of our troops were injured or wounded. It was always with great enjoyment that us more-seasoned troops listened to the sergeant cook as he recounted the story. He always had fear in his eyes when he told the story, and we always had tears of laughter in ours. He was a great person and a very good storyteller.

The battalion was making some serious preparations for our return to Australia. Some were to return by plane, but most would take the journey on board the Vung Tau Ferry, HMAS *Sydney*. A lot of work was required to 'sterilise' our weapons and equipment to the standard required by Australian Customs. All dirt had to be removed and vehicles and weapons prepared for a sea voyage and eventual short-term storage. Our one social engagement was to invite representatives from all fellow units and have a battalion farewell party and a 'Welcome 8RAR' party or '365 days, no one has that long to go' party. The officer's mess also had a separate party to allow the task force commander and the COs of some units who we worked closely with to say farewell.

This went well until most of the dignitaries went back to their lines and a group of the officers decided to 'hitch a ride' to Vung Tau on board a 9Sqn RAAF Iriquois which had just returned one of our field teams back to Nui Dat (which included a good friend Mick Bell). This seemed like a really good idea at the time but started to go wrong almost immediately when Peter McCauley decided to put a smoke grenade in his shirt pocket and climb up on the roof to signal the chopper to land on the roof and pick up a group of about six of us. As Peter rolled over the guttering, the pin of the smoke grenade caught on the lip of the guttering and dislodged. Logically purple smoke started pouring from Peter's shirt which had caught on fire. We eventually got it out and found another shirt for Peter although he had a huge purple burn mark on his chest for weeks later. In the meantime, I had rounded up Mick Bell secured his weapon and ammo and found somewhere for him to leave his pack, loaded him onto the chopper (he was still trying to work out what was going on, all he wanted was a beer and shower), and off we went to Vung Tau.

Now what happened at Vung Tau is a bit of blur, but somehow we purloined an American jeep, drank a gallon of beer, disrupted a restaurant enjoying entertainment, jobbed a Military Policeman, and escaped out the window of the Pacific Club. Mick, who had injured his leg on the last operation (liaison officer with a South Vietnamese Army group), was rounded up by the Provost (MPs) when he tried to catch a Lambro cab back to our accommodation and I was given local accommodation by 101st US Airborne who thought we were awesome. I actually took a Lambro cab and went to the lockup to see if Mick was there. They were just unloading him from a jeep and, as I didn't want to be locked up as well, decided to come back in the morning. Somehow this all occurred, and we all managed to get on a chopper that was heading for Nui Dat. Unfortunately, the Provost report was already on the task force commander's desk. Mick was called before the Brigadier, and I assumed that I would be next.

Everyone had become very cautious because of the proximity of our return to Australia as no one wanted to get killed or wounded this close to the end of the tour. Unfortunately, we did suffer a number of fatal incidents close to our return which were very sad affairs. One of our assault pioneers, whilst assisting on protection of a land clearing operation, was killed by a mine blast and several others were wounded. Also, one of our officers, Bob Convery, was killed in a 'fragging' incident whilst sleeping in the company lines. I was still designated as the A/Adjutant on this night and was woken by fellow platoon commander, Tony Daniels, who was the duty officer who rang me and advised me of the immediate circumstances and said, 'What do we do?' I answered by saying, 'I am doing nothing, you, however, must ring the battalion commander and the adjutant now and let them take the matter over.' This they did and the matter ran the full course with a duly constituted court martial which kept a number of our battalion members in the country to give critical evidence. Not a good way to end a tough tour of duty where individual sights were set on seeing families again in November and then being advised that the court martial might drag on to the new year, which it did. The final guilty verdict seemed to satisfy those involved that justice had been seen to be done.

However, for me, the Bob Convery incident was career saving, and I say that with great respect. I had known Bob from the School of Infantry well before I came to 9RAR. As soon as the CO had time to draw breath, he called me in, gave me a light serve, and said, 'Brian, there is an aeroplane leaving Tan Son Nhut tomorrow for Sydney at 2 p.m., be on it.' I saluted and left, almost at a run, Mick Bell had lost two years' seniority from his visit to Brigadier 'Black Jack' Weir, and I was sure to receive a similar award. I am fairly certain that Mick, Ray Lunney, and myself were on that same flight. I think the CO was rewarding us for having loyally served a full tour of duty although he got us out of the country whilst the task force commander was distracted with the formulation of a court martial. It was a good time to reflect on the year that we had just spent at war.

Front-line troops in jungle warfare do it tough. When patrolling, we were humping a pack, searching for enemy signs for about ten hours a day, covering up to twenty-five kilometres; if we were patrolling in bamboo, it reduced to about ten kilometres a day but took the same amount of time, and the continual bending almost destroyed my quadriceps because I was tall and we carried water and ammunition around our waists which put the weight on our quads. The weather was hot (around 38 degrees Celsius), most days in the dry, and sleeping when you weren't in ambush was difficult. The wet provided a different set of obstacles whereby you could go to sleep on the jungle floor and at some time during the night you would end up floating in 400 millimetres of water.

There was an endless stream of ants, bugs, and snakes (kraits and vipers in particular) that continually made your life a misery. Again you could go to sleep on the jungle floor and in the middle of the night, you would be covered by a thousand black ants trying to hack you into pieces. Snakes would seek the warmth of your sleeping silks or 'chomper' ants would eat the front out of your greens whilst you lay in ambush. Green ants were probably the worst as they would build their nests in tree leaves which hung down just so that you could walk into them or, worse still, drive into them if you were in APCs. Cavalry crews had enormous problems with these insects. Sometimes it seemed that the enemy was the last thing you were looking out for.

Water was probably the most sought after of resources—the harsh environment and physical nature of our trade meant that each man required at least six litres of water per day and some more. During the wet, there was plenty of water, but filling 360–400 plastic water bottles via the spout is both time consuming and noisy. In the summer, these had to be filled at the Task Force water point and dropped in by helicopter sometimes every day. Patrolling even half a day with no water completely exhausted all reserves of strength and endurance. Dehydration then became a medical problem that could not be treated in the field. Finally, the toll extracted from the human body when long, exacting assaults were required on bunker systems will always be remembered particularly if you were taking casualties and most bunker assaults did. These are the things that most will remember from an active tour of Vietnam.

The tour confirmed for me that no one who goes to war returns unchanged. Regardless of what role you played outside the wire, everyone witnessed many deaths and many people wounded and that has a profound effect on the human psyche. Processing the benefits of this year's worth of new information was a difficult thing to do; it may have been an adventure, it may have made you stronger, but it certainly brought about abnormal changes that our bodies were not always prepared for nor capable of adjusting to. My final assessment on these effects did not become obvious to me until many years later, but I did know straight away that adjusting back to a 'normal' life was not going to be easy. My immediate thoughts were that I was glad to be an Australian; I was extremely proud of the way the soldiers I had been associated with did their job. Many did not want to be there, many were very scared in action, but not one turned and went the other way. They did as they were ordered to and with every ounce of courage in their bodies. These same soldiers showed extraordinary resilience, suffered intolerable circumstances, fought with distinction, and complained very little. Personally, I grew mile high in this same period, being in command and undertaking this level of responsibility, particularly when human life was involved, it was very confronting and intimidating, and I don't pretend that I got it all right, but no one died because of any mistake or misjudgement that I made. I feel confident that I fulfilled my obligation without controversy or contradiction. My company sergeant major Bruce Sutherland summed up my performance rather well many years later when he said, 'You were never going to win the war, but you didn't back away from anything and you always looked after your soldiers.'

It would be remiss of me not to mention the very spirited and competitive rugby union competition we established in Nui Dat during the short duration we had between operations. I think all companies managed to provide teams with the exception of Admin Company, but A, B, and Support companies seemed to provide the most determination to always 'arrange' a game. These were great games with no training, generally no rugby fitness, almost always after a night on the grog, and were played on a field that still contained embedded rocks. However, there was no lack of enthusiasm, and I don't remember too many getting injured badly enough to get them out of the next operation. We even managed to select a battalion team who played a game against 161 New Zealand Battery which was a torrid match with a tenacity of test match proportion. I can't remember who won this game, but I know Doug McGrath was our captain and the result was fairly close, perhaps a Kiwi win.

CHAPTER NINE

RETURN TO AUSTRALIA

I T WAS A very subdued flight home surrounded by soldiers anxious to get back to a life they had known and enjoyed. I savoured the thought of not worrying about where I was putting my feet. I knew I was not walking into an ambush, and with some effort, I could identify every sound around me whilst I was awake.

Arriving at Mascot airport was as exciting as it was disappointing. We arrived late at night because it was thought we would attract less attention that way from protesters who were still trying to justify their unemployment status, however, there was a good crowd of family and supporters present. There seemed to be a few protesters trying to spit on us, but we had been through too much to let them even change our stride. Customs, Immigration, the staff from QANTAS, and all the remainder of the crowd were wonderfully helpful and accommodating and generally gave us a round of applause which we were not expecting. We were required to secure our weapons, pick up our pay, and then meet our families. This was all done with great expediency, and before I knew it, I was reunited with my wife, my daughter, and my mother-in-law and father-in-law. It was midnight, I was exhausted, and they were understanding. It was exhilarating, it was over, and I didn't really know what to feel. Time to sleep and sort it out in the morning.

I had returned to Sydney because that was where Carole and Nicole (our baby daughter) were staying with Carole's parents. I was granted six weeks' leave and then given orders to report to 9RAR in Brisbane on a certain date in early February. I was up early on that first morning home as I wanted to get to know my daughter and spend as much time as I could with Carole sorting out our immediate future. Carole's dad, Laurie, was already up and had Nicole dressed and fed by the time I got up. Carole emerged shortly after and advised me that good friends of hers had moved out of their Cronulla unit to allow us to spend a week there because of the turmoil in our life. This was truly a random act of kindness. This was also a great chance for Carole, Nicole, and myself to get to know each other again.

The week at Cronulla was pure bliss—much different from what I was used to but time to adjust, time to feel married again and time to become a father for the first time. What a contrast—where had I been? We soaked it all up answering to no one and doing as we pleased. All too soon, however, the week was over, and we headed back to Penshurst, completed my leave, and started planning for Brisbane.

CHAPTER TEN

9RAR BRISBANE

CAROLE, THE BABY, and myself drove through to Brisbane, gained the keys to a married quarter at Keperra in the South-western Suburbs, and moved in. The location was good only about ten kilometres from Enoggera Camp. We had almost no furniture, so we received what we did have (which took about two hours to unload and position), and then we had to start looking for some basics such as a cot, lounge, and kitchen setting. We purchased these basic items, met our neighbours (who were not military but were wonderful neighbours), stocked the pantry with groceries, and then I reported for work on the following Monday morning. The battalion had an Australian component of new officers, NCOs, and soldiers who had been living in the barracks since about November, so everything was pretty organised when I arrived, and many of the Vietnam veterans were returning from leave also and were slowly restocking the ranks. Only a limited number of weapons were held by the battalion at this time, so little training was taking place, mainly cleaning, and short days with early dismissals.

The new commanding officer LTCOL Eric Smith had arrived and was getting his plans in place for training the battalion for a subsequent tour of Vietnam sometime in the future. I was appointed as a company commander and was told to reconstitute the company and prepare it for training when weapons, ammunition, and equipment became available. In the meantime, all the major administration that the battalion didn't previously have time for became the priority—examples of this were the selection of a tune for the battalion slow march and the battalion quick march, standing operating procedures, a manual for battalion administration, etc. Many of these things had been done during our period in Vietnam but not officially recorded. Administration was a bit foreign to some of us at this stage, so life was actually pretty quiet by Vietnam standards, and we all started rocking backwards on our heels a bit.

Deja Vu

During our tour of Vietnam, I somehow ended up being the duty officer for B Company during a stay at Vung Tau. I suspect it must have been a B Company R&C. The B Company officers seemed to be absent and the NCOs wanted nothing to do with keeping the troops in line as an A Company officer had been appointed to do it. That A Company officer was me, why me?

I only knew a few B Company soldiers from playing battalion rugby, and I am proud to say that they caused me no concern over those two days. In fact, no one in B Company caused me any problems except Jock 'Bloody' Smith.

Jock was a wiry Scotsman, as his name would imply, who spent the whole weekend causing me grief. If there was a fight, he was in the middle of it; if there was a break out of camp, Jock would have organised it. He was permanently in a state of destructive motion and ensured that I had a thoroughly miserable weekend (this was my time off operations also). I didn't see Jock again for the rest of our time in Vietnam. I remain thankful for that, although I make no comment on his soldiering ability as these were exceptional times and I had not *worked* with him.

Living in Enoggera, purely by chance I ventured into the officer's mess one Sunday evening to buy some beer for home use. At one end of the bar was a group of the new young officers of the battalion talking to a young man who I couldn't see because he had his back to me. All were dressed in coat and tie. As I ordered, I heard this voice (from the person with his back to me) ask about 'Big Ives' (Ivan Clark) and John Langler. The new officers were taking a great interest in this conversation and obviously were caught up by the stories about Vietnam that were being told. As I completed my order, I thought I recognised the Scottish accent and turned the young officer around to face me. *'Private Bloody Smith'*, I screamed, *'what the #$&*@ hell are you doing in the officer's mess!'* I frog-marched Smith to the door and asked him whether he thought I should lock him up for impersonating an officer. *'We were having a few beers at the boozer, sir'*, he said, *'and they bet me fifty bucks I wasn't game to try; are you going to lock my mates up too?'*

Logically, I didn't lock up Smith because I really thought it was a gutsy thing to do. However, I still can't believe that Jock 'Bloody' Smith had come back to Australia to haunt me. What really made me chuckle, however, was how he had the three young officers actually believing he was an officer. That deserved applause. Jock passed away on the Gold Coast in about 2015; I hope he had a good life.

As the battalion built up, training became more progressive and the more senior positions were beginning to be filled. I was replaced as company commander first by Grahame Dugdale who was then a captain and later by Major Ken Moffat. This was an enjoyable time in the battalion because we were starting to train in earnest and were able to get back on the range and out into the bush. The fortunes of the battalion are included in a book I published at the behest of the 9RAR Association and called *Proud to Serve* and outlines many of the thoughts and reservations about the soldiers preparing for a second tour. This really no longer concerned me as my time, unfortunately, in the battalion was at an end. The CO visited my office one day in November 1970, handed me my promotion to captain, and advised me that I had been posted to the Jungle Warfare Centre at Canungra.

CHAPTER ELEVEN

THE JUNGLE WARFARE CENTRE

Background

CAPTAIN JAMES COOK recorded his sighting of Mt Warning (the mountain from which the name of this book is derived) just south of what was to become the NSW/Queensland border in 1770 on his voyage up the east coast of Australia. Fifty-four years passed, however, before the commanding officer of the Brisbane penal settlement explored beyond Morteon Bay and discovered the coastal entrances to what were later called the Coomera and Logan rivers and the Canungra Valley.

A year later, Alan Cunningham set out, also from Brisbane, to locate the centrepiece of Cook's discovery in 1770, Mount Warning. Cunningham found the mountain, but on the way, he traversed the Canungra Valley and was overwhelmed by its potential and majesty and reported to the commanding officer that it was ideal for settlement. By the 1870s, several settlements had been established along the Canungra valley including one that became known as Canungra township. Rainforests were discovered catering for all types of products, including homesteads, wagons, fences, railway sleepers, wharves, barrels, and many agricultural instruments. Cedar, in particular, assisted financially in the establishment of the valley. The introduction of the railway and the positioning of timber mills turned this valley into an economical stronghold for those bold enough to take the risk. The cedar, in particular, was in great demand in England.

Unfortunately, by 1920, much of the commercially viable timber had been worked out of the Canungra and Coomera valleys. Logically, the mills and the settlements adjusted, although many men were left out of work because of the closure of the sawmills. A variety of small farms emerged with beef and dairy cattle being introduced along with pigs and sheep—crops of maize, potatoes, cotton arrowroot, and sugarcane emerged although not all succeeded, and many sharecroppers were broken by the harshness of the country.

In 1885 Edwin Franklin married Ann Curtis and selected a property he called 'Glen Woolfit'. The eldest son, George, took over this selection when Edwin and Ann moved back to Henry Franklin's home 'Sara Vale' after Henry and his wife died in 1898. George worked 'Glen Woolfit' until the Department of Interior resumed it on behalf of the army in 1942 and established the Land Headquarters Training Centre (Jungle Warfare).

Establishment

In 1942 General Blamey, the Australian commander-in-chief, became acutely aware that all reinforcements for the battle that was occurring on the Kokoda Trail/Track against the Japanese should be trained in jungle warfare. Suitable sites were narrowed down to three: Canungra, Kyogle, or Murwillumbah in NSW. The recommendation by Lieutenant General Sturdee was for Canungra which Blamey accepted with alacrity.

Climatic conditions seemed ideal for the purpose intended. The decision was to set up a jungle warfare training centre to bring trained soldiers and junior officers up to the physical standards demanded of arduous operations, initially, in New Guinea and eventually the entire South-West Pacific area. The qualification for attending the centre before moving to the South-West Pacific became mandatory.

It has to be kept in mind that this was temporary-style accommodation with tents, ablution blocks, kitchens, and palliasses only needed to accommodate the troops most of whom came through in company-sized blocks. When the Second World War ended, instructional staff were reposted and a caretaker staff maintained the centre whilst another use could be ascertained for it. It sat like this from 1946 when Lieutenant Colonel F. P. Ted Serong (considered to be our foremost authority on South-East Asia at the time) was appointed commandant of the Jungle Warfare Centre in 1955 and told to rebuild a more permanent establishment with the purpose of training Australian soldiers in jungle warfare for operations in South-East Asia.

Jungle Warfare Training

This was the establishment where I was posted at the end of 1970. It was alive. Vietnam was supporting three infantry battalions, artillery, tanks, engineers, communicators, a Special Air Service Squadron, a Logistic Support Group, a Field Hospital, a Field Ambulance, a Dental Unit, a Postal Unit, and all the necessary supporting units, including a Field Workshop (RAEME), Light Aid Detachments (RAEME mobile workshops), transport, laundry units, and a field park.

Every replacement for every soldier that served in Vietnam had to attend a course (generally minimum of three weeks) before they were considered to be Draft Priority One, which was the minimum standard to be qualified to serve overseas in an operational theatre. Training for war gave the staff a real sense of purpose particularly as most had served in Vietnam and many in Malaya and Borneo during Indonesian Confrontation. There were still some who had served in the Second World War and a number who had served in Korea. Legendary names abounded; this was collectively the most experienced group of veterans I had ever seen. Even at this time in the Vietnam War, soldiers like Len Opie and Ozzie Ostara had completed four tours of Vietnam and formed part of the elite 'Purple Circle'—self named because they had all been members of the Australian Army Training Team which had produced four Victoria Cross winners. John Murphy and Rod Curtis were military cross winners from Malaya, and there were soldiers who had been in Long Tan, Bihn Ba, Fire Support Patrol Bases Coral and Balmoral, the Long Green and the Light Green—what amazing company. What staff to have the privilege of training with!

Fortunately, many of the instructors were captains and warrant officers that I had worked with previously from the School of Infantry and from my tour of Vietnam. I really felt that I had been posted to the heart of military professionalism. No wonder we rated ourselves to be among the best in the world at jungle warfare.

Carole, Nicole and myself drove up from Brisbane and were allocated a married quarter on the Southern side of the camp. These were relatively new quarters, one level, three bedroom, and seemingly adequate for our purpose. It was, at first, a bit daunting to see a fire in the lounge room with wood stacked for winter. This place might just be a bit colder than Brisbane. The other ranks' married quarters were on the northern side of camp and were also quite new. There was only one road on that side and it was called Boike Road, so it was easy if offering directions to where one of your staff lived; you would simply say, 'They live in Boike Road'. In our case, the same applied, petty much, with the road being called 'Corcoran Crescent' after Philomena Corcoran who had sold the property to the army.

We had little time to settle in although the houses were all in a row, so it was only a short time before we knew all the families and particularly the closest neighbours as this was a busy place and the men seemed to spend a lot of time training these thousands of soldiers, needing their qualification to serve overseas. The school/pre-school was on base with a public school in the township of Canungra.

Essentially, the establishment was built on two ridgelines with the first ridgeline containing the headquarters, transport unit, officer's and sergeant's messes, the Badcoe club (other rank's mess), instructional buildings where all officer and senior NCO courses, promotion courses and administration courses were conducted. Later the Intelligence Centre was also included having been moved from Middle Head in Sydney. The second ridgeline was where all the jungle warfare training was centred. This included the Headquarters Battle Wing, instructional buildings, the (dreaded) Confidence Course, the river, the tower, the messes for students, and the accommodation (all tentage). We, as group captains, had one corrugated iron building, which had four self-standing dividers in the middle, giving us each (four groups) very little room to carry out administration and brief our staff. We had one cupboard, one table, and six chairs. Somehow it seemed enough except when you wanted to express some anger at staff or students or support staff when everyone in all four rooms heard every word and expletive that you chose to offer.

From five in the morning, this ridgeline was a hive of activity. The instruction was done to two separate groups; those who came through as sub-units, i.e., companies, troops, squadrons, etc., who had their own rank structure and were expecting to maintain this in Vietnam, e.g., companies from battalions would go through set exercises and training based on the fact that they would travel to Vietnam as an integral group whereas others such as doctors, dentists, ordnance workers, cooks, or reinforcements, et al., would be grouped into individual platoons (simply called Groups) and go through the full range of instruction to prepare individuals for entering a war zone. Even battalions were subject to this drip-feed reinforcement system once the battalion had sailed for Vietnam. Again, a well-thought-out procedural system was achieved that constantly reminded the politicians and, for that matter, the parents of soldiers that their sons were, at least, fully trained for the traumatic ordeal that they were about to face. I do not recall any females being included on any of the courses nor involved in the more administrative tasks of typing, secretarial, or cleaning on Battle Ridge.

This was training at full speed. I was a group commander on Individual Training Wing, and we would work sixteen days straight (most nights also) and then have a five-day break, two of which were taken up on writing reports and preparing for the next course and generally one would be spent as duty officer or duty warrant officer/sergeant, thus, reducing your time with your family to little more than a weekend. Staff were required to do everything the students did, including range shoots, the Confidence Course, the water jump from the tower, route marches, bush exercises, and run-and-shoot exercises which were conducted at the end of each bush exercise. This consisted of a three-kilometre run (in full gear) after a five-day field exercise along a bush track to the Engineer Bridge Range (EBR), participate in a range practice and then a route march back to camp which was up Heartbreak Hill past the Boike Road married quarters and back to Battle Ridge (about another three kilometres). This was extremely testing, and many staff would end up carrying more than their own weapons back into the camp area. This really was a time when courage was tested and staff gained their credibility for enormous feats of strength and self-determination. This was certainly the area where staff, in particular, gained my respect.

Almost every day there was a story created. I returned from an exercise one afternoon to see a truck pull out from in front of the headquarters on Battle Ridge. In the back were four soldiers with rifles and my 3-year-old daughter in a pair of shorts who waved to me out of the back of the truck. Apparently, she had run away from our house, crossed the narrow wooden bridge in amongst the trees, and was running around Battle Ridge. My wife, finding her missing, called the centre and asked if they could have a look for her. The Ridge had just phoned my wife advising that they had located her when I rang in a bit of panic seeking clarification. She was quickly found, and the troops were just returning her when I turned up. Nicole was unrepentant and was quite unaware of the concern that she had caused. Our biggest concern was the number of snakes that were continually seen in and around the married quarters.

At this time Carole was also pregnant with our second daughter and although local doctors could check on her health and progress we decided that it was important to have the baby in a Brisbane hospital which was the closest city. We chose the Mater Women's Hospital in South Brisbane and the doctor decided to induce the baby to prevent us having to make constant trips to the hospital (70 kilometres away) if false alarms occurred. Planning went well and although induced the baby was a few hours late in arriving however both mother and daughter were well. Our second daughter Lisa was now part of the family and proved to be much better behaved than her free-spirited sister

Mainly for the benefit of the staff and students on Main Ridge, every morning an enormous morning tea was provided in both the officer's and warrant officer's and sergeant's messes. Whenever Battle Wing staff got the opportunity and the timing right, we would all sprint across the gully between the two ridges and hopefully get a shot at the scones before they were devoured by the student body. The officer commanding of our Support Group (provided services such as communications and enemy troops for exercises) was an ex-Kiwi with a wicked sense of humour who carefully cared for a large amethyst python. Quite frequently he would bring the snake with him to morning tea, and as all the students bogged into the cakes and crumpets, he would throw the snake onto the table in amongst the scones and strawberry jam and then calmly walk forward as everyone was heading for the exits and invite us 'Philistines from the other ridge' to indulge ourselves. It was hilarious, and he did it regularly but only if the commandant was not present.

This posting allowed everyone to test themselves against the soldier they thought they were, and no more was it tested than when it rained or when it was mid-winter. It was not a particularly wet location, but when it rained, it came in quickly and with great venom. However, winter could be bitter. Almost every morning there was a cover of frost over the ground, and if we were out patrolling, the frost would build up over the barrel of your rifle, and it was extremely difficult to get fingers and joints moving. By 9 a.m., however, everything would have thawed out, and the days would be beautiful although the ground remained damp until lunchtime, not the best way to get soldiers moving when you were training for tropical warfare.

As we entered 1972, it was obvious that the war was running out of pace. Australia had reduced its presence, and Gough Whitlam was about to be elected as Australia's prime minister. Quite a number of courses were cancelled, and all of a sudden, we had a fine group of instructors with no one to teach. The real beauty of Canungra was the availability of facilities. In the local training area, we had a custom-built 'VC Village', we had open training areas, we had dense training areas, we had mechanical ranges and classical ranges where any sort of practices could be conducted. We had a booby trap course, a Confidence course, a rope course, a grenade course/range, and a live fire course where everything was done with a Vickers machine gun firing live rounds three feet above your head. This was realistic training at its best. However, it was speedily coming to an end, and new uses for these facilities had to be determined, and in the meantime, staff had to be employed. These were challenges we were not fully prepared for.

Initially, it was foreseen that groups such as the Royal Military College and Army Reserve Officers courses would find great use of the facilities with a limited but well-prepared staff. However, they would only attend once or twice a year, so other student sources had to be found. It was decided that we would design and conduct survival courses for the RAAF based on the basic escape and evasion courses which forced the students to live off the land. Logically, to demonstrate how to live off the land, we had to learn the techniques ourselves and then be prepared to demonstrate these techniques to the students.

The first of these techniques was to purchase sheep and find someone prepared to humanely 'cut the throat' and demonstrate the skinning and preparing of the animal to eat. This technique, it was reasoned, could then be transferred to almost any animal including rabbits and cattle. Unfortunately, whilst waiting for this course to draw enough student interest to get started, the course was cancelled as was the second attempt. By this time, the sheep had become quite a family friend to the staff, and they had even given it a name. Consequently when the course finally got under way, the appointed slaughterer could not cut the throat of a family pet and the job therefore went to an unsuspecting member of staff who would have been referred to the Animal Welfare League if mobile phones were then in use. The demonstration, needless to say, went very poorly, and even though the task was eventually performed, it was quite messy and looked totally unprofessional. However, the course was under way, and there were parts of it that were extremely successful. I am not sure, however, that we ever ran a second course.

This was the end of my time at the Jungle Training Centre, clearly a place that legendary army ghosts came to rest. The quality of members from all corps within the army was, without a doubt, truly memorable.

CHAPTER TWELVE

DARWIN

SOME SIX WEEKS before I finished up at Canungra, I was advised that the family and myself would be moving to Goldie River in Papua New Guinea where I would take up the job of training officer of the Third Pacific Islands Regiment (PIR) which was about to be raised, and therefore, my family should have all our passport and inoculation requirements (for that area) up to date. I was also sworn to secrecy. This posting was a bit of a worry to Carole and myself as Goldie River was a bit isolated and our daughters were 'very blonde', which made them somewhat of a target for local, native bandits, but assurances were given, and we resigned ourselves to an enjoyable tour of the South-West Pacific. Transport arrangements were made and removal was booked with most of our furniture going into storage and a small amount travelling at the same time as us.

Ten days before departure, with all arrangements made, we were advised that 3PIR was not going ahead and therefore our posting to PNG was cancelled. We were completely stunned, taken by surprise, and did not quite know how to react. What was in store now? Our removal was still booked, and time was getting short—three days to go—and I was advised that my posting would be to the Seventh Military District Headquarters in Darwin and transport was being booked accordingly.

The trouble was that because of the late notice, there was not sufficient time to arrange for my pay or allowances to be paid before I left; initially, this wasn't thought to be a problem as we would be accommodated in Brisbane the night before we left, and therefore, I could catch a cab into the Brisbane pay office and get my allowances before I had to catch the flight. This would have been great except the public servant running the pay office refused to open the cage before 9 a.m., which meant that I would have been running very 'skinny' at catching the plane, so at 8.50 a.m., I left the pay office quite depressed, grabbed a cab, and met Carole and the kids at the airport without a bean in my pocket. No drinks for the kids until we got on the plane.

Whilst flying, I mapped out a plan to somehow get into the bank and draw out enough money to get us through the next couple of days. Great plan, we arrived in Darwin, on a Friday, in November, stepped out the doorway, and thought we were in an oven. Bloody hell, it was hot. Worse still, the driver who had been sent to pick us up informed us that it was Darwin Show Day and everything including the banks was closed—no ATMs or credit cards (for that matter) in those days, so no way of drawing any money.

We arrived at our married quarter with three suitcases and nothing else. We were climatically unadjusted, the girls were thirsty, and I had nowhere to go. We entered the quarter and, the place being unoccupied for a couple of weeks, was covered in dust. There was nothing in the fridge, and we had no linen until our furniture arrived which wasn't going to be that day. The girls were already getting filthy just playing on the floor. We were depressed. I decided that I would leave the house and go out and try to find a solution, no plan, just a determination.

At that moment, there was a knock on the door and there stood salvation. Our closest neighbour had seen us arrive and came over to say welcome. A young ordnance corps lieutenant, Colin Ward, greeted us with an engaging personality and a distraught look when he saw that we had nothing. I told him our tale of woe, and he immediately jumped into action. He lent me $50 and advised that the army canteen was still open and he would arrange a temporary account for us to get some food in (particularly milk for Lisa who was only 18 months old at this time) which we could pay for as soon as we got to the bank. Kevin and his wife later loaned us some towels and sheets and found us a six-pack of beer which was definitely not wasted. Logically, we became very close to our neighbours and saw a lot of them over the next twelve months—they had prevented our entry into Darwin from becoming a tragedy.

Monday was a new beginning. Already my family was adjusting to the heat. Canungra was in fact very hot when we left, so we didn't have to adjust as much as we first thought. The next day I walked across to the pay office (which was on the base) and drew my pay and allowances which allowed me to pay out all the costs from the day before and for Carole to fully stock the refrigerator. The layout of the base was very convenient for us with the headquarters (where I would be working) being only 100 metres from our married quarter. After I picked up my earnings, I walked down the corridor of the headquarters and introduced myself to everyone who was in their office including my new boss Major Dave (Darky) Couzens, RAA, who was to become one of the best bosses I worked for in my entire career. Dave arranged for me to have a quick tour of the Larrakeyah area (the base) and meet a couple of the unit commanders who were working there—a good opportunity topping off a very good day.

The evenings were hot, but the louvred and elevated nature of the houses allowed strong air flow which kept us fairly cool, and the wet season had commenced which brought spectacular evening thunderstorms which Carole and I began to watch over a beer from our small side veranda. Darwin was shaping as an interesting place.

I started work the next morning, a short walk only to the headquarters. Dave Couzens introduced me to the staff of Operations Branch which consisted of himself, myself, a warrant officer class 2 (military policeman), and an ops sergeant and an intelligence sergeant. We had access to a typing pool and an administrative pool who filed all our documents—small by any standard. Dave advised me that we had an Army Reserve Officer Cadet Training Unit (OCTU) which was autonomous but came under the authority of the headquarters, therefore, Ops Branch had the responsibility of 'keeping an eye on it' mainly for the purpose of ensuring that it was kept up to date with all operational matters and remaining up to date with training information. I, therefore, assessed my job as being the staff officer grade 3 (Captain) for Ops, Training, Ares, Intelligence, Welfare (I was also in charge of the amenities for the district and the picture theatre) and, as I later found out, interservice sport—bloody hell, when was I going to sleep?

Fortunately, everyone knew their jobs, and I had no shortage of help from other members of the headquarters when I was settling into my job. I did notice, however, that as soon as I sat at my desk for the first time, the chief clerk put this monstrous pile of files in my in-tray, gave me a smile, and said, 'We've been waiting for you to arrive, sir.'

I started to attack the mountain of files when Dave advised me that the commander had arrived at work and wished to meet me. That was a pleasant experience; the commander shook hands, sat me down, asked me a few questions about my history, explained briefly his philosophy, and suggested that this was a great place to work and he hoped I would enjoy it. I returned to my office which now had three people standing in it.

The first was the projectionist who wanted me to let him know what films he was to order and asked when we could speak about the amenities fund (which currently had over $6,000 in it), the second was the OC of the RAEME repair workshop who wanted to know when I was starting the volleyball competition (another officer who proved to be wonderfully supportive of my position), and the OC of the local ordnance depot (a senior major) who was quite adamant that I re-introduce the $600 sponsorship for 7MD members holidaying in Bali (which was quite close to Darwin)—a brisk start to my new job on subjects about which I had no idea. I asked them politely to give me a day or so to 'read into these matters' and I would visit their units and speak to them about it.

I decided I would try to reduce the overflowing size of my in-tray and then read up on the other matters that night. However, Dave Couzens stepped into my office and advised me that because of my security clearance I would also be responsible for reading and accounting for the Secret / Top Secret files held by the headquarters each week and make any appropriate reports to him as they occurred. He then handed me twelve salmon pink files and said, 'I would like these complete by lunchtime and handed back to me so I can lock them in my safe.' There went my first plan out the window. I shook my head thinking what a busy little place I have walked into. On day one, I made up my mind to work through lunch to catch up on my plan, and I don't think that practice stopped for the two years I was there.

The afternoon was just a grind to see how much I could get through, and it went well with the exception of a call from the mess supervisor who advised that I had been voted in as the mess secretary and I should call up and see him in the next few days as there were some functions coming up that I needed to organise. Groan, why me! I thought, well, it's 5 p.m., that's enough for one day (the working day started at 8 a.m. and finished 4 p.m.), so most had gone home or to the mess. I decided, being the first day, I would go straight home (having put a case of beer on the fridge before going to work) and thinking that a coldie would be ideal after a fairly gruelling though not unhappy day.

I got to the bottom of the stairs and headed around the laundry to grab a cold beer from the downstairs fridge when I was greeted by about eight new friends and a couple of wives who had dropped over to say welcome. There were no fences in those days, and privacy downstairs was provided by about 40 x 7 foot Uralia plants which grew around the base of the house. These guys had stopped at the first house on the way home, which was mine, and headed straight for the fridge. By the time I got there, there were only about half a dozen cans left out of the new case. Someone called out, 'You're nearly out of beer, Brian, perhaps you need to get some more!' I soon realised this was just a friendly ad hoc welcoming party, and in reality, it was great. It provided a very good opportunity to meet some of the wives and displayed the friendships that had emerged from living in this environment. I also learnt a lot about 'how things really worked' such as the need to 'get on' with everyone you worked with because when work ceased, these were your neighbours.

Darwin proved to be a wonderful environment for both Carole and the kids. The city was ten minutes' drive away, there was a barracks swimming pool, a canteen on base, and a very good public school directly outside the front gate which meant that Carole could walk Nicole to school each day and they could all go swimming in the afternoons—a great environment.

I thought I was actually getting on top of my job when the Intelligence WO advised me that we were also committed to spending a half a day a month teaching the Northern Territory Police the art of map reading and our first session was due on the forthcoming Friday. This I welcomed as I was always good at the subject and had taught it when I was an instructor at the School of Infantry at Ingleburn. It was also a great opportunity to meet the local constabulary and see how good they really were at their job.

This was a truly great experience, and I fully enjoyed the commitment. Whereas the police were very good at establishing their location on roads and along the coastline, they were easily disoriented once we took them into the bush. This became a fun experience with the police being keen learners and quickly realising the army weren't without skills. Our biggest problem was that we didn't get the same police every session, so we had to do a lot of revision, but nonetheless, it was great for us to get out of the office and great for the police to learn a new skill. We also made some very valuable contacts.

Whilst we were setting up the police instruction, Dave Couzens called me into his office and advised that we had another valuable role to play on the headquarters and that was to organise and orchestrate a continual update to the 'Military Directory'. In other words, we had to ensure that we knew more about the terrain and infrastructure of the Northern Territory than any potential enemy, and to do this, we needed to get out of the headquarters and explore the limits of our river systems. This would mean assembling a team of about fifty people to transport, navigate, carry (if necessary) several teams to the mouth of an identified river and update the information held on its condition, depth, accessibility, flow, and ability to provide food and palatable water. We recorded how valuable this river might be to a potential enemy.

Wow, this came as a surprise, and again I began to wonder how we fitted it all in. However, Dave displayed his great leadership and quickly showed me how to go about it, what we needed, and where to find the logistical backup needed to complete this exercise. The local unit commanders were used to these exercises occurring periodically and were very supportive and welcomed the opportunity to get their soldiers 'out in the bush'. We needed every truck, every Zodiac, every flat-bottomed boat, and every outboard motor we could get our hands on and the operators for these equipment. In addition, we needed food, water, and fuel and a lot of liaison prior to venturing into areas which were often private property, police regions, or indigenous leases. These were ten-day operations and provided almost the 'adventure of a lifetime'. We caught fish and prawns, observed some of the biggest crocodiles I have ever seen, were chased by buffalo, and slept under the stars. Needless to say, there was always hard work involved particularly when we had to carry the boats and motors over dry stretches of river and rocky outcrops.

During my time in the Territory (November 1972 until September 1974), we did five of these exercises, which included the Daly River, the Roper River, the East Alligator River, the Katherine River, and Groote Eyland. These were the experiences that made the posting to Darwin worthwhile.

Two stories quickly come to mind when I think about these exercises. The first being my first real experience with a crocodile. We were travelling from the source to the mouth of the Roper River (east coast of the Northern Territory) when night began to fall, so we pulled into a mangrove-covered bank and established a small camp lighting a fire and locating suitable places on the bank to sleep. We always slept with our feet to the water just as an added piece of security against being grabbed by a crocodile. During the night, I was sleeping about four metres from the young engineer who was our outboard motor mechanic when I heard several very loud, distinctive barks between us. I quickly jumped up thinking that we must be on someone's property for a dog to be amongst us. However, not so, a three-metre crocodile had come onshore and had positioned himself between the mechanic and myself, for what purpose I am not sure, however, my quick but unsure movement must have startled him and he turned and headed back into the water. By now the camp was awake and I advised them that perhaps we might need to run a piquet for the remainder of the night which we did with a much greater appreciation of the danger.

The other event that occurred on the Roper was closer to the mouth where we saw, on the southern bank, the remains of Vestey's Meat Works which was an abattoir and meat processing plant which had closed down about ten years previously. We assessed that it provided useful buildings that might be of assistance to an attacking force, so we chose to investigate on foot. Along with the buildings were a series of concrete ponds or pools which seemed to have been created to breed prawns. Now the interesting thing was that they were absolutely full of the biggest king prawns you have ever seen which were obviously living off themselves. You could almost walk across them, they were so dense. Logically, we drew out a mosquito net from our packs and proceeded to 'scoop' up kilo after kilo of prawns which we returned to the boats and decided on making camp early. Without ice, we could only cook enough for a couple of days, but they tasted beautiful and provided a great relief to hard rations after several days on the river.

These trips provided a magnificent view of the country with all of its beauty—wild birds, buffalo, crocodiles, reptiles of all types, and an endless supply of termites who built huge nests above ground and faced them east/west so that they protected themselves from the direct, intense heat of the sun. There were, of course, a myriad of hidden dangers, and we could not afford to have any serious injury because we had no immediate means of evacuation. Although the RAAF always provided people to accompany us on these trips (along with RAN, police, and Customs when they could spare the manpower), and therefore, we always planned on calling on the RAAF for a helicopter if we needed emergency evacuation. To my mind, we were never put in a position where we had to call on this facility.

We did, however, have a wonderful relationship with RAAF and RAN, Customs, and the federal police along with the Northern Territory State

Police, and they came into play in the most curious way. The other role I had on the headquarters was to be in charge of intelligence, and as such, I had to attend all investigations which were instigated by the RAAF for UFO sightings (unidentified flying objects). Logically, there were quite a few of these sightings, but most were dismissed by the local police or overflights by the RAAF which could explain the most likely reasons for the sighting. However, when an unexplained activity was thought to be occurring, it was important that we called the representatives of the border protection group, boardered a Douglas DC3 aircraft provided by the RAAF, and flew off to investigate. The police and Customs were excellent on these trips and had a large number of skills which saved us a lot of time which would have otherwise been wasted and were authorised to make decisions about the activity which set all our minds at rest and allowed us to return back to Darwin.

During these 'alerts', we travelled to Melville Island and Groote Eylandt, Alice Springs, Ayers Rock (now named Uluru), the northern parts of Western Australia (Kununurra, the Kimberley, Fitzroy Crossing), and Hall's Creek. Logically, at many of them, we met some wonderful locals who always wanted to share a drink and a story about their UFO experiences and many, of course, revolved around the infamous 'Mim Mim' lights. Indigenous workers in the outback areas had an almost 'absolute fear' of the Mim Mim lights—a group of lights, some big some small, that moved around the sky and often moved towards them if they were on horseback or walking at night-time. These were wondrous stories, but we never saw any Mim Mim lights nor found any evidence of their existence—however, the stories were great!

Seventh Military District Headquarters was only a small headquarters, but there were so many parts to every job that no one ever really got bored. Our family took great delight in drawing out a tent from the Amenities Store (which I was responsible for), loading up the eskies, and taking off 'down the track' (down the Stuart Highway) for the weekend. Our two main destinations were either Berry Springs or Howard Springs where there were great swimming holes, plenty of places for camping, and enough people to feel safe and secure.

Our girls would swim almost for the whole weekend, whereas Carole and I would read, walk, or sleep under the shade of some very convenient trees—very therapeutic, very relaxing. The nights were balmy and were mainly spent sitting around a central fire chatting to some newly made friends, many of whom were from units within Larrakeyah Barracks.

In Darwin, I played rugby league, Australian rules, volleyball, and basketball. I also was responsible for organising sport within Larrakeyah, so I recommenced the volleyball competition, started a basketball competition, and played golf in the funny little golf course that some adventurous soul had created within the barracks. On top of this heavy schedule, we also had a very competitive interservice competition where army and navy joined forces against the RAAF who had a base containing over 1,000 personnel. We played every sport imaginable with rugby league, Australian rules, volleyball, tennis, basketball, golf (played at the more suitably crafted RAAF course), and table tennis. These combined activities, particularly interservice sport, really brought all members of the base together which meant a very tight, loyal community, most of whom got on extremely well. Too well in some cases.

One Saturday evening, we were having a barbeque at Colin Ward's married quarter. The night was wearing on and we had had plenty to drink. At about midnight, the duty officer walked over from his office and advised us that there had been a major accident down the Stuart Highway and a lot of blood transfusions were going to be needed. The blood bank therefore rang the military to assist. The duty officer advised that he had rang the other ranks' contacts on the base and arranged a truck to take us into the blood bank. About six of us volunteered and washed our faces to sober up and got ready to give blood. The truck duly arrived, and it was already full of other ranks who had been having a similar evening as ourselves, only I think they may have been in slightly worse condition. They helped us aboard and off we ventured.

Now, the blood bank in Darwin was unique. In order to entice enough people to donate, they offered two stubbies of VB to anyone who donated blood. Well, we arrived, and of course, were very noisy and flooded the waiting room. One of the soldiers spotted the fridge, opened the door, and immediately started handing out beers. The locals were unimpressed at first, but when encouraged to have a drink with us, they came around, and by the time the nurse worked out what was happening in the waiting room, we had everyone singing some well-known song.

The nurse quickly worked out what had happened and was quite terse with the lot of us, but the soldiers quickly sweet-talked her and she realised she needed the blood donations, so she gave up protesting and got on with her job. Unfortunately, the blood bank ran out of beer before we had all donated, so we were grateful when the job was done and we could all go back to our parties.

Despite being a wonderful place to raise children, we did have one nasty incident which had a permanent effect on our eldest daughter, Nicole. We were having a barbecue downstairs and had the customary five or six couples attending. The kids (probably about ten of them) were playing in between a couple of the yards (no fences), and Nicole was nursing one of the neighbours' cats. Nicole was about 7 years old at the time when a neighbour's dog came bounding into the yard barking (probably at the cats). The cat that Nicole was nursing immediately 'arced up', exposed its claws, and ran over Nicole's head to escape. Shortly after, Nicole came to see me and said her eye was sore. I was at the barbecue and the light was not very bright. I looked into her eye and saw that it was very red but could not see anything else that might be inflaming it. During the night, Nicole continually mentioned the fact that the eye was sore. I eventually placed a patch over it and said that we would look at it the next morning. Carole also shared my concern but could not see anything causing the soreness.

Early the next morning, Nicole woke us with her sore eye. Immediately it was evident that the cat had scratched the eyeball (sclera and the cornea) and it was seeping. We quickly got in the car and drove to Emergency at the Darwin Hospital where Nicole was admitted. We then contacted a surgeon who was a friend of Dave Couzens and asked for his immediate advice. The surgeon wasted no time and rang the hospital and found out the diagnosis which was not good—micro surgery was necessary to save any level of sight in the eye. Carole and I were now confronted with a critical decision—give the go-ahead for micro surgery by a surgeon we had not previously met, nor heard of, but was the only eye surgeon capable of performing the operation in Darwin or risk a delay but catch the next plane to Adelaide in the hope of having more informed diagnosis by more experienced surgeons. We weighed up all the options we had on offer and decided we would have the operation done, in Darwin, immediately.

To their eternal credit, the surgeon and the hospital went into overdrive and Nicole went into surgery. It was a long and stressful wait, but eventually our precious daughter was returned to the ward and was restful and seemingly pain free. The surgeon called by, advised us that he thought the operation was extremely successful, and advised that Nicole would spend a week in hospital and then could return home and, because of the threat of infection, was required to keep the eye covered for several weeks before a final clearance would be given.

Darwin, in those days, did not have a specific Children's Ward, so the children were grouped down one end of the general Adults' Ward. Nicole was quite unhappy when we left her on the first night as she was not used to living without her parents; however, by the next morning, she was brighter and had made friends with those who surrounded her. One of these was a young aboriginal mother whose daughter had got too close to a fire whilst sleeping and had a burn on her arm, and another was a young boy who had received a dart in his eye and was in a similar position as Nicole. He was very quiet the first few days but was an absolute dynamo as he gained in strength and confidence. He was a wild boy (wouldn't stay in bed), but he was funny as a monkey and kept us all entertained—him and Nicole became very good friends, and they were good for each other. During the time we were in the hospital, we didn't see this young boy receive any visitors, so he anxiously awaited our visits every day, along with Nicole.

Within a week, Nicole was released from hospital and eventually the eye patch was removed and she started to adjust to the refraction in her vision. The surgery looked like it had worked, and there was very little physical indication that surgery had actually taken place. However, it had, and Nicole has had great difficulty with that eye ever since although never allowing it to distract her from her objectives. Subsequent visits to ophthalmologists have never suggested that the initial surgery was anything but the best available option at the time. Carole and I have often discussed whether we made the best decision at the time—we still don't know.

Darwin was referred to as the 'Last Frontier', and I have to say that every step taken outside the barracks was an adventure. The fishing was great, the people unique, and the experience for the whole family was refreshing and totally enjoyable. We were expecting that all this would end about Christmastime 1974, and we would be looking for a posting somewhere on the east coast of Australia; however, early in 1974, Brisbane experienced (once in a hundred years) heavy flooding, and the area most being inundated seemed to be the area where our furniture was stored whilst we were in our sub-tropical posting (furnished accommodation). As the drama of the event played out, I spoke to my superiors and asked if I may take some leave, catch a RAAF flight to Brisbane, and see if our furniture was okay. The commander did not approve this leave and said that I was to wait until the 'Brisbane Lord Mayors Fund' was finalised and I would be advised the result of the searches conducted in the storage houses in Brisbane. This occurred, and we were advised that most of our equipment was okay except one container which contained certain items (which they listed) and enclosed a cheque for $936 as compensation for those items which they found to be missing. We accepted the decision knowing that our big items of equipment/furniture were safe and we would have the basis of a full house of furniture for our next accommodation even if it might be a bit out of date.

As 1974 wore on, I was advised that because I had spent a very busy posting in Canungra and left with very short notice, I had about three months' worth of annual leave stored in my Record of Service and was told to plan on leaving Darwin early so that my leave credits could be cleared. No posting order had been received at this time, but Carole and I set a date for late September to leave as we would be driving out and we could take a look at the country on the way out. Just before leaving, I was advised that I would be posted to Brisbane (unit not identified), however, I would be required to do one of my 'career' courses in Sydney in January before moving to Brisbane.

So fully loaded and suitably farewelled, the family plus trailer set off for the East Coast via Adelaide. This was to become one of the most amazing ordeals we had yet faced as a family. Fortunately, I had prepared for the trip and loaded additional water, spare parts (including nuts and bolts, water hoses, etc.), and some dried food. I had also had the wheel bearings on the trailer renewed although I had not checked them for tension because it was only completed hours before we left—that was a mistake!

We were travelling well with the girls in the back seat singing along to all the tapes we had brought with us (*Bangtail Muster*, the theme from the Muppets, etc.). We were equipped for camping and had stayed the first night at the Daly River crossing providing me with one last chance to catch a barramundi before I left the Territory—failed. We packed up the following morning and were heading for Katherine. We were just approaching Pine Creek when I noticed one of the wheels off the trailer running down the road beside the car. I immediately pulled up, chocked the trailer (difficult because of the weight), and set off down the road on foot to collect the miscreant wheel. All nuts were gone from that wheel, but I had enough spares to cover it. I unloaded the trailer and checked both wheels feeling lucky that none of the bolts had (bar one) damaged threads, repacked the trailer, and got under way again—not exactly a good start to a long journey.

We travelled comfortably, stopping overnight in small camping sites along the Stuart Highway until we got to the Telegraph Station just north of Alice Springs. The nights were still quite cool (sleeping on the ground), so we decided to pull into the hotel (very old), have a meal, and see if we could get some accommodation. This we did with the hosts being a very nice couple who served the four of us pub meals at the bar. It was a wonderfully historical place and was great to sleep off the ground even if only for one night.

The next morning, we packed up and headed off for Alice Springs. What a great feeling to be back in Alice. I had visited there a number of times on military business which had included trips out to Ayres Rock (now Uluru), but Carole and the girls had not visited either place. We sought out a camping park, booked in for a week, and set up our tent. The days were still a beautiful 18–21 degree Celsius. Time to start exploring. This we did visiting Standley Chasm, Simpsons Gap, the home of the Royal Flying Doctor, the camel races, Anzac Hill, and the infamous Todd River. Each night we would return back to our tent and cook up our meals on our camp gas stove which was small by today's standards but adequate for our purposes. What really surprised us, however, particularly sleeping on blow-ups on the ground was how cold the nights were—they got down to –1 and –2 degrees by night, which encouraged us to purchase a mat to put under our blow-ups to allow us to sleep.

After a week, we left Alice and headed along the 350 km dirt road to Ayers Rock (only part of the road was sealed back in the '70s). Unfortunately, we got about 100 km out of Alice, and I lost a bolt out of the trailer coupling and was unable to find anything suitable to make it safe. The bolt had been severed and the nut lost. This was a real problem. I pulled into a cleared area and checked the map. The closest location, by my reckoning, was a farmhouse about 75 km south. There was a tourist bus parked in the same cleared area as us, so I spoke to the driver and asked him how long he would be there. He said about two hours, he had broken a fan belt, so I positioned Carole and the girls in some shade, provided them some water and a very small amount of food, and left them to watch the trailer.

I took off estimating it would take me about three hours to get to the farmhouse and back and hoping that the owners were able to assist me— in blind hope I had taken the measurements of the size and depth of the drill hole. I hit warp speed with the whole way being a surface of four to five inches of powdered dust (referred to as bulldust) and carrying a big dose of guilt for the solution that I had chosen, particularly if the farmer could not provide me with a solution. I continued also to hope that the bus would take longer to repair than predicted. Fortunately, my navigation skills were good, and I passed very few vehicles along the way.

I arrived at the farmhouse in about an hour and the owner was in the middle of afternoon tea. As usual, for those parts of the world, the family was courteous and understanding, and they asked me to just wait for them to finish their tea and scones and they would have a look for what was available. Sure enough, they had a workshop/shed that could build an aeroplane, but believe it or not, they could not find a nut and bolt that would meet the size I was after. My heart sank, time was moving on, and I was no closer to a solution. 'The solution is simple', declared the owner, 'we'll make one!' Without hesitation, he uncovered a metal lathe, produced some blank bolts, set the lathe with a set of callipers, and cut a bolt to the measurements I had provided. Just to be sure, he cut three of them and, then just as quickly, cut and threaded the hex nuts to go with them ensuring two nuts for each bolt so that I could lock them in place. My god, the guy was a saint! Logically, he wouldn't take any money for the task but grinned as I shook his hand and said, 'Good luck!'

Two hours had passed by now, so I was getting a little anxious but put the 'pedal to the metal' and took off in a cloud of dust. I arrived back at the clearing to see my trailer was in place and the bus was gone, but Carole and the kids were nowhere to be seen. I jumped out of the car as they came running out of their shady spot as anxious to see me as I was to see them. Carole said the bus had gone about thirty minutes after I left and they had been on their own for the past two-and-a-half hours.

Now was the test, to see if I had measured the bolt holes correctly so we could get going again. I took out the new bolts and they fitted perfectly, so within twenty minutes or so, we were on our way towards Ayers Rock.

The trip was a long one, but I wanted to reach the camping area before last light. It was almost completely a dirt road and was very typically Northern Territory scenery, but the blend of colours that seemed to change every fifty kilometres or so (with the movement of the sun) made the journey anything but boring. The colours gave great credibility and reality to Albert Namajira's paintings. There was also another dimension to the timing that we visited that area. Alice Springs and surrounding properties had recently received the most rain that they had received at that time of the year (mid-dry season) for fifty years, and as such, all the wild flowers were out in bloom. They provided a beauty that can hardly be described, desert flowers of every different colour. The rain, however, had produced a further implication which we were to find out about very soon.

We arrived in the Ayers Rock camping area just before last light and commenced to set up our tent, stove, beds, etc. Carole had some dinner going and we were just eating our meal when I felt a presence in the area and couldn't quite comprehend what it was, but as the light faded, I could see hundreds of sets of eyes surrounding our camp space. We were surrounded by thousands of field mice which were the direct result of the increase in food and water occasioned by the mid-season rainfall. Surprisingly, during our meal, the plague receded, and we set about preparing for the evening.

We had set up our sleeping bags outside the tent to take advantage of the advancing summer weather, and after the camp had been cleaned up, we retired and switched off the gas lamp. Within minutes, our bodies were covered with a flood of mice running all over us. Logically, this scared the kids, and Carole said that she couldn't possibly sleep under those conditions. We tried to move the sleeping bags inside the tent and secure it where possible, but this did not stop the penetration and invasion of this horde. Eventually, the girls were moved into the car, Carole into the front seat and the sisters into the back seat, and I was left to face the ever-increasing invasion. I tried pulling a parachute silk up over my body but could still feel the thousands of small feet running all over me and providing the odd nibble on my legs. Sleep was impossible, but I didn't assess any danger, so I lay there trying to see the night out. Somewhere in the middle of the night, the mice retreated, and I was able to get some sleep. When dawn arrived, there was no sign of them although any food that had been left out was gone. Eventually, the girls emerged having slept poorly in the car (an EH Holden) but satisfied that they didn't have to persevere with the mice problem.

We had decided to come to Uluru to view the changing colours and show the girls the magnitude of this wonderful monolith, but the mice plague convinced us that a long-term stay wasn't going to be pleasant, so we decided to head back to the Stuart Highway and continue on our way to the east coast. The trip was still well worth the effort and another experience we wouldn't forget although the girls were probably too young to remember it for long.

The trip into Adelaide was again a long one, and the road wasn't sealed for more than about half the distance (about 1,400 kilometres), so the family was starting to show signs of boredom (we had sung every song on our tapes about five times over except for the Muppet's theme which had been repeated about five hundred times), and the vehicle was starting to show a couple of rattles, so we decided that we would spend a few days in Adelaide and then Carole and the kids could fly to Sydney (to stay with Carole's parents) whilst I oversaw some minor repairs to the vehicle and trailer and then drove to Sydney. This took me about a week, but I think the family was glad that very long journey was over and they missed the extra journey from Adelaide to Sydney.

As soon as I arrived in Sydney, I booked a plane to Brisbane to get some indication of the state of our furniture and possessions since the flood damage earlier in the year had now been cleaned up and all the funds closed. The process was a simple one, but I had to catch quite a number of taxis to get me to and from the storage facility. I was expecting about five containers of furniture along with a fridge and a freezer; the attendant informed me almost immediately that the fridge and freezer were okay but only one container had our name on it. I immediately went into 'panic' mode and waded through the limited amount of items that were still held in the warehouse. Within minutes, I found our fridge (which was damaged beyond repair) having been left out in the open but no sign of the freezer; I quickly arranged for our one container to be opened and inside was an axe head, a steel trunk which belonged to me, sixty feet of garden hose, and a chair (broken) which didn't belong to us. I showed the attendant my letter which said all the other furniture (and listed it) was okay, ergo, where was it? We were missing about $30,000 worth of personal items. The attendant shook his head and said that it did not exist in the warehouse and must have been destroyed by the flood. I was shattered and wasn't quite sure how to advise Carole. I lodged my complaint with the warehouse, but they had no handle on insurance or compensation for that matter and didn't want to know about the matter. I got the same response from the Department of Defence and subsequent follow-up letters to everyone I could think of still left Carole and myself out of pocket for about $30,000—never to be recovered.

Life moves in funny ways, however. I was quite depressed as I travelled back to Sydney not quite sure how we were going to furnish our next abode with only a few possessions returning from the Northern Territory. No sooner had I got home when the phone rang and the Infantry Directorate advised me that I had been posted to Hong Kong on detachment to the Brigade of Gurkhas, specifically Seventh Duke of Edinburgh's Own Gurkha Rifles located in the New Territories. My family was also cleared to travel with me. I would attend my infantry corps major's course (captains qualifying for major) in January, and we would fly to Hong Kong in February. This was perfect and meant that we would not be required to buy any new furniture as the unit where we would be living in Fanling was furnished. Off to another adventure.

I attended the corps course at the Infantry Centre which had been relocated to Singleton in central NSW since I had last served there in 1967/68. Great opportunity to catch up with some old friends and, of course, make some new ones. Peter Cosgrove and myself had not seen much of each other since returning from Vietnam. He was required to stay on to attend a court martial and did not return until early in 1970.

We took the opportunity to re-acquaint ourselves, and Peter went on to demonstrate why he was later to become the nation's governor general. He was clearly the top military mind within our course, although there were others who challenged for the billing. Absolutely marvellous course and I enjoyed every moment of it and every person on it—more education on military matters.

CHAPTER THIRTEEN

HONG KONG

AFTER A BIT of running around the family, all had their health cards up to date, our passports were issued, our remaining personal items from Darwin were resorted and redirected to Hong Kong, a date was set and we were off. We flew in to Kai Tak airport absolutely amazed at how our aircraft didn't hit any of the houses we seemed to be so close to as we landed. The airport was crowded but we were met efficiently by Lieutenant Martin Brooks of Seventh DEO Gurkha Rifles and advised that he would take us to some overnight accommodation at Sha Tin which bordered on the New Territories and he would pick us up the next morning and take us to the battalion and our accommodation at Fanling.

This was done and we checked into a very Chinese-style motel at Sha Tin and got our first chance to 'feel out' our new home. The girls were absolutely bemused by the fact that there were very few Europeans present; everyone who was staying there or working there were Chinese. We ventured into the restaurant for a meal (we had arrived about 7 p.m. at the airport) as it was getting quite late. The menu was in Chinese as was the food—toasted sandwiches, etc., were not on the menu (not that we could read the menu). However, we were served efficiently, the waitress understood what we were after, and recommended a couple of dishes which turned out to be excellent. Breakfast was the same menu, however, we managed to find scrambled eggs on there somewhere, so with some juices, etc., we managed to eat without fuss.

The British certainly were no strangers receiving exchange officers. Right on time, the quartermaster Bill Williams picked us up and took us straight to the block of units where we would be living in Fanling. He had all the paperwork with him, his wife had stocked the fridge with those essential items we needed for the first few days, and an invoice was left on the table. The fishmonger had been arranged to call at our door every Friday, and milk would be delivered every day. Our arrival had been very well arranged, and after the problems we had when we arrived in Darwin, we were very relieved. Bill's wife soon called in and said that she had arranged an amah to call, advised us what was the acceptable pay, and outlined the jobs that she could be asked to do, including watching our children if we went out. Bill suggested that I leave Carole to get settled in and meet the other members of the block in which we were living and I should accompany him to meet the commanding officer. This I agreed to and set forth in the quartermaster's Land Rover.

The exchange that I was part of was between the Royal Australian Infantry Regiment and the Brigade of Gurkhas; it was not until now that I was discovering my time would be spent with Seventh DEO Gurkha Rifles, a proud battalion whose origins dated back to before the turn of the century when the battalion was part of the Indian Army. The commanding officer's name was Lieutenant Colonel Keith Robinson, and he was a very pleasant, no-nonsense sort of person who advised that I wasn't the first 'tame' Australian who had spent time in the battalion. He seemed most pleased to see me and, along with the Battalion 2IC, outlined my role within the battalion and told me what was expected of me.

Brian presenting a gift from the RAR to Sir Walter
Walker, then GOC Hong Kong Command

I was assigned as 2IC C Coy and my officer commanding was Colin Lees, an ex–British Army hockey champion who was naturally very fit. He was also extremely eloquent and very keen to educate me in the ways, customs, and idiosyncrasies of the Gurkha soldier. This was not unlike an Australian Infantry Company in structure, but I noticed that everyone spoke in Gurkhali (a military language catering for all Nepalese dialects) which I, of course, didn't know a word of, so this was going to be a testing hurdle. I quickly learnt, however, that most Gurkha officers spoke English and liked to practice it, and even though the soldiers didn't speak much English, they understood it. So communication got better the more soldiers I spoke to.

Colin Lees was quick to enquire about the family and asked how well they had settled in. He said that the company officers and senior NCOs were holding a curry luncheon as a welcome to us on the weekend and invited us to attend. Not quite what I was expecting as I was only a captain at this stage, and Carole and I were not used to a lot of fanfare when we moved. This soiree was the most unusual luncheon we had ever attended. We turned up to this well set-up series of tables and chairs on a hilltop, virtually in a paddock, however, everything seemed to be there, but everyone was dressed in long trousers, shirts, and ties. Fortunately, I had worn long trousers, but I wouldn't have thought to wear a tie to an outdoor luncheon (I later found that the officers even wore a tie when they mowed their lawns).

Within minutes of arriving, two young Gurkhas turned up and invited our girls to accompany them. We were a bit uneasy about this, but Colin said that they were appointed to the girls for the day and would look after them. We remained apprehensive, but the girls went off happily and disappeared out of sight. The remainder of the luncheon was extremely pleasant with the officers and NCOs being very good company and continually trying to entice us to try the potent chillies that they so much loved to eat with their curries. It was my first experience of a Gurkha curry (goat on this occasion), and I was overwhelmed by how good it was (as long as you didn't eat the chillies). At about 3.30 p.m., the OC advised it was time to pack up and almost immediately over the hill came the two 'babysitters' with our girls on their shoulders and all laughing loudly. Overall a superb welcome to the company and a great meal to boot.

The first week at work was a matter of getting used to routines, meeting as many juniors NCOs and soldiers as possible, and trying to fit into an established and efficient framework. Quite a number of memorable things came out of this week. Firstly, soldiers weren't referred to by their name (e.g., Tickbaharda Rai, Udembahada Limbu, etc.), but they were referred to by the last two digits of their regimental number. For instance, my batman's name was Jitbahadar Rai, but he was referred to as Artis which was No. 31. This meant that not only did I have to get to know all the names in the company, but I also had to learn their last two regimental digits (quite a feat). I also established that Gurkha soldiers have a very keen sense of humour and loved to laugh. On one occasion, I couldn't recall a corporal's number on the morning parade, so noticing that he had a bald patch on his head, I referred to him as 'Helicopter Landing Ground' and the whole company laughed incessantly. Gurkhas were also very keen and often very talented sportsmen, and during this first week, the final events of the battalion's sports competition were in progress.

The first event I was to attend was the basketball; I arrived about ten minutes late for the start, and the CO asked me why I was late and that it should not happen again. Apparently, every officer was expected to attend every event from the outset. I paraded to the CO the next morning and explained that I was being fitted for my uniform by the tailor and got to the game as soon as I was released. He accepted my explanation and repeated that I was not to let it happen again. Lesson learned.

Our company was doing very well in the competition, and the champion company would be announced after the drill competition on Friday. Our company sergeant major was very confident we would do well. Sure enough, on Friday afternoon, we were announced as the winners—great feeling to march into the top company in the battalion.

During that first week, the CO had announced that the Red Cross Mobile Blood Bank would visit the battalion at the end of the next week. I was a keen blood donor and was anxious for us to lead the battalion in donations. Colin Lee explained to me that the Gurkhas had little time for the Chinese (regional history disputes over centuries) and were concerned that if they gave blood, the recipient might be Chinese, so they were not keen to take part. I argued that we had just won the champion company trophy, and this might provide enough impetus for us to change the thinking of the members of the company. I further stated that I would lead the company and would provide the first blood taken. Reluctantly Colin agreed and had the CSM speak to the company. Colin advised me that everyone seemed happy with idea and would line up, but he would go first. I agreed to go second.

The appointed day arrived, and two thirds of our company lined up behind Colin and myself. Other companies were taking interest and a strong line of soldiers was now in place. The CO also complimented us on what was about to happen and went off to speak with the other company commanders. Colin was called forward, the line moved forward, Colin sat on the edge of the gurney, the blood bank staff inserted the canula, Colin fainted and fell off the gurney, blood went everywhere, the Gurkhas fled out the door, the blood bank ended up with only thirty units of blood that day, and most were from European officers. Nice try, fail.

Map of Hong Kong showing Fanling where we lived (New Territories)

It wasn't long before I found out what a magnificent job the British did in Hong Kong. We had just begun to settle into the block of flats at Fanling; Everyone in the block were officers and family from the military in Hong Kong but not all were Gurkhas. Some were from other Gurkha units, and they were paymasters, educators, and logisticians, but we all mixed well and I was able to gain a very good understanding of the role of the British in Hong Kong. There were also other young officers on exchange from other British units such as the Welsh Guards and the Irish Guards and from other countries such as Fiji and Papua New Guinea.

Every weekend there was a party or dinner at someone's place. I had also started playing rugby with the Kukris team and met many new friends from this very unique experience particularly Australian ex-patriots, many of whom I had seen playing rugby in Australia on television but had moved to Hong Kong because of work or business interests. The social life was very demanding.

Sadly, at the time, I still had to sit for an examination (Current Affairs) to complete my qualifications for major, so some study was necessary to successfully complete the exam. It was difficult, firstly, because Australia wasn't quite the international centrepiece of the world as many Australians thought, so I had some difficulty finding study material. This was resolved by getting the Australian Education Department (military) to send me some relevant references and getting the Australian consulate to arrange for delivery of the main Australian newspapers periodically. Not perfect but I thought enough. My newfound friends, however, did not see the need to pass the exam as being as important as I did.

One Saturday afternoon, Carole had accepted an invitation to afternoon drinks at our upstairs neighbours who were Welsh. Due to study commitments, I had declined. About one hour into my study (which mainly involved reading), I heard a noise on the balcony only to see a rope with a can of beer on it being lowered onto my balcony and the rope being pulled frequently to ensure it got my attention. I smirked at the intention, drank the beer, threw down my books, and charged up the stairs and joined the party. The main perpetrator was my Welsh neighbour who was 44 years of age, an educator who played rugby with us and ran like a 30-year-old. His invitation was just too good for an Australian to refuse. Luckily, I managed to pass the exam which took a bit of arranging through the Australian embassy and the education officer of Seventh Gurkhas.

Time had come for our company to do their tour of duty on the Chinese border. I think I was the only one in the company who had not done a previous tour, but again, to me, another wonderful adventure. The company moved into very basic barracks at Sha Tau Kok and Low Wu. The Hong Kong police also had a station at Sha Tau Kok so that is where the Coy HQ was set up with a platoon with another platoon going to Low Wu and the Third Platoon constantly patrolling the border on a rotational basis. A patrol was also positioned out on Ping Chau Island where many Chinese tried to reach by swimming. Unfortunately, the sea and sharks claimed most who attempted to achieve this. This was a time of great unrest in China, and every night, as many as fifty Chinese would be captured by the patrols, handed over to the Hong Kong police at Low Wu or Sha Tau Kok, who in turn would turn them over to the Chinese soldiers from the mainland.

The outpost at Low Wu had a commanding, expansive view of the gateway into mainland China. Soldiers patrolled the fields while peasants tilled the rice paddies with a few buffaloes but mainly by hand. The soldiers treated the peasants with open disdain and were often seen to be beating them with rifles or kicking them for little or seemingly no reason. This was a great learning time for me, and every night I would venture out with an escort and join the patrols along the border.

Every morning Colin Lees would debrief the previous night's patrols and collect any intelligence that may have been determined from them. Colin also had the task of liaising with the Hong Kong police at Sha Tau Kok and coordinating our military patrols with the police vehicular patrols.

Our tour of the border lasted about a month, and during that time, we had a number of visitors always accompanied by the commanding officer. Many were politicians out from the UK to determine how the British pound was being spent in Hong Kong. Others were visiting military officers who were keen to see what was occurring on the Chinese border. Nonetheless, they were all required to be escorted and briefed at each of the locations. They were all impressed by the way the Gurkhas went about their work—always alert, always active, and always courteous. This was a great experience for me.

On return I immediately applied to do an aikido course because I had seen on the patrols how aggressive and desperate some of the Chinese were in their bid to escape from the oppressive pressure of Chinese communism. I had seen rudimentary weapons produced and the preparedness to use them. I did not wish to get caught out on my next trip to the border. I had noted that many Gurkhas had done the course previously, and it was based on arrest techniques perfected by the British Army in Northern Ireland. The course was particularly physical and conducted by Gurkha instructors who have little sympathy for those less talented than themselves and are naturally very strong. Nonetheless, an enlightening, educational, and enjoyable course.

(L) Brian attending an aikido course at Sek Kong

Whilst I was on the border, Carole had received an invitation to visit the COs house for dinner the following Saturday evening. The time was set at 7.30 p.m. Carole and I were organised, arranged a babysitter, and arrived right on time, or so we thought. The CO opened the door in a bath robe and seemed a bit shocked to see us; he advised that he was just about to take a bath. I apologised and explained that I must have got the wrong night. 'No, no, no', said the CO, 'you just got the wrong time', and proceeded to explain to me that it was customary, in fact, courteous, for lieutenants to arrive half an hour late, captains to arrive forty-five minutes late, and majors to arrive when they thought appropriate. He added that he hadn't expected an Australian to arrive on time, so he apologised, poured us a beer, and said, 'Jan will be down shortly, please make yourself at home.' Jan joined us and nothing more was said about the matter—we had a very enjoyable evening.

It seemed that it was one thing after another in Hong Kong. The CO advised me that Colin Lees was reposted and would leave the battalion very soon, leaving me in charge of a company which I barely knew, however, I was extremely honoured and had no hesitation in letting the CO know. I was also advised that I was to commence a course in Gurkhali which was a week of face-to-face learning, part-time study, and then a final week for exams, etc. This suited me perfectly and would give me a chance to practice the language whilst leading the company.

I was just getting my head around the course when Brigade Headquarters advised that Seventh Gurkhas would be tested for Fitness for Role (FFR) by brigade staff in a further two weeks' time. The CO called me in and said that the British Army took FFR very seriously and he thought I might find it very hard to achieve good results with a new company in a series of very tough, physical military tests, so he had arranged with Brigade for me to be given the choice of tasks so that I had the best chance of succeeding. I objected quite stubbornly to this and said that it would not be fair on the other companies if I were to be given the softest option when, in fact, our future promotion/career might depend on the result. I requested that my company be drawn 'out of the hat' along with the rest, and whatever the task, I would attack it to the best of my ability. The CO reluctantly agreed, keeping in mind he probably had the most to lose as this was the test of his battalion's fitness for going to war.

As you might well guess, we pulled out the most complex of all tasks comprising a very difficult attack on a water-pumping, hydro-electric station which contained a number of terrorists and was heavily booby-trapped and which I was to secure before first light, combined with a secondary task of a route march and shoot immediately after the attack regardless of whether it succeeded or failed. Later a number of the fellow company commanders told me how relieved they were when the task went to C Company. Surprisingly, I wasn't overly concerned as my battalion in Vietnam was very experienced in cordon and search, and I always fancied myself at route marches, particularly as I had a much longer stride than the average Gurkha.

Unfortunately, my problems arose initially from familiarity of the location by my Gurkha platoon commanders and my daughter having an accident at school. My commanders told me they had all done this exercise before (having been stationed in Hong Kong several times) and they would show me how to do it. They outlined their plan, and I listened to it but without conceding any level of consent. I then told them I had to do a reconnaissance and they should come with me. I then made it quite clear that I would give my orders at 5 p.m., but their soldiers should be packed and ready to move immediately after orders. This really set the 'cat amongst the pigeons' as the Gurkha plan had them moving very early in the morning and they were quite concerned, angry even, that I was disregarding their solution.

The reconnaissance allowed me to get a closer look at the power station and, through binoculars, determine that there was only one main entrance which was a solid but narrow bridge over a very fast-flowing stream (that provided the power for the turbines). A major road ran past this bridge. The back of the station, however, was hilly but densely populated with shrubs and trees which separated the station from the closest village which was about 800 metres away. A single track seemed to lead to the village. The location from which I was observing the power station was directly opposite the entrance and across the road but elevated by a small hillock. My plan had begun to formulate in my mind.

On return to camp, I received a phone call from Carole advising that Nicole had had a fall at school and had possibly broken her leg. Nicole was now home from the medical centre, but they were awaiting the results of the X-ray which took a specialist radiographer to read. I was devastated but knew that once I had given my orders (which would take about one hour), the platoon commanders could take over and begin their specific tasks. I advised Carole that I would be home in two hours, and by then, we might have the results of the examination on Nicole's leg. I informed the CO what my plans were. The CO also had seen this attack done many times, many different ways, and was anxious to see what I had to offer, however, he said that he would judge my efforts on the basis of the results and he would be an umpire and therefore be inside the power station when the attack occurred. I saluted and left.

My plan was a simple one but totally unexpected by my platoon commanders. At 8 p.m. two platoons, taking separate routes, would leave under cover of darkness and make their way to blocking positions in the dense scrub at the rear of the power station. Their task was to capture anyone leaving the station. The Third Platoon would, during the night, rehearse driving a troop vehicle at high speed up to the front gate, dismounting at speed, and race across the bridge to prevent demolition of it. They would then secure the bridge. The remainder of the platoon would rehearse getting over the bridge quickly and commence securing the building and searching the power station for booby traps. H-hour was 5.30 a.m. I would set up my headquarters/communications opposite the bridge on the hillock and follow in the attack group. The platoon commanders were aghast at my plan and questioned why they had to leave so early in the night. I explained that any disturbance within the village by villagers or, in particular, dogs would have lesser effect early in the night, whereas if there was any unusual sounds early in the morning, they would be treated with much greater suspicion and our mission might be compromised. Reluctantly, they accepted the orders and commenced the execution. I headed home to see how my daughter was getting on.

My return home found Carole very relieved and much calmer than when I had spoken to her on the phone. The radiographer found no break but a severely swollen and sore leg which had been bandaged, and Nicole was sleeping soundly after a fairly traumatic ordeal. During my time as a soldier, I always found that family crises occurred only when you were in the worst possible position to deal with it. This was no exception, however, and I now had to return to dispatch my platoons to their precise destinations.

Two platoons were dispatched, and the third commenced rehearsals, under lights in the transport yard, to perfect their dismounts and sprinting with full equipment including first-line ammunition. The preparations completed the Third Platoon, and my headquarters moved off just after midnight to quietly get in position to prevent any of the 'enemy' leaving via the bridge.

At H-hour, our truck which had quietly got within fifty metres of the bridge screamed into action and drove violently to the bridge and then came to a dead stop. The soldiers dismounted and sprinted across the bridge and secured the other side. The attack troops followed on signal and commenced the task of securing the building. At this point, the CO (identified by his white armband) approached me where I had set up my headquarters. He seemed a little perplexed and disappointed.

'Brian', he said, 'I think you have missed the boat. An hour ago, I walked out the back thinking that you must have had blocking force out in the bush but I saw nor heard any sign of them. When you attacked, eight enemy escaped out the back and they have gone. Whatever your plan, I think you have failed.'

I had a slight sinking feeling that I must have indicated the wrong location for the blocking force, but my 2IC who I had sent with the force for coordination was very experienced, and although he doubted my plan, he had executed all parts of it, to date, with great loyalty. The only positive thing I could think of to reassure the CO was, 'Please wait'. The other umpires had begun to assemble and advise that the two remaining enemy soldiers within the station had been captured and all booby traps located.

Just as the CO was about to dismiss me as another dreamer, JB Sahib (2IC) radioed that they had captured eight escapees and had them secured.

Smiles all around, exercise complete. 'Round up your company and let's commence the next activity.'

The CSM quickly rounded up the company, broke up into our appointed sections, checked boots and socks, and commenced the 15 km route march to the range. We were given a time limit for this, so we had to make sure everyone kept pace, however, the company was fit, so getting everyone past the finish point on time wasn't really a problem. The shoot was a little more difficult as everyone was breathing heavy after a fairly gruelling march, so getting relaxed enough to shoot accurately was a bit of a stretch, however again, we had just won the battalion shooting competition, so I left it to the CSM (an excellent shot himself) to conduct the competition.

I was a little worried about my own ability having not fired a rifle for some time, but the results showed that I came in second on the day, so I sighed fairly heavily with relief. It was then back to camp, clean up, eat, and attend the Brigade debrief in the afternoon. Needless to say, the only real comment was, 'You can't do better than 100 per cent, therefore, we congratulate C Company on a wonderful and successful performance'. This, of course, provided great kudos for me, who had taken a risk with an alternative approach to a well-visited problem and was seen to be successful. My company was ecstatic that we had received such a clear and decisive endorsement of our skills, and it showed in their approach to me. Gurkhas like to follow proven leaders, and now every member was going out of his way to ensure that they acknowledged my acceptance during this difficult test.

Hong Kong was a wonderful place, and everything was new to our family who hadn't seen much outside of Australia. Both of our daughters were blonde, and everywhere we went (walking), the Chinese ladies would go out of their way to 'tweak' our daughters' cheeks. To the Chinese, this was a sign of good luck, and they didn't want to miss out on it. Our daughters, however, quickly tired of it, and we found we had to protect them a little more as parents from the onslaught of well-meaning citizens who were simply trying to improve their lot in life.

We lived very close to the train station in Fanling, and Hong Kong had a rail service that went directly to the island ferries and stopped at only about half a dozen places in between. A trip from Fanling to Kowloon only took an hour, and we always managed to get a seat so the girls particularly loved going on these trips where we would walk around the shops in Kowloon (which seemed to stretch for miles) or catch a ferry to Hong Kong Island and catch the rail up to the Peak which provided the most outstanding (360-degree) view of the island and its surrounds. On one occasion, we took the hydrofoil to Macau and stayed for the weekend. We also purchased a car which was a bonus and allowed me to get to work and for us as a family to explore some of the less-exposed areas of the territories. Sadly, I drove it out onto the island on one occasion, and halfway up a long, reasonably steep hill, the gear shift came out in my hand, and we were surrounded by traffic. Sweat formed along my brow as I (using the clutch and hand brake) eased the car backwards, downhill, towards the edge of this six-lane highway.

We got there safely, but then I was confused about what to do next. Mobile phones had not been introduced to the world at that stage. I walked until I found a phone box, rang a number on my NRMA (equivalent) card, and was delightfully surprised when a man answered in understandable English. This was a Sunday, however, the mechanic agreed to come out and pick up the car which he did within a couple of hours and advised me of his business location, quoted me a cost, and drove off, with our car into the sunset. Fortunately, we knew the routine for catching buses, so we caught a bus back to the ferries, reached home by train, and collapsed with relief when we realised how lucky we had been. I went back to the island in two days and picked up the car. Another unexpected adventure.

My pay and allowances were all arranged through the Australian consulate on the island, so it was customary for me to pay them a visit every now and again to stay in touch. I did this about every month or six weeks and got to know the staff well. They were excellent representatives for Australia and were always helpful and courteous. On one of these visits, I was advised that the consulate had a good-sized motorised junk, which had its own crew and catering facilities, and although there was a token hiring fee, it was available for booking via the consulate. This was a great platform for a day out with the officers from Seventh Gurkhas, and I knew my family would love it. Very quickly, I ran the idea past the CO and the president of the Mess Committee who thought it was a great idea and set about arranging the day out. This we did, and we had the most outstanding South Sea Island cruise you could ever want. We explored the inner harbour of Hong Kong and many of the small islands around it. The captain stopped wherever we wanted and anyone who wanted to jump off the boat and have a swim. We found a secluded beach on Lantau Island, ferried the food and beverages ashore, and had a wonderful lunch with some members exploring the close parts of the island on foot. This was another truly wonderful day with all the families, including ourselves, finding something different in their lives. At an appropriate time, we packed up and headed back for the new territories.

Our battalion also had to take their turn at public duties in the defence of Hong Kong. One of these tasks was for a company to provide guard duties at Victoria Barracks on Hong Kong Island. This was a demanding task, and the CO arranged for each of four companies to do a week each. C Coy was first off the rank, so we arranged a handover from the battalion who had preceded us and began this tiring week-long duty. Barrack accommodation was available to the soldiers, and I was shown to a room in the officer's mess.

I was just settling in when I received a message that the GOC Hong Kong Command, Lieutenant General Sir Edwin Bramall, had invited me to join him for lunch. I did a quick scurry down to the front gate to check that my soldiers were settled and on duty and the Gurkha QGOs had found their accommodation. They had all done this before, I was the new boy on the block! Everyone was happy and settled, and I quickly realised this was no different to the Victoria Barracks guards I had done in Sydney as a young platoon commander. I advised my officers that I had been invited to lunch and would see them shortly.

Sir Edwin was a very well-respected officer throughout British Army circles, and although I was keen to meet him, I was feeling a little apprehensive entering his married quarter for the first time. I was ushered into the dining room where Sir Edwin introduced me to his wife but stated that she wouldn't be dining with us because we were going to talk 'cricket'. Lady Bramall was delightful and was as courteous as she was attractive. Sir Edwin was very impressive and put me at ease immediately with his knowledge of Australia and particularly of our military chiefs. This was going to be an enjoyable lunch. Lady Bramall excused herself, and we sat down at this massive table to informally discuss 'cricket', fortunately, I was a cricket tragic and had played the game for most of my school days.

The first point Sir Edwin wanted discussed was the impending closure of the century-old Hong Kong Cricket Club (first established 1851). Sir Edwin was a respected member and loved the traditions and the history of the club. However, for planning, development, and economic reasons, the club was required to close down. It would reopen in another property some distance away, but Sir Edwin considered that it would never be the same again. I was only vaguely familiar with the club but at least knew that it had a proud history and had passed its location many times. Sir Edwin and the committee had invited a very elite list of Australian cricket players (past and present) to attend a week of celebration and commemoration in Hong Kong and had advertised these players as the Superstars of '75 (being 1975). They included Alan Archer, Doug Walters, Clarry Grimmett, Harold Larwood (who was now resident in Perth), Rod Marsh, Bobby Simpson, and a number of others as suitably notable. The committee had asked them to play 'the final game' on the hallowed turf, but Sir Edwin wanted them to see the colony in a bit more detail, and he was adamant that he wanted them to visit a Gurkha battalion for a barbecue.

I was delighted to have this opportunity and told the general that I would speak to the CO later that day for his approval. This event later occurred exactly as Sir Edwin had planned it, and I had a wonderful evening reliving some of the great games with Clarry Grimmett, Alan Archer, and Bobby Simpson. I didn't get to speak, at length, to all the cricketers as Clarry Grimmett was so entertaining (although I think he was in his late eighties then) that I listened to his fascinating stories and his life history for too much of the night—I was in awe).

Sir Edwin then moved on to his second question. Who was going to win the test series in England? Just prior to our luncheon, there was great upheaval in England because vandals had dug holes and poured a vast amount of oil on the pitch at Headingly, the venue of the third test on the night of the fourth day. Australia had won the test at Egbaston, drawn the test at Lords, and had a chance to win the third test on the last day. England was keen to draw level in the test series, and Australia was keen to finalise the series. As it turned out, the teams agreed to abandon the test, and the fourth test was a draw with Australia therefore winning one–nil. This was a great conversation/discussion which I enjoyed enormously and told the general so, however, I still had a job to do, so I excused myself at about 3 p.m. and headed back to my duties as the commander of the guard.

This was not to be my last long conversation with the general. Some weeks later, back in the New Territories, I received a phone call from Sir

Edwin. Major General Sir Frank Hassett, Australia's chief of the general staff, was a great personal friend of Sir Edwin's and planned to visit Hong Kong in the near future. Sir Edwin was enquiring as to whether I could attain the Australian consulate's junk for a day sailing around the islands. Of course, my wife and I were invited to come along as well. I was delighted and said that I would check the details but baulked at leaving my children at home without either of the parents and quite precociously enquired if there was any chance I could bring them along. The general's answer was, 'Only because they are Australian, and I will take your word that they can swim.' So a day out on the junk was arranged, and the general brought his personal staff to provide waiters and food preparers. There were about thirty people invited (mainly British service officers and their partners), most of whom were aghast at our daughters jumping from the junk every time we dropped anchor. This was my first opportunity to meet Sir Frank and found him and his wife to be wonderful, engaging, and interesting people. The whole day was a huge success, and somehow, I got the credit for it.

It was quite amazing what a huge role sport played in the lives of Gurkhas. At the end of every working day, almost the whole battalion would get into their shorts and runners and head for the basketball courts (all camps provided for this, but they were all constructed cheaply using the old surface of bitumen with painted lines), teams would be quickly arranged, generally in company areas, and someone would be appointed as the umpire and the games would commence until dark.

On Wednesday afternoons, depending on the time of year, inter-company competitions would be conducted in soccer, basketball, swimming (if a pool was available), and athletics (running, javelin, shot put, hammer throw, hurdles, and most importantly Khud running). There was never a time of year when there was nothing on. We also used to get visiting ships wanting to compete in a string of events, however, as the sports officer, I had to pass many of these off to other units as we did not have teams in many sports such as rugby. We did, however, have a good relationship with the Chinese population who also loved to play basketball, so often on a Saturday morning, we (myself included) would venture into the poorer areas of Kowloon and play basketball or soccer against local estates which were always well supported. I found myself refereeing many of these games because the 'lack of love' for each other quickly came to the fore and I needed to keep the games under control. There were many European teachers present for these games (working for the Hong Kong government), and one morning I met an Australian lady who had been one of my teachers way back in kindergarten. We had a great catch-up and shared a cup of water. Coffee shops were not in abundance in the areas where we played.

I recall we had a call from an American ship who desperately wanted to play basketball against Gurkhas. I advised them that this would not be a good idea as Gurkhas would be too short by comparison with the Americans who would all have an amazingly skilful basketball team. Anyhow, they insisted and offered to pay for an after-party, and the battalion team was keen to play, so I reluctantly agreed. The team turned up in a very high-priced bus and unloaded—as I suspected, they were 'loaded for bear'—they were all at least a foot taller than our players with professional strip and the latest in footwear. Our players had $2 T-shirts on and sandshoes. The Americans looked around and said, 'Right, where is the court?' I advised them they were standing on it and this was the best court in the battalion area. It was asphalt/bitumen, we did not have nets for the rings, and the backboards were hand-painted. The Americans held a group discussion, hopped back on the bus, and we never saw them again. The Gurkhas selected two teams and played on—most unconcerned that their opposition had departed.

We did, however, have a much better relationship with HMAS *Brisbane*, an Australian guided-missile destroyer who was often in Hong Kong as part of being in the Far East Strategic Reserve. They also had a good basketball team and often asked if they could come to the New Territories and play basketball and have a few beers with Gurkha teams. They were great fun, didn't complain about the courts, and generally beat us, but they were good games, played in good spirit, and always ended with a few beers and some nibbles after the game. The CO used to come along and watch most of these matches. Our relationship was so good that the sailors invited a couple of us to join them on Anzac Day on Hong Kong Island. I doubted the wisdom of accepting this invitation because on the day after, I had been selected to play in the Hong Kong Sevens (as part of the RAAF Koala's team). I invited my Welsh mate (upstairs neighbour) to join me and he (of course) agreed with lightning speed. We took my car and headed for Hong Kong Island.

This was a great day which started with an Anzac Service at Victoria Barracks attended by a large number of the ship's company. After the service, I followed the wave of sailors all of whom seemed to know where they were going. As it turned out, they had booked this enormous Chinese restaurant on the island which accommodated and fed all of us, and in my case, for no cost. The drink was flowing, and though there was some beer, most of it was rum or whisky.

Logically by mid-afternoon, the sailors started to get restless, and of course, the games began. A number of sailors shed their clothes, and the 'dance of the burning bums' began with many young men getting gamer and gamer until eventually someone got fairly badly burned, so they decided it was time to stop. There were hundreds of raffles and more food and beverage. Eventually, while I was still almost sober enough to drive, we decided it was time to leave.

As we bid our farewells and walked out the door, we noticed a couple of sailors had befriended an American sailor who was almost completely 'legless' with alcohol. The sailors kept the American in this inebriated state by continually offering him a drink from a large bottle of whisky they were carrying. We noticed that it was not long before the sailors escorted the American into a tattoo parlour. 'Dai' and I decided to accompany them into the parlour and see what they were up to. The result was hilarious. The sailors paid the tattooist some money and the American was laid on this bench, on his back, with his shirt open where he immediately went to sleep. The tattooist started work, and we could see this light outline of blood on the American's chest. The sailors had paid the tattooist to draw a large image of the Australian flag on the American's chest. As soon as they were satisfied that the American was not going to wake up during the ordeal, the sailors took a swig of whisky and left, looking for their next unsuspecting victim. What a surprise that American was going to get the next morning.

We picked up the car and drove back to the New Territories, not getting home until after midnight. I packed my bag for the next morning and went to bed. At 4 a.m., I got up showered and dressed, breakfasted, and set out to go back to where I had been only a few short hours before. I was feeling very ordinary and not really up to a game of rugby, particularly at this level. I arrived at the Hong Kong stadium at about 6 a.m. and proceeded to get dressed and warm up. Our first game was at 7 a.m. As it turned out, it was to be our only game as the remainder of our team was RAAF, and they, like myself, had had a fairly big Anzac Day and it showed. We were awful and were soundly beaten by a very young team who were probably not old enough to drink. Here was our big chance to play in front of thousands of people, and we didn't last long enough for the gates to open. We showered and watched the countless games until about lunchtime when I decided I had had enough and drove home to get some sleep. An Australian team won it that year but played under a club name. It was to be a few more years before identified national teams played at that tournament.

I previously mentioned Khud running as one of the battalion sports. I was a little bemused when the CO first advised me that the battalion Khud race was on, and I was expected to be there. Khud racing was mountain foot racing which was popular amongst many of the sub-continent nations. The idea was simple, a race to the top of a selected small mountain and then back down again. The only difference, as I found out, was the almost insane speed at which these runners travelled on the downwards path. They simply defied gravity. The course was only a couple of kilometres long, and as the runners were going uphill, a gentle, steady pace was the norm, but as they came back down, the pace increased almost frighteningly, and the slope did not seem to be a remote consideration—nor did there have to be a path. These runners were as sure-footed as mountain goats and ran at top speed to gain ascendency. What an event, with the winner being recognised by the whole battalion gaining kudos and adulation. I left the event shaking my head; I had just gained even greater admiration for these wonderful Nepalese soldiers.

One Sunday afternoon, I was on standby as the battalion duty officer when I received a call from the brigade duty officer who briefly advised me that a boatload of Vietnamese refugees had been taken on board by a Norwegian merchant ship and their obligation was to deliver them to the nearest port which in this case happened to be Hong Kong. The Hong Kong government had accepted their responsibility and now wished to process these people (about four hundred), but to do so, had to house and feed them until foreign embassy outstations could set up. The government had asked the army to assist by providing a 'tent city' on Sek Kong airstrip, provide sleeping facilities, eating facilities, and security by dawn the next morning. We had also been asked to provide initial processing. It was now three on Sunday afternoon. A meeting was set to be held at 5 p.m. at Brigade Headquarters. I immediately rang the CO and the quartermaster.

By 6 p.m., I was positioned at Sek Kong airstrip having been provided with a simple brief, taken delivery of a truckload of Second World War tents, and received a company of Seventh GR soldiers. I immediately started to lay out the tents and brief the Queen's Gurkha Officers. Truckloads of stores, star pickets, barbed wire, mats (for sleeping on), and soldiers began to arrive. I was beginning to feel overwhelmed; however, I managed to stay on top of it. I also remembered that the Duke of Edinburgh (the battalion patron) was arriving the next day, and both the company and myself were looking forward to his visit. I felt assured the CO would handle that one. I had assessed that, thanks to the timely delivery of stores, I could get the task completed and ready to receive refugees by 6 a.m.

It was at this same time that I received a visit from the brigade major who advised me that the Norwegian ship was close to docking and that the first refugees would now be arriving about 2 a.m. We could not work any faster or any more efficiently. I would put priority onto the security fence and then complete the tentage. I would put six to each tent rather than four. The brigade major then dropped another bombshell. There were senior army officers amongst the refugees up to the rank of major general, and there were also rumours that there were some troublemakers. Great, just what I needed, a bunch of ungrateful Vietnamese refugees who were expecting entitlement. Thank you, sir, leave it to me. At this time, I had not seen another officer other than my CO and the brigade major (who kept expressing that we were going well), everyone else was preparing for the Duke's visit tomorrow and were not available.

It was time for me to set up the receiving point and determine how I was going to organise the arrival. I briefed one of my QGOs that I wanted one soldier with a loaded rifle to be at reception and another ten with pick helves to accompany refugees to their tents. I had the quartermaster's staff to lay out the items that I thought were essential for one night's accommodation. The engineers were still erecting the security fence and the last of the tents were slowly being put into place. What a gigantic effort. It was just after 1 a.m. None of my workforce had received any food. Food was also not expected to be available for the refugees until noon the next day.

Almost without warning, a vehicle turned up. It was a Hong Kong police car. A single officer got out and walked over to meet me. He was a young Chinese officer, who spoke reasonably good English and was very smartly turned out. He asked me if I was ready to receive the refugees to which I replied no quite emphatically, at which he smiled and said, 'Well here they come', and pointed to a couple of buses approaching the airfield. He quickly provided me with some essential details and advised that many of them would be carrying sheaf gold which they had organised before they boarded the boat, I was not to touch it, he would search all personal luggage. He also advised me that I should not show weapons unless there was an incident. I immediately asked my work section to line up at the reception point without pick helves but make sure their kukris were on display. I really was in no mood for any nonsense from this lot. I began to rehearse my reception speech, keeping it short because I did not expect them to speak much English. The policeman also reinforced that he spoke no Vietnamese. It was now 2 a.m.

The young policeman was terrific. As each bus pulled in, he boarded and told the driver not to let anyone off unless he authorised it. He called for one person who could speak English to come forward. On each bus, he somehow found that one person. He briefed the spokesman who got the refugees off the bus and into one line where he searched their personal luggage (by this time, two additional policemen arrived and assisted with this task), and then they came to me six at a time. I remember clearly the briefing I provided, 'You will walk to this point, you will get a mat, a bowl, a pair of chopsticks, and you will accompany this young man to your tent, food will be provided tomorrow'. This was understood and the system was working well even the police were happy with the arrangement.

The sixth bus arrived, and I could see that there was disruption. Someone was causing dissension. A well-groomed refugee busted through the group and came directly to me, screamed at me, and advised that he was a general and that his wife was put on another bus and he demanded they be reunited and put in brick accommodation. My response was almost too immediate. I said, 'You will get a mat, a bowl, a pair of chopsticks, and you will accompany this young man to your tent, food will be provided tomorrow.' Unexpectedly, he continued to complain. I was getting tired; it was around 3 a.m. I stepped forward and grabbed the general by the front of the shirt. At this point, two Gurkhas stepped out of the shadows in support. I repeated, 'You will get a mat, a bowl, a pair of chopsticks, and you will accompany this young man to your tent, food will be provided tomorrow.'

The message sank in. The general realised he had no power as a refugee and dutifully, though reluctantly, collected his items. At this point, I turned to brief the next group, and there standing in my path was the brigade major (Major Miles Hunt-Davis who later became the CO of Seventh Gurkhas) who had obviously witnessed my altercation with the general. I thought I may have overstepped the mark and he would berate me, however, his comments were very welcome. 'All going well here, Brian, I see, I will catch up with you tomorrow, good night!' and he departed. The rest of the night went fairly smoothly with the local police being very helpful and the refugees being very exhausted. At approximately 5 a.m., my commanders were reporting in that all the fencing was complete and the tentage had all been erected, the refugees were sleeping peacefully. The buses had finally stopped arriving, and the Hong Kong government had arranged for a delivery of portable toilets.

At 6 a.m., an officer arrived from Seventh GR and advised that I was relieved and I was to return to barracks by 9 a.m. to be on parade, with my company, to meet the Duke of Edinburgh. Bloody hell, that was not a lot of time. I was hoping that my gear was all cleaned and needed nothing more than a touch-up. With the exception of one cup of coffee, I also had not eaten since lunchtime the day before. Logically, this was all a scramble, however, somehow I managed to get to the parade minutes before they marched on. The CO met me and asked how I was feeling. He offered for me to stand off the parade if I was too exhausted. I quickly notified him that I was fine, and he told me to take up position.

In due course, the Duke came to my company and the CO advised him that I was the 'tame Australian' and I had bags under my eyes because I was still getting over Anzac Day, no mention of the fact I had spent the whole night housing refugees. It was a very pleasant experience, and I was grateful and honoured for the opportunity to meet a member of the British royal family.

Brian accompanying HRH the Duke of Edinburgh as he inspects the Battalion

After the parade was over, the Duke had morning tea with the CO and some other dignitaries but advised that we still had obligations to the brigade at the refugee camp. In the few hours that I was absent, much had happened. The battalion 2IC Maj Charles Henderson had taken command of the camp and fellow company commander Maj Alan Forrestier-Walker was his deputy. Embassy staff from many foreign embassies had begun to set up tent offices and were beginning to interview refugees, carefully selecting those with the most potential to become first-class citizens or those who had academic or trade qualifications. Canada was first, I think South Korea second, sadly (to me) Australia did not set up for another two days.

The camp was getting very tense as no food had yet been provided. Food was to be provided by the Hong Kong government along with some cooks and portable cooking equipment (similar to a mobile kitchen). What they weren't required to provide, however, was 'dish pigs' people to help prepare the food, serve it, and then clean up. The kitchen duly arrived, was positioned, and the cooks commenced boiling the rice and preparing the food. The refugees began to line up in their hundreds. Charles Henderson received the request for people to assist with the serving of the food. He located an interpreter and wrote out what he wanted and provided a microphone for the interpreter to call for volunteers. The interpreter obliged, but no one came forward. Charles prompted the interpreter to make the call a second time, the interpreter obliged, a couple of volunteers reluctantly moved forward. Charles had the interpreter advise that this was the last chance for volunteers to come forward. No one did, so Charles ordered to cooks to switch off the gas, called for the driver, and drove the mobile kitchen out of the camp and ordered them not to return until the next day. This went close to causing a riot, and many of the social working staff present lodged strong complaints. Charles would not budge; however, when the kitchen arrived the next day, volunteers were in abundance. Everyone ate and an uneasy peace ensued.

Foreign embassies quickly made the choices of the refugees they wanted and moved them out. Many who remained gained the confidence of the military members who worked there daily and small purchases such as lollies and toys started becoming available. Care and social groups such as Red Cross, etc., quickly set up small groups of tents and a few merchants, selling small goods and some food, were allowed into the camp. Stories also started emerging about the bullying and extortion that went on during the boat ride and the dictatorial role the general played during the voyage. He was reported to be carrying a gun which he used to threaten fellow refugees on the trip. This was all reported to the local police who eventually came and picked him up, and he was never sighted again. The Hong Kong police also confirmed that many of the refugees were carrying sheet gold (easy to hide) and were, in fact, quite rich.

Eventually, the size of the camp was reduced by at least half, so Brigade decided it was time to free up some of the space that had been used for the purpose of housing refugees and move the remainder to a disused barracks closer towards the Chinese border. This was done and provided many with better accommodation although less room for the kids to play. The camp at Sek Kong was removed and allowed to return to an airfield. It took some time, but eventually, the responsibility for the refugees was handed over to the Hong Kong government and control of the camp to the Hong Kong police.

Carole at this time was getting to know her neighbours very well and was quickly learning about the art of playing mah-jong, which is a tile-based game that was developed in China during the Qing dynasty and has spread throughout the world since the early twentieth century. It is commonly played by four players. In the area that we lived (modest population but mainly Chinese), all through the afternoon and into the night you could hear the clack of tiles from the myriads of locals who played mah-jong. Our neighbours were mainly British, but they still loved playing mah-jong, so Carole joined the group and learned the game.

Quite unexpectedly, I was called to a meeting in Sek Kong at the brigade officer's mess and fronted a meeting of senior officers and some others that I didn't know. They formed the Hong Kong Colony Rugby Union Selection Committee. I was advised that I had been selected to play in the Colony Rugby side who would be playing the Welsh National side as it was on its way to play Australia. I said I was deeply honoured to be selected and was prepared to drive the hour each way to train on the island for the next couple of weeks. Then they gave me date of the match and immediately my exuberance changed to disappointment. Our battalion was due to go back onto the border three weeks before the game, so I would not be able to train. The group advised me that my CO would understand if I chose to play rugby and one of the QGOs would fill my role within the battalion during the period. I was torn between personal achievement and commitment. I knew the CO was genuine in his offer, but I also knew that he would be disadvantaged if I chose the personal route. Housing great personal disappointment, I advised the group that I would not be able to play, my commitment was to the battalion and my job was to patrol the border. The selection group expressed their disappointment at my decision but understood my position. I left without any further discussion.

I recall sitting out on a large rock the night the game was played. We had no radios, so I couldn't even listen to the game, but I had a few army mates who were also selected, so I silently wished them well. I recall it was raining lightly. The Welsh side beat Colony 50-3 which was to be expected with Gareth Edwards having a blinder and the Welsh fielding their top fifteen for a good hit-out before they landed in Australia. My mates later informed me that it was a spectacular feeling playing against such a superb side.

This was to be my last tour of the border as 7GR had been advised that they were to replace one of the other battalions in Brunei in December. This caused me some anguish as I had been authorised to spend my tour in Hong Kong for a two-year period. I did not know if this meant I would have to change battalions and stay in Hong Kong or I could accompany 7GR to Brunei. To my knowledge, this change of locations had not been challenged before. I immediately wrote to my directorate, advised them of the situation, notified them that there would be no costs for removal as we did our own packing and our boxes would be removed as part of the battalion removal. My only concern was my allowances which in Hong Kong were excellent, allowing us to employ an amah for the kids and still live comfortably. My directorate seemed to have the same level of confusion. No one answered my letters. I also spoke to the consulate who advised that they would continue my pay into an agreed account, but they were not authorised to pay anything but the most basic of allowances until authorised otherwise from the day I left Hong Kong. That ended up being the story, I received no correspondence and my allowances would drop to almost nothing when the battalion left Hong Kong. I simply made the decision that we would go to Brunei and informed the CO. He was delighted. We began packing. On 28 November 1975, we emplaned in Hong Kong for Bandar Seri Begawan in Brunei.

CHAPTER FOURTEEN

BRUNEI

ON BOARD THE HMAS *Sydney* on the way to Vietnam we had negotiated the Sunda Straits (between Sumatra and Java) and observed local Indonesians going about their business, but other than that, I had not been anywhere near Indonesia and never heard of Bandar Seri Begawan which was the capital of Brunei, an oil-rich sultanate on the island of Borneo. All of Borneo was Muslim, but ownership was shared and contested by Malaysia and Indonesia. Brunei was independent (although still Muslim) and was likely to remain that way as the vast majority of oil deposits in the South China Sea seemed to be located off its coast—these oil deposits making the Sultan of Brunei, for many years, the richest man in the world. Fortunately, the Sultan and his family (he had several brothers) were very pro-British and he welcomed a British military presence in his domain.

Enormous wealth ensured that Brunei was a tidy place with rice (the major consumable) being totally subsidised for all the residents and the military being given a free ride for accommodation and barracks for the soldiers. Again, for Carole and myself, this was a whole new world looking, smelling, and feeling nothing like Hong Kong. We didn't do a guided tour of Bandar Seri Begawan, however, two noticeable icons stood out as we passed through. The first being a huge mosque which had a domed roof which was completely encased in gold—quite ugly really, but totally acceptable to the locals and worth a considerable amount of money. The second was a huge statue (maybe ten metres high) of Sir Winston Churchill cast in bronze. Apparently, the Sultan (who himself had been a student at Sandhurst Military College in England) admired Churchill. Brunei was, in fact, rated as the second largest collection of Churchill's memorabilia outside of London. Our trip to our new home seemed like an endless procession of palm trees and rice paddies.

Brunei located on the island of Borneo

The ship with all our personal belongings had already arrived when we flew into the only airport, and by the time we had been transported to Kuala Belait (north-western region of the state) about 50 km away, the advance party had our boxes unloaded and delivered to our houses. We were able to immediately commence unpacking. The house we had been allocated was a wonderful four-bedroom free-standing house which was built in a square with the centre being open and a small lawn and garden being enclosed. It had a veranda all around the inside of the house. What was immediately noticeable was the very deep 'monsoon' drain that ran past the front of the yard. Also attached was a one-bedroom (with toilet) unit if we chose to employ an amah. We were ecstatic this was beautiful and tropical and was situated amongst married quarters where all the other officers and their families were housed.

The young single members of the battalion were housed at the Sultan's summer palace just up the road which also served as an officer's mess. Somehow we had also arranged to bring our car from Hong Kong, so we had transport to get both to the mess and to the barracks which was about ten minutes away. The other item that we had purchased before leaving Hong Kong was a rather small coloured TV, a rather rare commodity in those days but proved to be useful for the very small amount of watchable television available in Brunei.

It was still the dry season in Brunei, so we were able to get straight into training as a battalion. I was moved from company commander to operations officer within the battalion structure and had an RQMS (colour sergeant) attached from one of the British battalions as my training warrant officer and a Gurkha sergeant clerk to assist me. The RQMS was a wonderful fellow who had great experience as a soldier and was an expert at rifle shooting, so he was perfect for the job he had been assigned. This was a good team, so the job had great prospects.

The CO briefed me on what he required of me and accentuated the fact that he wanted good public relations with the locals, particularly the police who had the final say in all the areas we used for training. I understood my role, knew what the CO wanted, and was determined that our battalion would do well in the rifle shooting again this year. My first job therefore was to find out what the company training programs were going to be so that I could book ranges and training areas. I also had to book in battalion exercises (which the CO outlined), external commitments, and of course, sporting contests. Fortunately, 10GR had most recently been the residents in Brunei, so a lot of areas were already available, I merely had to coordinate their use. My operational team and I jumped into this with great enthusiasm, and within a week, we had the basis of a good plan, with some flexibility, that I could take to the local police planning committee for consideration and approval.

My first visit to the local planning committee was extremely unique. I thought it would be a couple of policemen and myself and they would merely 'rubber-stamp' any reasonable proposal I put forward. Not so, there were about three policemen headed up by the local chief of police, a political adviser, a religious leader, and about three others whose identity I never did get to know nor did I ever find out if they could speak English. The meeting started off with sweet cakes and tea and the police chief chaired the meeting. He spoke good English and seemed a very fair and reasonable leader, he certainly was always charitable and understanding to me, but I could see that I had to come prepared to every meeting (monthly) if I wanted approval. Every new or doubtful proposal I made was questioned and discussed in Malay, and it wasn't until the group agreed that approval was given. It seemed that our approach and format were different from that of 10GR, and, therefore everything had to be reconsidered. This seemed fair enough to me, and I advised the CO that preparation for these meetings would take much more time in the future. I also arranged for the CO to meet the chief of police as an act of courtesy. Jungle training was now set to commence for 7GR.

Already guard systems were set up for the barracks, localised training had commenced including briefings on the new training areas, courtesies to locals, and details about parades and duties. Sport had also commenced. Every afternoon after work, I would visit each of the company areas and see basketball being played by almost the whole battalion until dark. Everyone got a game, there must have been twenty courts throughout the area and all were being used, absolutely amazing.

On the home front, Carole and girls were settling in very well including attendance at school. The British military travelled with their own teachers, so we had at least two teachers (husband and wife) who moved into the school provided and produced an education program for anyone who attended—great system. The only problem was that the house next to ours was set up as a pre-school, and there were many calls for it to be opened but no teacher/supervisor could be found. Some of the ladies gathered together and asked Carole (particularly because of her nursing background) if she would consider running the pre-school. Carole nervously accepted, and instead of reading or watching television of a night-time, I found myself cutting up cardboard, colouring in, pasting, etc., in preparation for the next day. Carole loved it and, in turn, so did the parents who showed their true appreciation when it was time for us to leave Brunei. This also proved very convenient for us financially as I had still not heard back from my directorate and my allowances had almost dried up, so the additional income proved valuable.

It is strange, but every time I drove towards the capital, I had this strong feeling that this country would be ideal for a hash house harriers club. I had never done a 'hash' but had read about the plantation owners in Malaya having invented this comical system of staying fit by running through the jungle 'with rules'. I read up on this and convinced myself that the area was ideal, and we should start a club in Kuala Belait. Gurkhas loved running, so I included a group of them in my planning, but also there was a number of ex-patriot Brits and Aussies living locally, so I thought with the addition of a few of the officers from 7GR, we could get this started. I had also heard that a schoolteacher from Bandar Seri Begawan (British) was part of a hash that was very strong in the capital, so I encouraged him to come down and give me a hand to get started.

Surprisingly, this all fell into place, and before long, we were getting sixty or seventy people every week attending. I appointed a hash master, a treasurer, and a president which of course was me. One of the Aussie guys from Shell even agreed to write a newsletter each week, and it was written in a very good-natured way that it appealed to everyone. He even got it printed by Shell which saved us the cost. Every month we would put on a Gurkha curry at one of only three European clubs we had in Kuala Belait which was the Motor Car Club. The locals thought it highly amusing to see sixty to seventy runners in different groups, running in all directions on a Monday afternoon. Our most regular runner was the CO; he loved his running and he encouraged the Gurkhas to attend.

It is amazing how a good idea will find a life of its own. In 1982 I was sitting in my office in Sydney when I received a phone call from the editor of the Kuala Belait local radio station who announced that she was Valerie Whitehead (who was the wife of an officer who used to run in the hash when I was involved in 1976). They had decided to quit the army, and her husband, Don, had taken up some job or other in Kuala Belait. Valerie advised me that she had tracked me down to do a live radio interview as that particular week represented the 1,000th hash for the local hash club, and she thought it appropriate that she should notify me publicly. I was 'chuffed' to say the least. What an honour that the club had persisted after I had left, apparently as strong as ever.

Strong friendships (which persist today) were formed with the local group of Australians and their friends who were working for Shell. We were quite lucky, in that soon after we arrived in Brunei, an Australian lobbed up to our door and advised that the local Australians were meeting at the Panaga Club (the biggest club for Europeans in our area) to listen to the Australian federal election results on Radio Australia on Saturday night and we were invited to attend. This was a good opportunity to meet some of the fellow ex-patriots, and I was always interested in political results.

Carole and I both attended, and we were openly welcomed and forged some really friendly relationships which as I mentioned still hold strong today. The first person we met was Ray Phillips who I had gone to school with and had lived at Burringbar not all that far from Murwillumbah. Ray was the regional manager for Carrier Air Conditioners and had made Kuala Belait his headquarters, so whenever he was not travelling, he would return to Brunei, and this was one of those times. The night progressed steadily and logically, awash in alcohol, and at some stage, someone announced that Malcolm Fraser had won the election. Everyone seemed happy with this result, although Brunei was quite divorced from Australia in political terms and I don't think anyone cared too much.

I found out that most of the Australians employed by Shell were on contracts of five years or more and were accountants, draftsmen, divers, and labourers. It was also pointed out that most of the complex diving was done by Italians. There were many British, Indian, and Dutch workers employed as well—many of these had children who attended the pre-school where Carole was to become the teacher, so eventually we also got to know many of these.

The Australians asked us what we were doing for Commonwealth Night which was simply a huge party where every different nationality built a bar and offered either traditional food or beverages. Brunei being majority Muslim had banned alcohol, but the Sultan provided exemptions for the officer's mess and the Panaga Club, and of course, Gurkhas were permitted to drink their rum within the barracks and their married quarters area. I informed the Australian group that the CO had decided that because 7GR had a 'tame' Australian attached, our theme this year would be Botany Bay and our bar would be constructed as a jail. Costumes would be in the form of convict uniforms. I recruited several of them to do a 'shift' behind the bar and ordered a suitable amount of Foster's Lager to be shipped in for the night. Someone came up with a contact from QANTAS Airlines and they agreed to fly in fifty dozen meat pies—not very original but a luxury in Kuala Belait. My mouth watered just thinking about them.

Our carpenter to build the bar was our doctor from 7GR who took some hoarding from some other party that had been held previously and, with meticulous calculation, cut and moulded the pieces to fit together in the space at the club that we had been allocated. It was then up to us to paint it to make it look like a jail which we somehow did, and on the night, it looked pretty good. The night was magnificent with several hundred people attending of mixed nationalities enjoying the food and the beverage and myriad of games that were arranged for our entertainment. The 7GR officers all did shifts in the bar and the workload was divided pretty evenly. Only one fight for the night and I was involved in that and it was over pretty quickly, although I ended up with fourteen stitches in my face—bit of a misunderstanding really, fortunately, it had no effect on the party.

Whilst living so close to the sea (about 100 m from our house), we used to go swimming in the South China Sea although the water was always coloured brown and was about the same temperature as bathwater, but the girls enjoyed it, and it was not dangerous. The fortunate thing about the area was that it had a small yacht club which held competitions in the mouth of the local river every Saturday. I immediately paid a small fee and did a sailing course which was held over about three weekends and I was awarded a ticket of authorisation to sail 'moths'.

It was at this time I discovered that Regimental Funds somehow, over the years, had purchased a number of 'moths' for recreation purposes for the military members of Brunei and housed them in a private shed about five kilometres along the coast. We had no transport for these craft, so we decided that there was enough of us now qualified to sail that we would run our own little competition in the area of the sailing shed. This we did on Sundays, and it provided great fun and enjoyment.

I was quite surprised to see that the Sultanate fostered a rugby union competition—a game that I enjoyed enormously. British ex-patriots in Bandar Seri Begawan seemed to be the administrators of it, and it boasted four teams and lots of enthusiasm. The Royal Brunei Malay Regiment, which was the Sultan's private army, had two battalions of locals who produced a team with the commander being a British colonel who was very fit and still played rugby and, of course, captained one of them. 7GR only had one Gurkha who played rugby (Tekbahada Rai) who learned the game when he attended Sandhurst as a student and became a British officer. The rest of our team was made up from British officers from 7GR and some other ranks who were mechanics and tradesmen from Headquarters Brunei who were a group of soldiers who provided the necessary administrative backup for the battalion, e.g., administration of married quarters including refurbishment and repair, vehicle repair workshops, canteen and food supplies (for us to buy our food and beverages, including milk), postal services, etc. Somehow we managed to scrape up enough players each week and a couple of referees. Linesmen were probably a bit of a luxury, and one of the spectators usually got this job from each of the teams.

I realised the value of Headquarters Brunei when I fell through the roof whilst trying to install a television antenna. They sent out a repair team which included replacing about ten tiles on my roof (probably asbestos now that I think about it). No charge, Sultan to pay. We also managed to get Foster's beer (which I preferred in those days) and vegemite because my girls didn't like marmite and didn't really eat much else. Their taste buds were not adjusted to curries at that age.

The British military had a marvellous jungle warfare training camp at Sungai Petani in Malaysia which used to cater to military forces from all over the world. For either economic or strategic reasons, the camp was shut down in the mid-1970s, but a smaller, more sub-unit-specific camp was set up in Brunei at Seria which boasted basic field accommodation and instruction facilities for about 120 students and staff. The staff levels were small, and equipment was limited, however, once organised, the courses seemed to run very well.

My interest was always high about the content of these courses because I had spent a lot of time training, fighting, and instructing on jungle warfare. I ventured down to a course and was immediately attracted to the course program. The staff were excellent and treated me with great respect, so much so that I was asked to attend one of the classes within the next week (before the squadron of students went back to the UK) and do a two-hour presentation on my time in Vietnam. The lesson was scheduled for a night-time, and I approached this thinking that I would be judged harshly (being Australian) by the squadron and taking up a night when the squaddies could be getting some sleep. How wrong I was, I delivered the lecture, questions lasted at least thirty minutes and the students were sensational—their interest was high and their knowledge was deep so much so that the SAS Warrant Officer who ran the course (and later became a very personal friend) advised that there would be a barbecue on the beach, with beer, and I had been invited. This came as a bit of a surprise, and having been up to do physical training with 7GR that morning at six and having instructed for two hours, I was starting to get a bit weary, however, I could see the leadership being displayed by 'Jordy' and I didn't want to interfere with that. So we sat in the sand, ate steaks and drank beer, and relaxed and the questions didn't stop coming.

These wonderful soldiers were insatiable for knowledge—again another wonderful, entertaining evening and I made another 120 friends.

I was invited to attend every course that came through after that and attended many lessons just learning new approaches to jungle warfare. Jordy and I became very close friends; he sat through every presentation I gave, and one evening, I asked him why he sat through all of my presentations, 'They are all the same', and his response was spontaneous, 'No, sir, your presentations are never the same!'

One afternoon I was rung at work by the RSM Headquarters Brunei and asked if I would come to his mess for a drink. I agreed always feeling somewhat privileged to be invited to a WO and sergeant's mess. When I arrived, I was immediately introduced to the RSM of 22 SASR—what an honour! Probably the most famous regiment in the world. We had a beer and the RSM of 22 SAS cut right to the chase.

'My CO has sent me out here to recruit you for 22 SASR.' I was gobsmacked. He outlined the terms and conditions particularly that we could take a six-week holiday in Australia to get things sorted and the fact that I would not have to take a step down in rank (which is a usual condition for joining the senior British regiments) nor would I have to do a selection course. I could not understand how I was even in their data bank until I recollected that Jordy was a very senior member of 22 SAS and obviously had been keeping an eye on me and reporting back to the regiment. Jordy was also a spectator at all the rugby matches we played having been a player himself not so long back. I needed to speak to Carole about this massive career step. My commitment was probably going to be ten years.

After hours of consideration and discussion, we decided that we would not take the offer and I informed the RSM. The final decider was probably the fact that my knees were shot from playing rugby, and being an infantryman particularly in SASR, I would not be given any sympathy if I couldn't keep up or I couldn't parachute. I was concerned that the offer had come a couple of years too late. Reluctantly the RSM accepted my decision and headed back to the UK. My vision of ten more years of active soldiering faded, but how nice to be considered worthy.

The wet season had started, and it was truly monsoonal. Regular daily rain came down in torrents for several hours and flooded low-lying areas and filled the monsoon drains. Much of the battalion training had to be restricted to local training areas as many of the jungle areas soon flooded and became impossible for overnight training. However, with planning, this was soon easily accommodated, and many individual skills were still practised and perfected. Each afternoon, after training, basketball was still played by most of the battalion. In fact it was whilst playing basketball, in the wet season, that I badly sprained my ankle. After an X-ray, my ankle was put in plaster, and I was told that I had to rest it for ten days. This was too pedestrian for my active lifestyle, so I arranged for my sergeant clerk to bring my 'in-tray' to my house and come out and clear it every day. I set up a table and the phone in our lounge room and got to work. Being the training officer, I had to ensure that battalion events (such as the annual route march) were planned and organised. This set-up worked surprisingly well, and everyone soon got to know that I was still available but my phone number had changed. Essentially, I was still being useful, and anyone who needed more detailed discussions simply hopped into their cars and came out to my house.

I need to tell of a very funny event that happened in the middle of the wet season whilst I had my leg in plaster. It was a Saturday night and I was at home with the family watching television and listening to the rain tumbling down. The rain was particularly heavy this night and, as such, had overflowed the monsoon drains and was covering the road at the front of our house which was directly opposite the CO's house. Next door to us was a house occupied by an Irish Ranger and his wife, and they were having a dinner party (Fred and Sue). I heard a car drive up and stop in front of our house which was somewhat unusual in such trying conditions. I heard some voices, so I ventured into my garage which was elevated and overlooked the road. I soon observed that the CO had been out to a party with his wife, obviously had a few drinks, and because the road was covered in water, had missed the turn into his house and had the rear offside wheel stuck in the monsoon drain. The CO was dressed up to the nines, and his wife was still in the car. The CO was in no state to be making serious decisions about moving the car and I was still in plaster. I called out for him to get back in the car and wait.

I rang Fred, the Irish Ranger, who was just finishing dinner with friends and outlined the circumstances. They too were well dressed up but quickly threw off their shoes and headed out into the night. Gallantly they carried the CO's wife to her front steps and returned for the CO who insisted on helping but accidentally fell in the drain and had to be helped out. Four young officers lifted the car out of the channel, started the motor, and drove it into the CO's garage. It should be pointed out that the quartet was laughing their heads off the whole time, and the CO, great guy that he was, was showing suitable embarrassment. Fred joined me in my garage, and we had a great laugh before he re-joined his party for port.

It was about this time that the CO advised me that we had a requirement to fly to Hong Kong and provide an 'enemy' party for a quite punishing exercise conducted for the British Army in the Far East. I was to lead the party with about half a company of Gurkhas. The exercise was to test the stamina, fitness, and general infantry abilities of section groups within the units currently posted to the Far East. I think there were about twenty-five groups who took part, and they were mainly tested for navigational skills over a three-day period, but they didn't get much sleep in that time. The groups were courageous but totally exhausted by the time they finished—so was I for that matter.

We returned back to Brunei, and the wet season was over and again it started to get hot. During my absence for that couple of weeks, the battalion held its annual route march which I had walked and measured out before I left. I thought I had it well organised, but the CO was quick to point out that I had made a mistake walking the battalion for about five kilometres along the railway line as it was difficult to get more than about four wide, so no rhythm could be established and there were many stones on the paths, so tired soldiers were turning ankles on them, etc. He also pointed out the miscalculation that I made with the water and the water trailer wasn't enough to fill all the water bottles on a day that required about ten litres per man. For me, this was a big fail and my first real lesson in logistics. This simple lesson was to serve me well in later days as my last posting was commanding a logistics battalion.

The CO had encouraged and approved for me to visit Nepal for a couple of weeks in September. Gurkhas were provided with flights to get to Nepal and were given a rotation every eighteen months instead of annual leave. They would leave the battalion for six months. These flights were therefore going every month out of Brunei, so it was easy to book on a flight, at no cost, and hitch a ride to Kathmandu. Many soldiers had given me the names of their villages so that I could visit them if I had time. I had mapped out a small plan of the closest villages I might be able to visit and was getting ready for this adventure of a lifetime.

I was due to fly out for Kathmandu on that Monday. On Sunday afternoon, Carole and I decided to have a game of tennis on the courts at the back of our married quarter. I was feeling a bit sluggish, and it was my time to serve. I threw the ball above me head and went to hit it, but my arm wouldn't lift. I tried again, and again, I had no energy. I started to feel quite ill. I went back inside and told Carole I needed to lie down. All of a sudden, I started to sweat, profusely. I got up and went to the shower and stood under cold water for a short while, but I still continued to sweat. I returned to my bed and spent the rest of the night sweating.

By morning, I had saturated the mattress (and as it turned out, I had lost ten kilos in weight). Carole quickly called the doctor and advised the CO that I would not be going to Kathmandu. The doctor gave me a quick examination and commented that it might have been malaria. He wanted me to rest for that day and see if I could come into his surgery the next day—after lots of hydration. The next day, I still felt lousy but got myself into his surgery. He was a very deep thinker and had given my situation a lot of thought. He asked me to strip off all my clothing and he took out a magnifying glass and started examining my body. It only took him a few minutes before he asked me what the spot on my waist was. I quickly looked down and identified the spot he was talking about. I told him it was the first time I had seen it. The doctor looked very satisfied with the discovery and said that he could not be sure, but he thought I might have scrub typhus. This immediately rang alarm bells for me because we had been briefed on the dangers of this disease before we went to Vietnam and had always put a special solution around our waistbands and where we bloused our trousers to prevent the penetration of the mite that carried scrub typhus.

Jim (the doctor) knew that I had been to Hong Kong recently, and even though the health authorities had denied the presence of scrub typhus in Hong Kong (for tourist reasons), twenty-two cases had been reported within the past twelve months. Jim advised me that the Committee for Tropical Diseases met quarterly for meetings in Brunei, and luckily, there was a meeting within the coming week. This was a high-powered group of the top British and Asian doctors majoring in tropical diseases in Asia. They met for exactly the purpose of identifying, locating, and curing tropical diseases. Jim approached their representative and notified that he had a patient with the correct identifying marks and the right incubation period for scrub typhus. They contacted me straight away and asked if I could be present at their next meeting.

This was hilarious, I felt like a male model in a painting class. I was asked to strip off and stand in front of a very serious-looking group of doctors, both male and female, who professionally pushed and prodded me and discussed possibilities and theories all of which concluded that I had scrub typhus. However, the group was almost certain that Chinese authorities would not accept this conclusion because of the damage it would do to their dependence on the tourist trade. It is also interesting to note that no record was made, in my medical records, that notated I had contracted scrub typhus. I know I lost close to 10 kg during this two-week period.

We only had one lot of visitors the whole time we were in Brunei and that was Gary and Gai McKay who stopped off on a holiday around Asia. They stayed about ten days, and there wasn't a lot to show them other than the boundaries of the very rich state in which we lived. However, during this time, I got Gary to run a 'hash' with us and share a Gurkha curry, play a rugby match, and get a sail in one of our 'moths'. Gary was quite an accomplished rugby player and added a lot to our team, so much so that the opposition thought we had imported another player—alas, it was for one game only. Gary was keen to visit Kota Kinabalu, but getting passport clearances to enter Malaysia at that time was a slow process, so time beat us to achieve this.

Time was drawing close for the end of our tour, so Carole and I both organised farewell parties along with our friends organising farewell parties for us, so leaving Brunei seemed as though it was going to be a long process, and this proved to be correct. The rule at the officer's mess was that parties were required to invite all the mess, but the host only had to pay for drinks consumed 6–9 p.m. It seemed that every member of the mess turned up for our farewell—not quite sure how to interpret that—and at 9 p.m., we were having such a good time that I agreed to pay for the night. As it turned out, this doubled our budget for the night. Not only that, but after the party, we decided to go to the local village (kedai) and see if we could get a steak. I drove my car which I had sold and was due to be handed over in two days' time. Unfortunately, I missed a turn and drove it into a stormwater drain and blew the front two tyres, replacement of which managed to clean out the bank account we had accumulated since being in Brunei and meaning that we were going home 'skint'. I replaced the two tyres the next morning, but they were very expensive in Brunei, and I was lucky to have enough left in the account after extending the length of the party the previous night.

Carole was also farewelled by a large gathering of parents who were sorry to see her leaving the pre-school. This was particularly rewarding for someone who had no experience as a teacher. She had done a very good job.

What a marvellous adventure serving in Brunei and, in particular, ending two years with Seventh DOE Gurkha Rifles. The ironic thing about the end of this tour was that the CO, now LTCOL Miles Hunt-Davis, had just completed my annual report and had yet to get me to read it and sign it. We had been booked on a Cathay Pacific flight to Hong Kong from where we would return to Australia. In those days, Australian officers and, therefore, their families travelled first class, so we were assigned seats at the front of the aircraft. The CO, who also was travelling to Hong Kong on the same flight, was not entitled to the same privileges as I was, so he sat down the back of the plane. I reminded him of the need to provide me with my annual report and suggested he ventured up to first class to deliver it. 'Be buggered', he said, 'if you want your report, you come down to the back of the plane.' This, I, of course, did and we had a drink and a laugh. I signed the document, and we said a final farewell on the aircraft.

Carole and I and the family stayed over one night in Hong Kong to allow me to finalise matters with the Australian consulate and say our final round of farewells. We also attended a party for Steve Rabuka who was a Fijian Army officer who took my place as the exchange officer with the Brigade of Gurkhas. Steve later became quite a unique figure, in that he played rugby for Fiji, became the country's first Olympic representative, and held a coup because of the unjust ownership of all small businesses the Indian population had taken in Fiji—a separate story on its own, but not for this book.

CHAPTER FIFTEEN

HOME AND 5/7RAR (MECHANISED)

RETURNING HOME AFTER two years was great, but we were returning with only a handful of furniture and nothing remaining from our initial storage. We stayed with Carole's parents whilst I investigated what plans the Directorate of Infantry had for me. Logically, we were owed some leave and we had to find a place to live.

My new posting was as a company commander with 5/7RAR (Mechanised) at Holsworthy. This was essentially an experimental unit designed to assess and train soldiers in the art of mechanised warfare. This required a total change in thinking and tactics to that which I was used to having spent most of my military career in jungle warfare. This was certainly going to be a challenging couple of years.

We still had to find somewhere to live. Married quarters were scarce, and the little we had saved overseas would need to be spent on furniture. However, a little bit of luck came our way. When I returned from Vietnam, Carole and I had bought an unimproved block of land at Indooroopilly in

Brisbane. We had to arrange a friend, Wayne Aitkenhead, to keep it mown and tidy as the blocks around it were all being built on and neighbours ensured that the council were informed every time it got a bit overgrown. While we were in Brunei, somehow a real estate agent contacted us and made an offer on the block. I, having no idea what land was now worth in Brisbane, knocked back the offer, added $5,000, and expected not to hear from them again. Just as we were leaving Brunei, I was advised the offer was accepted, and all of a sudden, we had a deposit on a house. Carole and I found a suitable house at Campbelltown (twenty-five minutes from Holsworthy), and it proved to be a lifesaver.

I called in on the battalion during my leave to spend an afternoon with Peter Cosgrove who I had seen very little of since returning from Vietnam. Fortunately, he hadn't changed a drop and was currently adjutant of 5/7 RAR but was soon to leave to take up a company commander's role in another unit. The CO was LTCOL Jake O'Donnell at that time, but he too was being reposted before Christmas, and the new CO was to be LTCOL Murray Blake who I had the privilege of meeting in Vietnam after he had been involved in the battle of Binh Ba with 5RAR where he was awarded an MC. I called in his office early in the new year before I took up my post to pay my respects before the working year started. Certainly one of the toughest people I have ever worked for, but clearly one of the best.

My first day at work didn't really go well for me. The CSM read out standing orders on parade which advertised the position of a dog handler at Oakey in Queensland, and twenty-two members of the company applied for it. I consulted with the CSM and he agreed we had a problem. I got the CSM to round up the twenty-two applicants and advised them that whatever their problem was, I thought we could resolve it within a month. I asked them to hold off with their applications for thirty days, and if they still wanted a transfer out after that period, I would look to release them.

The vacancy for dog handler was still a couple of months away. This satisfied the men, and they seemed pacified at present. The CSM and I worked hard in that thirty days to ensure we had a company that was organised, competitive, and working to a plan. It seemed to have worked as no one re-applied at the end of the thirty days.

Unfortunately, by the time I paid the deposit on the house, I had very little left for a car, so I arranged through my brother-in-law to buy a twenty-year-old Hillman Minx. Unfortunately also, it mostly needed to be cranked (with a crank handle), and as I drove from my company office to the front gate, it dispensed enormous amounts of white smoke, causing much mirth and jesting among the soldiers. The RSM called me aside one day and said, 'Really, sir, I think you need to fix it.'

Fortunately, on this matter, I was able to again call upon my brother-in-law, who was a motor mechanic, and asked him to regrind the valves for me. This he did, and when the 'blue machine' next made an appearance within the battalion lines, I received a hearty round of applause.

The first year in the battalion was spent getting everyone qualified for their jobs in a mechanised role and getting our tactics sorted out to company level. Essentially, every soldier had to do a driving course, and all NCOs had to do a crew commander's course. This was time-consuming when we were trying to keep the company proficient in their infantry skills and minor tactics (weapon handling, shooting, fitness, navigation, etc.), so there was an enormous balance of training required particularly as myself and the CSM both had to qualify in both these courses as well. All was going swimmingly until one of my APCs ran into a high-voltage metal stanchion (carrying thousands of volts in electrical cable) and brought it down. Thankfully, no one was injured, but it must have cost a lot of money to be repaired and the investigation went on for months. The cable wasn't ruptured, so I don't think we blacked out Liverpool.

Mechanisation proved to be much more difficult than I had initially imagined. Every tactic had to change, troops had to be disgorged, troops had to be deployed, and any firing by the APCs had to done with the realisation that they had ground troops in support, so angles of fire became very relevant. Night movement became particularly 'hairy' along routes or paths not known. Seatbelts were not worn by troops in the rear and any tip by an APC because of an unknown or unseen creek could spell disaster. Speed by night was filled with fear. Refuelling of APCs was sometimes a logistical nightmare, and wet weather could cause disruption due to bogging, flooding, etc. The simple life of an infantryman had changed severely. The smell of achievement and ambition had changed to the smell of diesel.

Our first year as mechanised infantry therefore went very quickly with many new skills being learned and practised. The year probably would have gone unnoticed in our memories except that the CO had accepted an exchange program with a mechanised unit from Fort Carson, Colorado, in the United States, and C Company was chosen to provide the nucleus of the mechanised group. Vehicles or weapons were not to be taken and would be provided by our host unit. The CO had decided to go, but the group was to be led by myself. Our total number was 120 which comprised C Company plus supplements from other companies, a public relations officer, a paymaster, an ordnance rep, a padre, and a signals officer. This was seen by many as being the highlight of their year. This was the reward for soldiering in peacetime.

Preparation had to start immediately. We had about two months' notice, so we had to make sure of a number of things. Firstly, we had to be super fit, then we had to be right up to scratch with our basic skills, and finally, we all had to have a reasonable knowledge of our own country. We, as a battalion, already had a fitness program, but with the trip as an incentive, I decided to 'step' this up a bit, and after some consultation with the CO, it was decided to determine a list of two hundred questions that might be asked of any of our soldiers. This was totally subjective, but there was some data around about what questions Americans wished to know about Australia, so we lent heavily on that list. We distributed the list to our soldiers and suggested that they learn as much of it as they could. We then included the questions from the list in our daily workout. For instance, we would run a kilometre, stop, do some basic calisthenics, and whilst doing them, I would ask individuals questions from the list in a quick-fire fashion, then run on for another kilometre asking for the answers along the way. This didn't go down well with soldiers initially, as a few of them had a clue to the answers, but as the weeks wore on, more correct answers were forthcoming, and it became obvious that the troops had been learning more of the list.

By the end of the two months, we all had a pretty good idea of a bit more about our own country (population, major sports, major features, e.g., height of Mt Kosciuszko, etc., attitudes towards light, but limited political events or personalities, e.g., 'Who was the leader of the federal opposition?' etc.). We thought we were pretty well prepared except that I worried about the physical state of a couple of our attachments, e.g., the paymaster who hadn't done any physical work in the past ten years and smoked about twenty cigarettes a day, but to his eternal credit, he kept trying his best to meet our standard.

Finally, it was critical that we all knew the words to our national anthem and a couple of other songs such as 'Tie Me Kangaroo Down Sport'. Platoon Commander Gary Bornholt undertook to produce a number of these songs on a sheet of paper and distribute to the whole company so that we didn't get caught out if called upon to sing a couple of tunes. This later proved to be a lifesaver.

The trip commenced with the usual amount of military precision. We made our way to the airport and were loaded on to an American

255

commercial flight with our group being the only passengers. The staff were all female, and I knew I would have to be watchful of the group once a few beers had been consumed. I passed this on to my platoon commanders and CSM. We were subjected to the usual protocols of air safety, flying over water, etc., and then the bar was opened. Logically, because we were all known to each other, everyone moved around and chatted as they drank—not quite sure where we refuelled, but the staff told me that they had to restock with beer as we had almost consumed their complete stock and reserve. We closed the bar down early in the morning so that everyone had the opportunity to get some sleep and reopened after everyone had shaved and had breakfast.

The excitement was still evident with some of our group never having been outside Australia in the past. The aircrew approached me and said that the captain had asked if we could sing a couple of Australian tunes for him (he would leave the door open so that he could hear). He particularly wanted to hear 'Waltzing Matilda'. Without really meaning to, I hesitated before speaking to Gary Bornholt about this. The aircrew took this as a request from me for them to provide something in return. They consulted with the captain, and without hesitation, he offered to divert the plane and show us a close-up look of the Grand Canyon. This was an enormous concession, and it was a long way out of our way, and I was concerned that the captain might be up for a big explanation. However, who was I to worry? I asked Gary to get a group together, move up to the front of the plane, and work out what songs they would sing leading with 'Waltzing Matilda'. This took a bit of organising and a few reluctant soldiers came forward, were handed the song sheets, and the music began. At first, we were a little embarrassed at this soiree, but as we passed a couple of beers around, the group launched into the songs and completely impressed the captain and crew when we provided more than a couple of songs and eventually got the whole plane singing.

The view of the Grand Canyon from down low was stultifying, absolutely magnificent—already the trip was a success. We did hear later, however, that the captain was stood down from flying for diverting the trip and flying inside the 'no fly' zone over the Grand Canyon. I suspect he knew the outcome when he took the risk, such a wonderful, kind man.

We were well received at Fort Carson. Everything was in readiness for us, and we were shown respect and courtesy. The diggers' eyes bulged when they saw the size of the Coral Club which was the 'diggers' boozer', big enough to hold a ball in. After orientation, the company settled in, and I did the required rounds of courtesy calls which included the brigade commander and the CO of the Fourth US Infantry (mechanised) who were hosting us. An amazing stroke of luck was the fact that the battalion 2IC was a British major on exchange who was extremely helpful particularly when it came to interpreting local rules, etc.

Almost immediately, I was invited to a seemingly endless round of dinners and parties and quickly received a first-hand insight into American (and British) hospitality. I was smart enough to have brought a trunk load of Australian wine, and the Americans were delighted to even think we produced wine let alone of a drinkable quality—were they surprised when I presented them a bottle at each visit.

On my reconnaissance to Fort Carson several months earlier, I noticed that every month, every unit in the Fort Carson area was required to conduct a run with everyone in their unit attending. The units would be given a time to be a the 'starting gates' and would be timed on the basis of the first man leaving and the last man arriving at the finishing gates. It was only a couple of kilometres, run in T-shirts, trousers, and boots, but the determining factor was that Fort Carson was 6,000 feet above sea level—a fact I acknowledged on my first couple of runs and proved to be one of the reasons I was so keen to get our company fit before coming to the States. This run was taken very seriously, and the reward for being announced the winner was that that unit got to hold the Fort Carson Battle Guidon (flag) until another unit shook it loose. My understanding was that 101st Airborne (a celebrated unit I knew well from Vietnam) had controlled ownership of the guidon for quite some time. I also noticed that all American units had to sing when they ran, or their structure would disintegrate and people would fall out and start walking. Singing seemed to provide them with the necessary cadence—interesting.

Our hosts provided us with a very basic training program on arrival which was designed to allow us to integrate quickly with our hosts and start sharing ideas and comparing training methods, etc. I was fairly quick to notice that the monthly run was about four days into our program and we were invited to participate. It was therefore critical that we got our soldiers running daily so they learned how to better use the oxygen that was provided at 6,000 feet. I was concerned that this might not be enough time.

The day came and we attended the running gates right on time. This was really the most organised athletic test for soldiers I had ever seen. There were only about five or six gates, but your time was taken from the time the first member of your team was passed through the gates (turntables). We had 119 starters with our last man being our less-than-infantry-fit paymaster. We quickly reformed once we were through the gates and started running four abreast, in cadence. We started with the paymaster up front with the instructions that he was to be telescoped to the rear if he couldn't stay in step. There were American groups all around us, and they were all singing their marching songs, which I found incredibly boring because it seemed like I had been hearing that same tune for thirty years (I had actually). However, we got on with our job taking a bit of flak from some of the huge members of other units running occasionally alongside of us, quickly identifying us as the visiting Australians and making sure that we knew our position in the pecking order. Most of the direct comments came from Afro-Americans, I might add. We were wearing our 'Charlie Coy' T-shirts, and I remember one big soldier coming up to me and saying, 'Is that Coy or Boy?' I was hoping I didn't have to fight him at the finish.

We were nearing the finish line, and sure enough, our paymaster had dropped to the back of the pack. I quickly dropped back and ran beside him but didn't say a word. He was trying to keep up and he did. When we reached the gates, he was still in touch and caught his breath whilst he was waiting to get counted through the gates. We had finished as a group, in the time I had set for the run, based on our training back in Australia, and we felt good. Time to get back to the lines, shower, and get ready for a day's training.

CSM broke the company into three groups, and we were just about to head out when the CO (Fourth Mech Bn) said, 'Brian, remarkable job, and I think your company has won.' There must have been a thousand soldiers (men and women) running that morning, how could we have won? Well, we did, and I was given a copy of the results to prove that it wasn't a set-up. The guidon was later formally presented to us by the Brigadier sadly advising that it has never gone to a unit outside Fort Carson previously. Well it had now. We proudly flew that guidon on every parade we attended when we arrived back in Australia, and it was still housed in the Charlie Company display case last time I visited the battalion. We were the champions!

Brian receives the keys to Colorado City
during his visit to Colorado in 1977

The trip was everything we wanted it to be. We did some courses with the local Ranger battalion (mainly escape and evasion/interrogation, etc.). My men were not too happy with the fact that I arranged for very little chance to escape. I wanted to see what their reaction was to 'capture' and interrogation, and it proved to be a very interesting exercise with the men themselves finding out a lot about themselves. I was able to view all the men during their internment and their interrogation and was able to reveal some startling information about their performances; those that told lies, those that gave up the truth too easily, those that tried to tell lies but were not practised enough at it. The big advantage I had, however, was that even the exercise interrogators didn't know the truth whereas I did. A report was provided by the Rangers at the conclusion and then I held a debrief with the officers and soldiers who attended. It was hilarious and, as I said before, very revealing. At first, the men were very angry they wanted the opportunity to escape and evade, but I had them placed almost immediately into capture. However, as we talked the exercise through and I pointed out relevant observations (both good and poor) and finally revealed what the interrogators thought was the information we provided, the men were quite relieved to see how highly they had performed without any training in this area. The officer on the course, Gary Bornholt, had perpetuated this amazing lie and kept building on it, somehow managing to make it sound truthful to the extent that the interrogators (highly qualified in this art) had actually confirmed that he was telling the truth—Australian leadership, what an art. The end result was that all men who attended came away feeling that they would not have volunteered had they known what was going to happen to them, however, they were satisfied that they performed with strength and courage and acknowledged that with some training they could have achieved even better results.

We attended a battalion exercise which went fairly slowly by our standards, but we manoeuvred well and met our missions on time, and the CO (Fourth US Mech) seemed happy with our performance. The interesting thing we found about the exercise was the way they fed their troops (us included). No hard rations were drawn, all meals were fresh and were provided by a logistic train (US term for support vehicles) that went to every company and fed the troops fresh meals; the problem was that by the time they got around to us on the first night, the only thing left was boiled cabbage. This did not go down well with us after fourteen hours of eating dust (we didn't get our cabbage until after 9 p.m.), so I had to arrange for that system to work a little better, which it did.

Our CO LTCOL Blake seemed happy the way all this was going, so he took the opportunity to visit some fellow Australians in Texas and left us for about five days.

We were about three weeks into the trip and some of our soldiers had made very good friends with their equivalent US counterparts who invited them to an afternoon game of 'Murder Ball' which was fascinating to watch. It was played on available patches of grass within the battalion lines and consisted of a large rubber ball about seven foot high. Two teams of ten were selected from each of the nationalities and a whistle was blown. I don't think there were any other rules. The teams simply had to charge this huge ball forward until it crossed the end line and that constituted a point. This was played for about ten minutes and then substitutes were allowed. This was hilarious, bodies were strewn everywhere, and of course, the Australians loved it. The Americans just wanted to win, the Aussies wanted to show their prowess and winning was secondary. They charged at the ball with great resolve, some bouncing off it, others getting rolled under it. I don't know that anyone was ever declared the winner, but all participants seemed to enjoy the contest. I made sure I was never close enough to get an invite to play.

We did, however, have a fairly robust rugby team, and we were invited to play a friendly match against a local Colorado team (not military); rugby was just gaining momentum in the US at this stage, and although a little rough around the edges, the local team played well enough to beat us although we did find the lack of oxygen at 6,000 feet a little unsettling. During a few beers after the game, we were invited to join a rugby carnival the following weekend in Colorado City. This we did thinking that it might comprise about ten teams and we would have to play only about three matches (including a final if we made it). We were advised that there were sixty teams nominated, and our first game was quite early on the Sunday morning (knock-out competition, all games played on the one day, twenty minutes each way).

Unfortunately (?), I had a serious drink the night before and declared myself unavailable. This upset the team a bit, but I really didn't think I could survive the low oxygen intake. However, we still made it to the first final, and it was about three o'clock in the afternoon when we played the final. We were pretty exhausted (having played three matches), the team we were playing was very fit, and we had watched them win previously. The game went pretty evenly, but the opposition was continually hitting our team with late tackles and the referee was doing nothing about it. My men were tired and getting very irritable about the late tackles. At half time, I spoke to the ref and advised him that if he didn't stop the late tackles, I would walk the team off. He got very offended at this and told me to stop complaining.

About ten minutes into the second half, we got hit with a very strong late tackle which severely hurt one of my players. With this, my big second rower was overcome with how unfair this game had become and who was responsible, so he walked over and belted the referee. That was it, our competition was over, Claude was sent off, so I called the rest of the team off the field, and we returned to Fort Carson. We probably were not spoken well of after the carnival, however, the local team forgave us and invited us to their club on the following Saturday night where anyone who spoke with an Aussie accent had ten new friends and free beer all night. Although we did have to sing a few versions of 'Waltzing Matilda' / 'Tie Me Kangaroo Down Sport', etc. Nonetheless, an outstanding night.

The trip proceeded well with a few problems. The padre did approach me and advise that he was worried about the number of married men, known to him, who were spending a lot of time with American ladies and he wanted me to stop it. I advised him that whereas I fully appreciated his observations, I was not prepared to police every soldier in his off-duty hours, although I would speak collectively to the company and convey his sentiments and support him. This I did but unfortunately to little avail as after return to Australia, the padre advised me that many separations had occurred as a result of this trip. In fact, two of my platoon commanders married girls they met on the trip and, to my knowledge, are still happily married. This should not detract from the padre's point, however, he was referring specifically to the married members of our group and he was doing his job. The padre clearly held me responsible for this situation, and we parted agreeing to disagree.

The trip home looked straight forward enough, and we had all our administration in order. As a parting gesture, the local newspaper wanted to do an interview on the success (or otherwise) of our trip. I asked Murray Blake if he would like to do it, but he declined and asked me to do it. I took the public relations officer with me who was a very mature and experienced journalist (within Army circles), and we commenced the interview. Questions seemed normal although I did have a habit of speaking in 'one-liners' or 'throw-away lines' which neither I nor the PR officer took much notice of. The interview concluded, the journalist and my PRO and myself all seemed happy with how it had proceeded. Nothing really controversial had been discussed, and although I pointed out a couple of differences in our training systems, I raised no criticisms of the trip, in fact, I praised it and said how fortunate we were to have been given the opportunity to visit. Now, this article would normally not have been released until the next day when we would have been airborne and heading back to Australia. Unfortunately, the airline had gone on strike for three days, and we, as a group, had to occupy a further three days in Fort Carson which we planned to fill in with trips to the Coors Brewery, the Mint, and several other local institutions to prevent 'idle hands' from getting into mischief.

At 7 a.m. on the second day of our extended tour, the CO (Fourth US Inf [Mech]) called me and advised that I was required to parade to the Brigadier's office and be prepared to explain the newspaper article, for which I was the feature component and apologise for comments made. My heart stopped beating, I rang my CO and the PRO; they made it clear that they wanted to distance themselves from it and left the explaining to me. At this stage, I hadn't even seen the paper, so it was somewhat in the dark, but knowing the word 'sensationalism', I feared the worst. I was paraded into the Brigadier's office, and there was a committee as solemn as the Spanish Inquisition. They were not happy, and I was the reason. I could see a copy of the newspaper on the desk and was trying to speed read it upside down, I could see the lines that I had spoken, and I could see how they were completely bastardised to mean exactly the opposite to what I had actually said. Logically, the Brigadier was having none of it regardless of my explanations. He gave me a massive spray and told me he wanted me to write a paper apologising to all the NCOs and men involved that I had insulted and explain to them how I saw the US 'fixing' their army. I saluted and 'fled' angry that I had not been given any real opportunity to defend matters referred to in the article. The Brigadier would not be getting a paper from me on any subject. I quickly got myself over to the Post Exchange where I purchased half a dozen copies of the *Colorado Times* and carefully read every word of the two-page article. I visited Murray Blake as I wanted him to be aware of the truth of the matter, as my future might depend on it. Murray read the article and laughed quite loud, saying, 'Not a bad article but you made the mistake of using "throw-away lines". This will get you into trouble every time because you allow latitude for your words to be misrepresented.' These are words that I have remembered all my military career. I don't think this matter has been brought up ever since; we simply walked away from it.

The plane was leaving the next morning, so I made my round of farewells but was treated very coolly by the senior ranks and the CO. My parting words were simply, 'Don't believe everything you read', and left them to draw their own conclusions. A great trip tainted at the end by a sensationalised newspaper article. I personally felt deflated, however, it didn't seem to affect anyone else in the group with the possible exception of the padre.

We returned to Holsworthy, and after a couple of days' leave, we were back into it. Our two years mechanised was in fact a two-year trial to determine the suitability for an infantry battalion to sustain and maintain a mechanised capability, permanently. Therefore we had a number of goals to achieve at unit level, and we had just been delayed by a further six weeks with the trip to the US (fortunately, with a mech unit, so our skills did not deteriorate).

We attacked the remainder of the 1977 and 1978 with great enthusiasm and some very cold days at Puckapunyal working with the tanks and our direct support artillery battery. These were good but hard days, however, our skills were elevated well above where we expected they would be. During all this training, we still maintained our basic company and unit sporting competitions. My company was eliminated in the finals of the rugby competition, ran second in the shooting competition, and the battalion won the rugby shield and the AFL competition (morale was high), so overall a magnificent effort, but it would come to nothing if we were not successful in completing the mechanised trial. The final trial for this was a lengthy night navigation and battalion attack scenario using tanks and of course engineers and artillery. It was run over about a week and Task Force Headquarters (including the Brigadier) provided the assessment team. We were the lead company and almost got off to a bad start when one of my tracks (vehicles) backed onto a very solid tree stump which managed to suspend our running gear off the ground and starve us of traction. Some practised recovery drills allowed us to get under way about ten minutes late with the CO casting some doubt about my heritage and offering to replace me or the company if we didn't get mobile with great haste.

Eventually we got under way, and as previously mentioned, movement was slow using tracked vehicles, sometimes off road. It took most of the night to get the whole battalion into their various attack positions and conduct the necessary reconnaissance, in the dark, to ensure our role in the attack was precisely as planned. We also had to position our engineers to ensure the wire was breached before we moved forward. Daylight was approaching, and we needed to be rolling by first light. So far, all was on track, and because we were maintaining radio silence, it was impossible to know how fellow companies were going. Tanks and mech infantry take up a lot of real estate.

H-hour was signalled at first light, and the attack began on a fortified village constructed for the purpose and communications were great because of the support vehicles—a wonderful conclusion to a tough couple of years. The whole attack felt great because every person knew their job, and seemingly every company was in position. Logically, some areas of the attack bogged down (thanks to the directing staff) and various commanders were appointed as casualties (to test the back-up system), so the whole exercise took all of the morning and some of the afternoon. After which the CO advised the exercise was complete and we should return to camp and commence cleaning vehicles, etc., whilst we waited for the result of the attack which would probably provide the final outcome of the trial. Surprisingly the result was in quickly, and the CO called his company commanders in almost as soon as we got back to camp and advised that both the attack and the trial had been outstanding successes and we could now go to the Christmas break knowing what our role would be in the new year. Unfortunately, for me I was also advised that I would be leaving the company and taking up a position as the senior instructor Field Wing at the Officer Cadet School at Portsea in Victoria, and I would have to leave within a week to view the graduation processes and procedures that were contingent to my job. I would then return to arrange for the movement of my family which involved finding new accommodation, arranging a removalist, and transporting them to Victoria.

It is interesting to note that most civilians that I spoke to in my army career firmly believed that all that was done for you and you moved into available rent-free accommodation, not so although our accommodation was capped, essentially making it subsidised although far from free. Moving frequently, in our case about every two years, it meant that you didn't get attached to houses and you didn't keep anything you didn't need. However, it also meant that you didn't always get a phone and linoleum was the more likely floor covering rather than carpet.

Portsea was an exciting posting for me as I had gone through the national service system at breakneck speed and didn't really get the time nor the opportunity to examine the system other than by experiencing it. My recon was time well spent listening to the assessments given on each of the graduating cadets after the final field exercise which in future I would be responsible for, keeping in mind that the class we were assessing was within a week of graduating as young second lieutenants in the Australian Army. What an exciting week I was experiencing. The Officer Cadet School was established at Portsea in 1951 and saw its first intake in January 1952. The Royal Military College in Canberra was already established at this time and its graduates were heading straight to the war in Korea. OCS continued graduating young officers until after the Vietnam War when it was integrated with RMC in 1985. Both proved to be very honourable places graduating many very highly distinguished names such as Peter Badcoe, VC; Sir Peter Cosgrove, AK, AC, MC (governor general of Australia); Michael Jeffries, AC, CVO, MC Governor General of Australia; David Hurley, AC, DSC, FTSE (governor general of Australia); Reg Beesley, AM (governor of Tasmania); John Sanderson, AC (governor of Western Australia); Peter Arnison, AC, CVO (governor of Queensland); Ron Grey, AO, DSO; Peter Leahy, AC; Jim Molan, AO, DSC; and the list goes on.

Portsea was, in essence, a sausage factory turning out young officers capable of leading an infantry platoon of thirty-three soldiers into battle within twelve months. However, we turned out some fantastic young men, highly capable who would remain personal friends for life. In order to achieve this, we had to have some outstanding young officers and warrant officers to do the training and these were from all corps and backgrounds. I was lucky to have inherited such a competent bunch of dedicated instructors, and whereas this may have made my job easier, it still didn't relieve the amount of time taken to run such a brutal schedule. Integrated into this heavy training program was the need for sport, and of course, the inevitable training of sporting teams. The major teams being part of civilian competitions. This even became harder when the cadets had their mid-term break of seven days; staff would be required to make up the numbers so that our teams did not forfeit.

Courses commenced every six months, and it therefore followed that we had two graduations each year. Grand affairs with a full parade and an opportunity to meet parents/partners/family who constantly thanked the staff for their role in the training of the cadets. In some cases, extolling their disbelief that we could actually make such changes in the young men who marched in to those who graduated particularly if the members had entered with chequered backgrounds.

Cadets had to have some knowledge of many facets of the corps of infantry. Special to corps training was done after graduation. The amount of subjects was vast, and of course, there were always written confirmation tests and concept papers that cadets were required to write during the course of their year of learning. Seventy-hour weeks were the norm with study additional to that. Then came the field tests with cadets getting the opportunity to demonstrate their leadership skills, or otherwise. The areas used for this were Yarram State Forest or the Puckapunyal Military Training Area. Pressure was increased with the addition of responsibility and activities varied to ensure that all skills were tested. This is where the benefit of good staff became paramount. The degree of experience and knowledge the staff brought to the field was inestimable. This was also a time when the cadets gained respect for the staff and the standard that they demonstrated and demanded. The sum of all this training, testing, and assessment boiled down to the one thing that mattered and that was passing the final Board of Study. The Board of Study was a meeting of all instructional and training staff listening to a summary of the cadet's year and deciding if he/she was to graduate or not. These were long-winded conferences determined to give every cadet a chance of demonstrating the ability to command an infantry platoon at war. The only other options were repeating a term (three to six months), repeating the course (an unlikely option) or failing, and marching out with the qualifications to march into a chosen corps with the qualifications of a corporal. Staff were often left deflated if the cadets for which they were responsible did not graduate. The Board of Study was an opportunity to make a final plea based on redeeming features or setbacks in the cadet's training year.

Nonetheless the system was a good one, honed by time and improved by some wonderful minds and some good leadership. This was a very professional establishment. This was a year that stands high in my memory of military experience. Towards the end of the second year (1980), I was advised that I had been accepted to attend the Command and Staff College across Port Phillip Bay at Queenscliff, which was a qualifying year for promotion beyond major. I was overjoyed at being selected, and it meant that my family and myself would remain in Victoria for one more year even though the journey was only about ten kilometres across the bay, it was over 150 kilometres to drive around, accompanied by our furniture.

Another tough year of study and presentations but again surrounded by smart, energised students mostly of the same rank (major), many of whom I had known previously. The demands on us as students was fairly severe, although the really smart ones seemed to 'breeze' through. I worked until about midnight four to five nights a week, played in the volleyball competition on one other and then socialised on the Sabbath. The wives cleverly nicknamed our existence 'the mogadon experience' because 80 percent of the students put in, at least, the same amount of time as I did and the wives were left to watch television. Even during our seven-day mid-term break, Carole and the kids caught a bus to Sydney whilst I stayed in Queenscliff and wrote my ten-thousand-word defence paper for assessment.

The course had its lighter moments of course when we, as a student body (separated into two groups), were flown halfway around Australia in order to learn about resources, infrastructure, demographics, etc., which was done by civic lectures in places like Mt Isa, Darwin, the Kimberleys, Perth, Alice Springs, Weipa, Thursday Island, RAAF Base Richmond, etc., and of course, the presentations were opened up for questions. Now, we did have some 'thrusters' in the group who always liked to hear the sound of their own voice, so we knew that no one had to have prepared questions, but we also had some larrikins who never missed an opportunity to turn serious presentations into hilarious situations. This always lightened the mood and kept everyone from becoming a little overcome by poor deliveries. These destinations were all reached by RAAF C130 aircraft, so we were able to travel fairly comfortably and with access to beverages. Logically, all movement was done to the sound of ring pulls being opened on cans of VB and pity help anyone who wanted to read or have a doze. There was certainly no shortage of things to chat about over a coldie. Whilst we were enjoying this sojourn, the other half of our class was covering the other half of Australia. In the second half of the year, we swapped over and pursued different objectives covering the other half of Australia. Valuable trips with a lot of fun thrown in. A great learning year with a lot of personal and professional contacts gained. Time to move on.

I was posted back to Sydney but this time to Victoria Barracks, an Australian Army base in Sydney, New South Wales. Victoria Barracks is located in the suburb of Paddington, between Oxford Street and Moore Park Road. It is just north of the Moore Park, the Sydney Cricket Ground, and Sydney Football Stadium. The land selected to construct the military barracks was on the sandy scrubland covered slopes of what was to become the suburb of Paddington. The land at that time formed a small part of an area of around 1,000 acres, which was reserved by Governor Macquarie in 1811 for a 'Sydney Common'.

The main planning considerations for its construction largely revolved around the fact of its remoteness from the town centre and its unsuitability for agricultural purposes, as the terrain presented high ground, stunted trees, sand, and scattered outcrops of stone. Additional advantages included its proximity to good drinking water and the availability of sandstone, which would be used in the construction of the barracks. The Commanding Royal Engineer, Lieutenant Colonel George Barney, was familiar with the water supply from the Lachlan Swamps in what is now known as Centennial Park and the line of Busby's Bore to Hyde Park. As colonial engineer, he had carried out extensive investigation of the bore prior to its completion as a water supply to Sydney Town in 1837.

Approval for the construction of the new barracks was granted on 3 August 1840. The initial design of the barracks was accredited to LTCOL George Barney, Royal Engineers. Barney's initial plan and cost estimates for the new barracks were based on using locally produced bricks. The availability of sandstone readily on site for the new barracks gave him the opportunity to save on the cost of manufacturing or buying bricks. All the stone used for the barrack buildings was quarried in the vicinity.

Victoria Barracks, built from 1841 to 1847, was the third barracks built to accommodate military personnel in colonial Sydney. Having initially housed British regiments, it became home to colonial New South Wales units and up to 2016 continued to provide accommodation for Australian military personnel.

Victoria Barracks in Sydney hence became a beautiful sandstone military headquarters with loads of history. I had first become acquainted with Victoria Barracks when I was in 1RAR at Holsworthy. We were required, as Sydney units, to rotate through guarding the barracks and I recall being the guard commander there on two occasions I think I was there for two weeks at a time. One of my duties was to be the guide for casual visitors who gathered each day at the front gate at 10 a.m. for a tour. This duty was particularly demanding with my job requiring me to visit each of the sentry posts at least twice each day and no days off for the two weeks I was there. I was, however, able to be absent for periods of up to four or five hours as long as I was contactable by phone. I took advantage of this on two occasions and caught the bus to the Town Hall Hotel for a couple of beverages.

Visiting the sentry posts was sometimes a scary task with Paddington and particularly Moore Park being frequented by some of the greatest weirdos imaginable. Even the sentries were threatened from time to time, and on one occasion, I had to double up the sentries for their own safety. There was also a large number of very attractive prostitutes patrolling these streets and there wasn't one night where I wasn't propositioned on my rounds. I was also concerned on some occasions that the sentries weren't taking advantage of the offers, but I was unable to catch any of them in compromising circumstances, so I assumed that they were remaining true to their employment.

I was now posted to these beautiful barracks serving as a staff officer on Operations Branch for Headquarter Field Force Command later to be named Land Command. This was the headquarters that controlled all land operations conducted by the Australian Army. I served as staff officer (Plans) which was the centre for planning all evacuations or support operations of Australian military personnel around the world but more specifically around Australia and its sovereign states and neighbours. These evacuations could be for bushfire, police emergencies, civil war, etc., none of which I decided but all of which I would be instrumental in arranging if we became involved. I had direct access to the RAAF and the RAN and frequently held conferences to determine our state of readiness. I was somewhat horrified to see the state of the written plans but quickly determined that the template was in place and all they needed was an update. RAAF and Navy seemed to be much more aware of the plans, so our biggest arm wrestle was fighting over responsibilities.

This was soon overcome, and by the time I left the job, we were starting to get some shape about our roles and responsibilities. I was then actually posted as the staff officer grade 2 (Operations), which was the next-door office (so I moved a whole six feet), and after six months and due to some leave and a posting, the staff officer grade 1 (operations) vacated his office (which was again next to mine, another six feet), and I was advised that I would be doing both jobs for the next six months. All of a sudden, my job became a serious burden. This became the busiest year of my entire military career. During this year and mainly centred around my office, I had to conduct a TEWT (Tactical Exercise Without Troops) for MAJGEN Kelly who was the general officer commanding Field Force Command. This entailed reconnaissance and writing the exercise (with very little help) which involved deploying and fighting a battle with a brigade in the Northern Territory.

Of course the exercise was conducted on the ground for all the operational leaders within Land Command and their operational staff which involved the movement and accommodating about seventy officers from major general down to lieutenants, provision of vehicles, provision of aids to assist presentation, allocation of space for reconnaissance and lectures, and the issue of the tactical problems. In addition to this, we had to provide aviation fuel, diesel fuel, standard fuel and oils plus water and meals for all involved—an enormous exercise with the smallest exercise headquarters I have ever been part of. However, we made it work, and the GOC was seemingly happy with the end result, not that he ever told me.

It was during this time that I made the decision to purchase a sandwich/coffee shop in Coogee which really did seem like a very good idea at the time. When I made the decision, I was working fairly hard but was stationery therefore able to allocate some of my time to 'out of work' activities. I would go the shop early in the morning (5 a.m.), slice all the meats and salads, turn on the coffee machine, and prepare the shop for Carole and the staff who would come in later. I would have coffee a toasted sandwich with Carole for breakfast and then change into uniform and head into work at Victoria Barracks. I would then return at 6 p.m. and clean the floors and pack the fridges.

During the periods that I was away, Carole's dad, Laurie, would stand in for me, and the staff would pack the fridges and mop the floor. This double life worked for a couple of years, but eventually Carole had had enough; my knees were in need of repair, and the pressure of running two jobs was becoming too stressful on me and therefore the family. The business was well established with regular customers and a steady income but was in need of being completely refurbished. It was ready to be sold. It was in fact sold to a family who turned it into a pizza shop which is still running today—so much for my good idea.

The year that we went into the shop was also the year that the Third Battalion, Royal Australian Regiment, became an airborne battalion. They were stationed at Holsworthy and were training to a three-year plan that was due to materialise during this year. This meant that we as the headquarters were due to scrutinise their preparedness for this role, check that all their soldiers were parachute qualified, report to the general that this was about to happen, conduct a final exercise, and plan a changeover parade. Holy shit, why me? Logically, the CO from 3RAR rang me and invited me to a conference where I could explain my timeline for these events to his staff. I was horrified, nothing had been done. The file had been sitting in the bottom of the safe for a couple of years unattended. Logically, I paid the CO a visit, and thanks to his total professionalism and many hours of work, we managed to piece together a pretty good plan that somehow succeeded. At last the Australian Army had an airborne battalion.

During this same year, SASR advised that they wanted to run another field exercise at unit level. We had run one the year before in Tasmania, I had been the exercise director, and it seemed to go well, so the CO decided he wanted to run another this time in North Queensland, so he asked that we find him an area in which to operate and get the necessary clearances. This was not an easy task, and I had clear my desk for a couple of weeks and make all the necessary bookings to get up to North Queensland, find suitable location, and then check with the landholders to gain their permission to exercise on their property. I put together a small party, and we flew to Cooktown in a small aircraft provided by the Aviation Regiment, booked in at the local motel, hired some vehicles, and made a plan. Fortunately, the major area we wanted to use was owned by one farmer, so we flew to his property first. He met us in his ute and in a couple of loads took us back to his house where his wife made us a big heap of roast lamb sandwiches for lunch. We outlined our plan to the owner, and he was hesitant, he was concerned that we would have an effect on his cattle. We reassured him that we would be moving slowly in small groups and contacts would only occur sporadically.

This was, after all, an SASR exercise where their role was intelligence gathering and silent extraction where possible. The farmer was still not convinced. I had an idea. I said to him, 'Have you ever seen your property from the air? Would you like to?' His face lit up. I turned and spoke to the pilot (a major) and asked him if this was permissible. He was not happy about the prospect but said, 'Only if you can get the authority provided by the SO1 [Operations] at Land Command.' With great relief and alacrity, I informed him that I was the SO1 (Ops) Land Command and I could approve. The pilot was great; he recorded his authority and then took the whole family for a look at their property from the air—what a change of attitude, the property owner could not agree to our proposal quickly enough. He signed our prepared letters of authority and we were off, back to Cooktown to plan the remainder of our reconnaissance.

The remainder of our time in Cooktown was mainly done in four-wheel drive vehicles trying to find locations and areas where specific events could occur. We assembled the information and prepared to head back to Sydney. We loaded into the aircraft and were away. Unexpectedly, we ran into the mother of all storms, the pilot tried to fly around it then under it, but radar showed that it was as wide as it was deep and we started to get one hell of a ride. The plane was bucking and dropping 40 to 50 feet at a time and the five of us in back were all looking a little worried, a little pale. I decided to listen in to what the pilot was doing (he had an airframe mechanic travelling with him in the off seat). I was previously frightened, now I was terrified he was no more reassured than we were. I switched off the headset and told the others nothing. Given what seemed like an eternity, we flew into clear air and everyone was very relieved. I again put the headphones on and congratulated the pilot on a good effort.

Land Command was the centre of the universe for me. This is where all the warriors came for rest. I met and worked with many of the legends of our time. Great leaders who many only got to hear about, but I was able to meet them and in some cases work with them and in all cases share a drink with them. Life was pretty good, however, in the army, every time I got to a point where I thought I was on top of my job. They posted me to another and, in this case, promoted me to lieutenant colonel. Again, the distance was short. I was to take up a job with Training Command which had offices down Oxford Street closer to the city which meant I could still park my car at Victoria Barracks and walk to work each day. We were living at Randwick at this stage, so there was no disadvantage to Carole or the kids in terms of work or schooling. Everything remained pretty much the same. My posting, however, did cause me to be on the back foot a bit as I was now working at the lower end of Oxford Street which boasted a large population of homosexuals and brothels and my position was designated as the staff officer grade 1 (Aids and Devices). To the army, the position referred to provision and supervision of any equipment to do with training—too good a title to be missed by my fellow workers. They gave me a tough time particularly on Friday afternoons when I would go for a drink at the Victoria Barracks officer's mess.

For about six months, I would receive a round of applause for being 'the officer with the most hands-on job in the army'. This was always good fun particularly when MAJGEN Neville Smethurst took over Land Command, he didn't understand what the applause was for, and I had to explain the joke. Incidentally he was one of the best officers I had ever worked for and laughed along with everybody else.

Training Command provided excellent opportunities for me to visit many of the military training establishments that I had never been to along with those where I had spent some time. My role was to analyse the training requirements of these units and speak with the commanding officers and the staff and try to ascertain a priority for their needs and a budget. The units were quite a mixed bunch and trying to determine between 'needs' and 'wants' got a bit difficult. The schools ranged from Command and

Staff College, the Officer Cadet School, the School of Infantry, School of Artillery, School of Aviation, School of Signals, Ordnance Centre, Land Warfare Centre, Parachute Training School, Training Groups in Brisbane, Sydney, Adelaide, and Tasmania, and the School of Health. My budget and the time available did not allow me to visit training groups in Perth or Darwin, but I managed to visit all the other schools at least once during my two-year term. These were fascinating trips where I met fellow officers who I hadn't seen for years and got the opportunity to listen to what the schools were trying to achieve and more importantly how I could help.

Because each of the schools always provided for at least a couple of foreign students, e.g., PNG, Singapore, Malaysia, US, Canada, or the UK, we were able to access some foreign aid funding, purchase much-needed training equipment and take it with us (I generally took one staff member with me on each of these trips), and deliver it unexpectedly, making us look very much like a late visit by Santa Claus. Prior to this period, even our biggest schools had the barest modicum of training support equipment only, particularly for indoor instruction. Most schools were issued with several overhead projectors (vu-graphs), an occasional opascope, and a couple of film projectors. There was no modern tape or disc projectors, no curved screens, laser pointers, basic sign writing systems, ceiling projectors, nor photographic systems for quick reproduction of lettering or photographs. Their needs were great.

As a result of this close liaison with the schools and their training staff, we were able to make major changes to an existing proposal for a dedicated allocation of training equipment to military schools. The proposal which was over a year old had been written in isolation, in that subjective judgements were made about what each major school should get and what each of the smaller schools should get with little thought to the fact that they all had different needs. Essentially, I spent the first twelve months getting to understand the individual needs of the schools and the second twelve months fighting to change the proposal for their future needs into a realistic inventory. This worked in well with my posting finishing at the end of 1986, it allowed me to finish the job, however, when I marched out in December, I had not seen one item of equipment delivered to the units. It was pleasing, however, to have seen the program through and set it in place for the future. Eventually, the equipment was received and delivered to the schools.

During this time, I was contacted by the director of Infantry and offered a posting to Washington—a posting I would have relished with the exception that my daughters were in their critical years of high school and were doing well. I was given twenty-four hours to make the decision, and Carole and I agonised over the possible outcomes. We were offered the opportunity to put the girls in a full-time boarding school of our choice or take them to the United States. Our final decision, after hours of consideration and discussion was that, for once, I would put the family first and decline the position. Disappointing for us but we thought, over time, beneficial for the girls. It was a decision that didn't impress my masters and, effectively, ended my career, however, I have never been unhappy that we chose that path, in fact, inwardly I felt quite noble about it.

I was also aware that the job as chief instructor at the Infantry Centre, now at Singleton, was becoming vacant and threw my hat in the ring for that job thinking that I would be well qualified for the job. However, although I was considered to be the number one contender, my recent non-acceptance of the US posting was taking its toll. Revenge is a dish best served cold. The commandant of the School of Infantry informed me over dinner at our house that I had not been accepted and a more junior LTCOL had been named to be the new chief instructor. This left me numb but accepting.

I received a phone call from the new director of Infantry who questioned why I had not been given an infantry battalion to command. I advised him that I didn't make those decisions, but it might help him to understand if he read my file. Two days later, he rang again and offered apologies for the way I had been treated and stated that I had been incorrectly denied command of an infantry battalion, however, he said that it was now too late, and he could do nothing to recover the situation. The best posting he could offer me was the command of the Logistic Support Battalion (1LSG later to be renamed IALSG). This was a composite battalion with a limited number of permanent headquarters staff (about twenty) with all its units and additional staff 'shadow posted' to the battalion and made available for release on thirty days' notice. This made it difficult for the relevant COs because effectively it meant that they had two jobs and therefore two bosses, and in the case of units like Engineers, they were always busy, so they had very little time for updating the information that I needed to be an effective Support Battalion if members of the ADF were committed to operations. However, I had my job to do and my boss was the Deputy Commander of Land Command and his office was right above mine. Additionally, I had a warehouse out at Frenchman's Road at Randwick where I stored the equipment and stores needed to set up a headquarters in the field. This warehouse became very useful when the 1987 'Welcome Home Parade' was arranged in August of that year for Vietnam veterans.

It evolved to be much bigger than ever expected and very close to the event veterans who hadn't booked accommodation realised that Sydney was booked out for that weekend and only desperation would save them. My staff and I ended up with a car transporter, ten standard vehicles, and twenty-eight people (including some RAN guys) sleeping on stretchers on the floor of the warehouse. My RQMS was very sympathetic to these veterans as he had been unable to go to Vietnam himself due to blood compatibility problems with his sister who had a disease requiring compatible blood platelets every four weeks. The RQMS therefore treated all of these veterans as brothers and catered to all their basic needs, including food, transport, and beverages. I was committed to my own unit (9RAR) and, therefore, left the administration of the temporary accommodation to my RQMS who handled it admirably.

I had always been a pygmy when it came to logistics, and it was extremely ironical that I could have landed such a job, but the logisticians saw that it was preferable that an infantryman be at the helm because of the knowledge of the forward units when planning of convoys, etc., was employed. The need for basic knowledge of ammunition usage, water requirements, convoy protection, and provision of rations was better left with someone who had experienced it and the more technical elements of the logistic support could be left to the staff who were trained in road speeds for convoys, time past a point, and capacities of vehicles/planes/helicopters and roads.

I had tendered my resignation and was due for discharge in May 1988; however, I had planned and was very keen to execute a meaningful logistic exercise before I finished up. I had submitted a budget and knew I would have to keep fighting to keep it in the training program. To fully test our ability to move to a foreign country and be prepared to support a brigade at war, I knew that we had to move some distance and both RAAF and RAN had to be involved. I therefore decided that we would move from Sydney in NSW to the Cultana Training Range in South Australia and we would engage the services of RAAF air transport out of Richmond and HMAS *Tobruk* (RAN transport ship) out of Garden Island in Sydney. This would require the loading of all stores and vehicles (those not going by road), rations, water, and surplus personnel (loadmasters and work party), so logically, there were numerous conferences and work groups working overtime to plan this move. Fortunately, I had excellent staff and their contribution was outstanding.

The task I had set was huge, not only did we have to move all this equipment tactically, but we had to unload it securely at the other end in an operational environment and we had to construct suitable accommodation (under tentage) for all units which included the erection of a field hospital to include an operating theatre (sterile) along with wards and an emergency room for day-to-day (real) casualties along with those provided by the exercise. This also meant that a complete exercise scenario had to be written (my job) including running sheets for units, i.e., their daily requirement and an 'enemy' group to provide disruptions to any set routines, etc. We also had Naval Diving Team to provide below-water protection to HMAS *Tobruk*, so I had to write a number of scenarios which included them. The workload was becoming overwhelming and even I doubted we could make this exercise work. However, with an amount of adjusting and some very good cooperation between the services and eleventh-hour approval of my budget, we launched.

This was to be my military 'swan song'. It was important for this exercise to work. Whilst the staff commenced the loading and dispatch of units from around Australia, I visited the mayor of Whyalla who was a very experienced, very tough lady who left me in no doubt about what she expected from the 'invasion' of troops in her shire and just who she would hold responsible if anything went wrong. Despite this tough approach, I warmed to her strength of character and calmed many of her fears when I advised the number of local food and fuel contracts we would be taking out with local businesses. I also reassured her that all of our physical activity would occur on the range and in the water with as little disruption to Whyalla locals as possible. We did, however, have one little clash over carrying rifles in the town when we went in daily to pick up fresh rations, as the mayor was worried it might concern the locals about some sort of military dictatorship. We resolved this quickly.

Brian hands over his final command (First Logistic
Support Group) to Ron MacKay

It was with great relief the road convoys began to arrive on time and with no major incidents on the way. The *Tobruk* arrived, and security and unloading began to occur. This was an amazing feeling and revealed an absolute masterpiece in staff planning. Within three days, we were set up and fully operational which included the field hospital with doctors and nursing staff. Now was time for me to set the 'dogs loose' and create some operational scenarios to test the security and defence capabilities of a unit set up to support a brigade at war. I had just commenced the first serials of my operational scenario when Ron Mackay (a member of my planning staff) was given authority to be promoted to LTCOL and take over the LSG from me in the field. The photo above shows Ron on the left assuming command. Logically, Ron, being a logistician by corps, wanted me out of there as quickly as possible. I agreed to hand over all my responsibilities and ideas and leave the following day. This all went very easily as Ron and several other staff members had helped me plan the whole exercise, so wholesale change was not likely.

I said farewell to the mayor and travelled by staff car to Adelaide where I booked into a hotel, had a hot shower, bought a pie and pea floater (a lasting bit of nostalgia to remember my time in Adelaide from when I was preparing for the trip to Vietnam) for dinner, and wandered across the street to the Adelaide Casino where I settled in for a relaxing night. I could almost feel twenty-two (plus) years of military service drain from my body. I only had to report to Field Force Command on the next day, sign my discharge papers, say my farewells, and I was unemployed for the first time in my life—age 47.

CHAPTER SIXTEEN

END OF AN ERA

DURING MY PAST six months, I had put out a few feelers to people who had said to me, 'Brian, when you eventually get out of the army, look me up, I will find you a job.' They were interested in employing me, but all said, 'Just knock out a short CV so we have a record, and I'll start looking for a job for you', until they saw that I had no education. All of a sudden, behaviour, work ethic, and achievement had nothing to do with my employment. It all came down to education, so I was left stranded and jobless. I always had a penchant for creative drawing/signwriting, etc., so I bought a couple of businesses that I thought would suit me and allow me to exercise my creative juices.

The first was a screen-printing business, which had a good steady turnover and potential for expansion and development. It also came with a huge four-foot square Kodak camera which was ideal for this type of work. I entered Sydney Tech at Ultimo (as a mature aged student) to do signwriting but was denied because it still required an indentured apprenticeship which I, of course, did not have, so I opted for the next best creative class which was ticket writing.

I found that I had a natural talent for this and ended up fifth in the state at exam time. In fact, I found it a bit too easy, the teachers took umbrage at the fact that when we had a half-hour break for a cup of tea, a mate and I would slip to the pub next door and have a couple of schooners. Most of the students, being young people, would beaver away (most didn't drink tea or coffee), grab a can of Coke, and still at the end of the night would not have finished the project. Warwick and I used to come back to class, work feverishly for about forty minutes, put on the finishing touches, and head out before the class finished. Only one student really impressed me, and he ended up being first in the state in the same exam I sat for. His work was extremely good. This skill helped me enormously doing the artwork for the screen-printing business which I had moved from the north-western suburbs of Sydney to Marrickville in the south. This better suited the targeted businesses I was seeking for the future marketing of our business.

I approached Warwick (my mate from the Ticket Writing course) to see if he was interested in working for me with a view to becoming a partner. With similar interests, he agreed, and we started a partnership that endured for over ten years despite some initial teething problems and being under-capitalised. Warwick was a good calligrapher, and at that time, he was the secretary of the NSW Calligraphy Society and was learning signwriting from a very good friend. These were skills that few people had, and we thought we might be able to capitalise on them. It wasn't long before we started to think that we could print anything. We took on another staff member and accepted requests to print T-shirts, banners, flags, plastic bottles, vinyl, and do sublimated prints. We got good orders for T-shirts, so we purchased an automatic printing machine ($100,000) and employed another six or seven staff. Despite a good working relationship and working sixty hours a week, we still didn't 'quite make it'the Chinese cheap prints were just gaining a foothold and we found it difficult to compete.

Warwick started working for the Calligraphy Society on Saturdays, and I started signwriting after work (night-time) doing window splashes and fluros in my spare time on the weekends. Carole was also working doing casual nursing jobs around the Eastern Suburbs. Fortunately, we had a safe unit for our daughters to come home to. They were being schooled close by in the Eastern Suburbs also.

Just about everything that could happen did happen in that business. We got ram-raided, we got burgled (three times), we got raided by the federal police. I was taken away by detectives to police headquarters in Goulbourn Street and questioned as to why we were printing copyright designs. This was in fact quite a fascinating experience, and as an army officer, it was the most incompetent raid I had ever seen. In fact, I told the female detective in charge that if I had conducted a raid that badly as an army officer, my own men would have lynched me.

Our factory frontage had a ten-foot (three-metre) roller door, about two metres of glass frontage, a sliding glass door, and a wooden door which led upstairs to our storeroom. Warwick and I had started work early (3 a.m.) because we took on printing a very intricate, indigenous design onto Christmas cards, by hand, so we were using very fine mesh and quick-drying inks, six colours, and it was the middle of summer. To keep as much coolness from the night air coming into the factory, we had the roller door up and naturally the lights on.

At about 5.30 a.m., our staff started to drift in (mainly Chinese) and go to work. I said to Warwick that I thought I heard a noise out the front and walked out the roller door to check it out. I looked towards the wooden door and there were two burly detectives with a door hammer about to smash the door open. I yelled out and asked them what they were doing. Immediately I was surrounded by men in suits with a search warrant shoved in front of my face and the usual questions of identification asked. I said I was the proprietor and they should come in via the roller door, which had been open for hours, and do what they had to do. The police couldn't do this, they had to race in as a group, yelling as loud as they could and try to gather up the staff. The staff, however, had never seen this sort of behaviour in Australia before, so they all bolted out the back door and headed in all directions. They were terrified.

The detectives told me to round them up. I quickly told them I wasn't going to go searching around Marrickville at that time of day; there were too many known bad guys living in the suburb. I sought out the leader of the raid, who was a female detective, and asked her what the purpose of the raid was and could I read the warrant. She told me we were suspected of printing copyright designs and using illegal staff to do it. Despite my protestations, the search of the premises resulted in our factory being wrecked, my artwork being thrown all over the place, and all our books of accounts being impounded. I was loaded into a police car and taken to police headquarters.

This in itself was quite hilarious because I was a coach at Randwick Rugby Club and a lot of police played for our club. As I was being led down this long corridor, all these young policemen were appearing out of offices saying, 'Hey, Brian, what are you doing here?' 'How are you going, mate?' 'See you at training', etc. The particularly galling part for my escorts was when Senior Detective Ian 'Speed' Kennedy (one of the senior investigators in the Anita Cobby murder) pulled us to a halt and asked the escorts what I was doing there, and they burbled out a pretty unconvincing summary of why I had been arrested. 'Speed' was the coach of the Australian Under 21 Rugby Team at the time and ex-head coach of Randwick Rugby Club, so I knew him well. He steered me into a room, pointed to the phone, and said, 'One call.' He knew who I would ring. The manager of my rugby team was a barrister and ex-army LTCOL. I rang him and carefully listened to his instructions.

'Speed' and the two detectives re-entered the room and the inquisition began. After about two hours, they left the room, returned about half an hour later, and told me that I was free to go and a car would take me back to Marrickville. Warwick and I laughed a bit about this for a few days to come, but in reality, the police had left us in a dire position. Our staff had gone and the police had all our books of trade, we had no copies of orders, invoices, pay, etc., and therefore had to use memory only to be able to submit a tax return that year and they had taken about twenty of our printing screens, several of which were a new design for a customer. This was a loss of about $1,200.

In about twelve months, the director of police prosecutions wrote to us and told us we had absolutely 'No Case to Answer'. I rang police headquarters and asked for the return of our books of trade and our screens. Their answer was that they couldn't be found. Fortunately, all of our staff returned and would have been cooperative had they not been scared off by the bullying approach used by the police. We had also always made it policy to view a copy of visas before we employed anyone, so we knew they were all legal. As it turned out, the trader who we had been selling our screen-printed shirts to was also dealing with about four or five other screen printers. One of these must have been printing copyright designs and we just happened to get caught up in the net.

Warwick and I battled on for a few years always on the lookout for new ideas to get us into the comfortable bracket, but we always seemed to be 'a pound [weight] light and a dollar short'. It all really came apart when I had an accidental fall when delivering T-shirts about nine o'clock one night. My legs just gave away on me, and I fell down into the loading dock, awkwardly landing on the tow bar on my van. Not a soul in sight, so no witnesses and more importantly no help. I managed to get to my feet, got into my van, and drove home.

Over the next few weeks, my back got progressively more painful to the point where I would have to lie down on the floor just to get some relief. The end result was an emergency trip to Prince Henry Hospital at Randwick where Dr Bernie Kwok, an Eastern Suburbs neurologist, was operating and agreed to see me as soon as he left theatre. Dr Kwok concluded that I had a ruptured disc (L4/L5) and would need an immediate operation. I was admitted straight away, and he operated that afternoon. I doubt that I have ever experienced that much pain, however, recovery from the pain was fast, and because we lived close to the hospital, Carole was able to visit when she was free. Long-term recovery, however, was slow, and I was unable to return to work for a year. During this time, Warwick and I discussed the handover of the business to him. Eventually, he and his wife, Katy (who was Chinese), bought the business from me, and when I was able to go back to work, I took on the casual role of designer/artist and essentially did artwork to suit the business.

Warwick and Katy developed the business well and eventually moved it and themselves to Shanghai where Katy's parents lived. At the time of writing, Warwick and Katy were still running a very successful business. In fact, we paid them a visit in Shanghai and were hugely impressed with the way they had advanced the business. Warwick and Katy remain our very close friends.

Carole and I decided that our final retirement location would be somewhere up near the Queensland/NSW border probably between Noosa, Queensland, and Ballina in NSW. Our daughters, Nicole and Lisa, had finished up at school with Nicole pursuing an arts degree and Lisa attending business college in the city. Carole's parents were ageing, and Carole was driving across the Southern Suburbs to visit her mother at least once per week. It wasn't long before it became necessary to place

Doreen in a nursing home where she passed away with Laurie agreeing reluctantly to go and live with Carole's brother (Phil) and his wife, Mary, in the NSW country town of Coonabarabran. This was a big ask of Phil and Mary, and I applaud them for the effort. They too were eventually forced to place Laurie in the local nursing home where he also passed away a number of years later, aged 93.

During the period that Doreen was in the nursing home, Carole and I entertained no thoughts of moving, but when Laurie went to Coonabarabran, we decided to think about it particularly with Lisa planning her marriage and Nicole living independently.

Lisa duly got married and also went to live in Coonabarabran with Nicole packing up and driving to Melbourne when her degree was finished. Carole and I decided to look for somewhere for us to settle. Eventually, we bought a house at Banora Point (Oxley Cove) on the Tweed River, not far from where I was born. We loved the house and the location, and both Carole and I started to re-establish ourselves in our new location. Our neighbours were great, and we became involved in local organisations, I in the Banora Point Residents Association and the Cudgen Headland Surf Life Saving Club and Carole in the local book club and the garden club.

My association with the surf club became a very busy one as I could immediately see there was a lot to be done. Some very willing members but few visionaries and they were very short of funds. I was initially very hesitant to make suggestions but soon found there were a number of members who were thinking the same way that I was. It was critical that we expanded the capital base, exploited the available grants for basic club equipment, and embraced the local government dignitaries so that our name stood out in the public arena. Of course, to do this, we, as a surf club, had to continue to be competitive as a club and be seen to be up there amongst the leaders in our local branch competition to give us credibility.

You don't make an omelette without breaking some eggs, whereas I had been absent for over thirty years, many of my schoolmates had stayed in the area and established themselves in the surf club (I had known many of members since we were 4 years of age). They filled all the positions from chairman of the board to president of the surf club right down to the senior competitors, so my forthright approach caused a lot of angst amongst the most senior men in the club who incorrectly assessed that I wanted to take control of the club and institute all the changes that I had outlined. My aim was simply to join the senior executive and offer them the benefit of my experience, particularly as an administrator, and steer them towards the next ten years rather than the next twelve months. However, fear of the unknown 'spooked' the board into a state of intense dislike and caused them to form an 'us and them' group within the club.

It only took me a year or so to demonstrate how easy it was to raise money for 'not for profit' organisations and also to gain support from some very strong, dedicated, and courageous members who provided the nucleus for the club's future. Some of those in support were Gary Cain, David Field, David Cahill, Brian Lewis, Sue Furlonge (now Sue a'Court), Adam Mills, Mark and Barbara Buckman with a number of others with divided loyalty but not opposed to change. I kept arguing points of difference at committee meetings, and tension began to build until the president stood up at a general meeting and resigned and took the whole committee with him and advised me quite strongly to see if I could form another committee—so I did and that committee was strong and forward-thinking for the next ten years. That wasn't the end of the story, however, as within a couple of months, the chairman of the board (who had also been the president of the Surf Club Committee) closed down the board at an AGM and quite wryly advised me to see if I could be so successful with the board. So I accepted this challenge.

An unsuspecting member was elected as chairman, but he was a fair person and held the chair for a year. Other members mentioned above filled the remaining vacant positions with one member staying on. I was not allowed to join as a board member because of the draconian rules put in place to protect the club from external takeover (which was never attempted, I might add), but was really a nasty attempt to 'get even' for me taking this stance. The new chairman, however, invited me to join the board as a consultant, allowing me freedom of the board but not allowing me to vote. I was more than happy to accept this offer. I held this position for two years and then was voted onto the board as a qualified member, remained on the board for six years, and during that time, became deputy chair.

In my time with the executive of the surf club, I raised over one and a quarter million dollars in grant money and secured a loan for a kitchen to be put in the club to complement the bar. Strong management since my time on the board has allowed the club to progress exponentially without the support of poker machines. The board always considered that if we were to call ourselves a family club, we couldn't promote gambling. That philosophy remains in place today. I also formed a strong apolitical working relationship with the local council Warren Polglase and John Griffin (mayor and general manager), the state member for Tweed who at the time was Neville Newell, and the federal member for Richmond who was then Larry Anthony. They and their successors have all proven to be wonderful supporters of the surf club since.

This period almost became overwhelming for me as I also, somewhat reluctantly, agreed to assist resurrecting the Kingscliff Sub Branch of the RSL. I turned up to an Anzac Day service, in Kingscliff, in 2002 and 2003 and was disappointed with both the service and particularly the small, partisan crowd. I spoke to the president Mr Joe Peoples (later OAM) who advised me that he was exhausted, 81 years of age, and received very little assistance. He said it would be a great help if I could take over the Cudgen Dawn service. I was unprepared for this and answered 'no!'. My view was that the whole sub-branch needed review, and I was prepared to offer my assistance but did not want to 'take over'.

After attending the 2004 service, I was approached by three sub-branch members (one of whom was in the same battalion as me in Vietnam) and strongly advised that if I did not take over the sub-branch with some urgency, it would implode as they would not stay on as members. I replied that I had been having discussions with an ex–warrant officer from Murwillumbah who I knew during service and if he would take on the role of president (I knew he was keen and he had just moved to Kingscliff). I would accept the role of vice president and reconstitute a committee.

Rod Lees duly took over as president and brought a friend and Ares officer with him (Wayne Quested) as secretary. I joined the sub-branch and became the vice president (a role I have held now for over fifteen years), and we had the basis of a sound committee. Tom Quayle, a wonderful supporter and sound accountant, remained on as the treasurer, and Bruce Peate willingly stayed on as the pensions officer which was a blessing for us as he achieved excellent results for almost everyone he represented. At that stage, the sub-branch still had an active woman's auxiliary, which was supportive and provided valuable assistance to the committee.

Our path was clear, and we had three areas that had to be addressed immediately. The first was recruitment of new members, providing priorities and systems for the administration, and making our sub-branch more attractive and more available to the general community (this, of course, included Anzac and Remembrance days). Rod took on the task of recruitment, Wayne the administration, and I immediately discarded all reference to the conduct of previous Anzac and Remembrance days and rewrote all the Orders of Service.

Our first year proved to be extremely successful with the old committee being our greatest supporters. We increased the membership from 62 to 120 members, we gained grants for a computer and a printer and some indoor games equipment, instituted a systematic filing system, and took our Anzac Day crowd from 400 the previous year to 1,500 in 2005 with a standing ovation at the main service with 400 people attending the Dawn Service at Cudgen. This was a healthy new start.

Since 2005, we have had five presidents, two vice presidents, four secretaries, three treasurers, one pensions Officer. We have introduced a number of events which has included a third Anzac Day Service at Kingscliff. The Dawn Service at Cudgen has been conducted since 1928 and always at 4.28 a.m. to coincide with the firing of the guns at Gallipoli in 1915 when the first troops went ashore. However, the Second World War veterans argued that to get to the Dawn Service at 4.10 a.m. for the preceding march was too big a task for veterans over 80 years of age, so they demanded a 6 a.m. Dawn Service for Kingscliff. I took the demand to the Cudgen Residents Association to argue the case for a compromise on timings for the Cudgen Service; it was my intention to move it to 5.30 a.m. The Cudgen Committee stacked the meeting and refused to budge on the timing. I now had a dilemma which I solved by approaching the principal of the local high school. I asked that the Dawn Service at Kingscliff be run (with support and assistance from the Kingscliff RSL Sub Branch) by the student body of Kingscliff High School with the captains (male and female) and the vice captains providing the principal speakers including the MC.

This service has now been running for six years and attracts around 1,000 members of the community and provides one of the few opportunities the school captains get to speak publicly. The high school principal and staff are fully supportive. Needless to say, a very rewarding success.

The sub-branch is the seed sponsor for the Kingfisher Day Club at Cabarita, a task that we take very seriously to ensure we keep it afloat. We also inherited a walkway, which we share with the Tweed Shire Council and the local Feros/Wommin Bay Nursing Home which provides a concrete path for ambulant members of the nursing home to travel to a platform overlooking the ocean. Kingscliff RSL / Tweed Shire Council turned this into a Memorial Walkway by providing plinths containing plaques highlighting the different operational areas Australians have been represented in at war. At the time of writing, we had twenty-six of these plaques, and we try to add two new plaques each year. They are rather expensive and sometimes grants are denied and local funding has to be raised.

We support DVA Health Week by organising and conducting a barefoot bowls morning with trivia and a light lunch. We conduct a very good Remembrance Day service which is generally attended by 200 to 300 people. We organise and sponsor a visit each year by the First Regiment RAA band and invite the people of the community to join us in a free concert. This is very popular and is held in the Rowan Robinson Park (Afghanistan veteran who was killed in Afghanistan in 2011 whilst serving as a Royal Australian Engineer) which is in the centre of Kingscliff and faces the ocean. We make the point that it is our donation to the community of Kingscliff for the support that they show the RSL during the year.

Finally, we have proudly provided over sixty RSL tributes to veterans (when requested) at their funerals. Personally, I have done fifty of these tributes—sometimes removing the coldness from services which attract few family or friends.

At the time of writing we, the RSL Sub Branch Kingscliff, are undergoing the transition from the Old Guard (Vietnam War) to the New Guard (all wars since which include Rwanda/Timor-Leste/Iraq/Somalia and Afghanistan). I cautioned that this had to be a period of patience as the New Guard wasn't convinced that we (RSL Australia) had got it right—certainly not under current conditions, e.g., pensions, etc., but my view has always been that they are better to take over a strong and successful organisation and change it from within. This way the New Guard will develop its own direction and policies but not have to establish the funds and power base that currently exists. There are some very smart young men and women out there who could re-ignite the RSL even if it results in some form of name change and direction. I helped carry the baton to this point and am proud of what we, the committee, have achieved. I really do hope the organisation persists.

It was during this period where I was seemingly trying to 'change the world' that Carole, Nicole and I faced another unexpected, frightening experience that no one can be prepared for. We certainly weren't. Nicole, had been running a juice shop in Coolangatta. Matthew had returned to Melbourne with the boys in anticipation of the shop being sold and the family returning to Melbourne where they found the weather much more agreeable and work more was available for Matthew. Nicole stayed with us, putting their house into rental. This was all going well although the sale of the business was a slow process and buyers seemed in short supply. Matthew had secured a job in Melbourne. Nicole was missing the boys, and it was decided that they return to our house for a short holiday.

Shortly after arriving, Carole noticed that Tysen, the eldest boy, had a red mark on his forearm and it was slightly swollen. Nicole rang Matthew and asked if he had noticed the mark on Tysen's arm. Matthew replied in the affirmative and said that the boys had been playing in some grass clippings and he assumed, quite logically, that an ant had bitten him. Carole, having been a nurse for forty-five years, expressed concern and suggested to Nicole that he should visit a local doctor and 'just have it checked out'. This we did and the doctor, who was largely unknown to us, measured the arm for swelling, prescribed anti-histamines, took a blood sample, and suggested we return in two days' time for a check on the swelling. This was good advice, however, the result of the blood sample came back the next day, the doctor rang for Tysen to be brought down immediately, and Nicole was advised that Tysen had a form of bone cancer (Ewing sarcoma) and had to be taken to Royal Children's Hospital in Brisbane immediately.

This was a shock we were not expecting, and it took some time to sink in, however, we reacted instantly and made the preparations for the trip to Brisbane. Some more exact tests and closer examination revealed that the situation was very serious. We were overwhelmed. Personally, I lost all control of my emotions. Tysen was 3 ½ years of age and was given very little chance of reaching his fourth birthday.

Tysen did survive this horrendously traumatic ordeal, and by chance, so did we, but there were some very thin tight ropes to walk and many sleepless nights along the way. We had difficulty finding accommodation close to the hospital, and Nicole still had the shop in Coolangatta to run. Tysen had major surgery to remove the forearm bone (radius) in his left arm and replace it with a bone from his left leg (fibula) and was put on chemo. Every night he was in hospital, we (Nicole, Carole, or myself) slept in the chair beside his bed. We started a system of 'hot cars' whereby Nicole would stay with Tysen, and we would return to home. We would drive up at 4 a.m. the next morning, and Nicole would take the car and return to run the shop at Coolangatta and return to relieve us the next day. Matthew, his mother Lorraine, and Jett flew up to visit on a couple of occasions, and we hired a unit next to ours for them to stay when Tysen was allowed home.

This was a very tense time, and everyone was getting very tired. Sometimes when staying at our place, Tysen's temperature would skyrocket, and we would have to take him to Tweed Hospital in the middle of the night. Other times, he would have massive nosebleeds, and we would have to take him to Tweed Hospital to have his nose tubes refitted. Eventually, we prepared ourselves for this and learned how to deal with it ourselves, including the changing of complex chest dressings and the replacing of feeding tubes through the nose passage. Tysen was the dearest little boy and, even though in pain, offered no complaint and tried to be as polite and cheerful as his little body would let him. He proved what a champion fighter he really was.

The Family: (L) Nicole, Tysen, Lisa, Jett and Courtney
(R) Ben and Courtney

Although cancer treatment is free for all children, the external costs of travel, accommodation, and medications were astronomical, and Nicole spoke to me about costs and how their finances were just about exhausted, and she knew that Carole and I had helped with the costs along the way and had little in reserve. Nicole said to me, 'Dad, what are we going to do?' and I recall replying, 'Nic, we still have about three weeks of reserves left, let's not panic until then.' Nicole shook her head and said, 'I hope your optimism is justified.' I replied that I also hoped that it was justified. Nicole had been so strong and flexible through this whole ordeal, but the strain was starting to show, and she seriously began to doubt my optimism.

One week after this conversation, I was contacted by the Cudgen Headland Surf Club. They were offering to put on a benefit night for Tysen. I spoke to Nicole and then advised the surf club that we would agree as long as I could assist them in the preparation as my family would be the beneficiary and I was an active member of the surf club. As all members of the committee for the benefit were in full-time employment, they readily agreed. The committee as I recall it was Cheryl Cain, Phil Davis, Scott Polglase (secretary manager), Lyndel Small, and myself. Many other people offered assistance as the date drew closer. What a wonderful, generous collection of people. Donations came from everywhere, helped enormously by Crystal, a *Daily News* photographer who did a double-page spread of Tysen for the paper. Some army mates from Brisbane hired a bus and notified the club that they would be down for the night. More mates from Canberra put on a dinner in the Federal Capital and did their own fundraiser, and fellow Vietnam veteran and mate GEN Peter Cosgrove AC, MC, rang us with a personal donation. I was becoming an emotional wreck with the extreme generosity of the people who surrounded us.

The night was a huge success. The next day, however, was a chemo day for Tysen, so we had to rise early and drive to Brisbane. The surf club benefit provided us with some seriously needed cash, and they also set up a fund with the local service station so that we could fill up our car with fuel there every time we had to drive to Brisbane. We were still completely overwhelmed as we made our way up through the Spring Hill traffic. Nicole had also been advised that we had finally been given permission to use Ronald MacDonald House for accommodation. This reduced our daily costs by about 60 percent. Tysen's treatment continued.

August rolled around before Nicole was given the 'all-clear' for the completion of Tysen's treatment and our divorce from the Royal Children's Hospital on a regular basis. There was much relief and joy but still much to be done. We still had to get the juice shop back under control and then pursue the sale of the business. Nicole also had to get her family back together as they had been separated by distance for almost a year. It was decided that Nicole and Tysen would return to Melbourne, and I would supervise the running of the shop and follow up any leads for sales.

I didn't enjoy the 5 a.m. rises, but within a few months, we had the shop running smoothly and profitably. The staff, selected by Nicole previously, were all good to work with, and everything was harmonious. Several sales leads appeared, but nothing that satisfied our basic criteria emerged. We were also trying to keep the staff employed, but it was not the over-riding factor. We sold the shop right on New Year's Eve, and although promising at first, the new owners chose not to keep the staff on. Fortunately, we had paid up the staff, including their gratuities, so some of those friendships that were developed then still persist today. Another adventure with a lot of energy expended and not a lot to show for it at the end. However, we left debt free, so there was no looking back.

2009 provided our family with an unexpected surprise, I was advised that I had been awarded the Medal of the Order of Australia (OAM) for services to Surf Life Saving and for service to veterans particularly those of 9th Battalion, The Royal Australian Regiment.

This was a great honour and was acknowledged by many of the local community and similarly many of my ex military friends and colleagues. Carole and I were flown to Sydney where I was invested by the NSW Governor Dame Marie Bashir AD CVO – it was also extremely interesting to see a number of colleagues and friends who were also being invested many years after I had last seen them or they had left the service.

*Brian and Carole in Hyde Park in Sydney; Brian was
the guest speaker on Remembrance Day 2015*

CHAPTER SEVENTEEN

SEEKING RETIREMENT

ENTERING MY TWILIGHT years, I attempted to ease back on my commitments in order to ensure that I wasn't saving for a day that I was not prepared to take. Carole and I organised a couple of very good cruises which included the top of Australia, another to view the battlefields of the Coral Sea, a family cruise to the South Pacific, and a bus/motel/hotel trip around the North Island of New Zealand. In doing this, I was demonstrating the surf club could survive without my contribution to its administration and fundraising.

Three successive years at the AGM, I resigned from the major roles on the committee. No one took any notice knowing that I was unlikely to turn my back on any genuine request. However, domestic issues (such as a flooded unit) and a step down in my personal health helped bring a closure to these somewhat demanding duties. Fortunately, the gap closed quickly with some wonderful young people stepping forward and filling the void. Not always the way I had done it, but once you take the final step, there can be no recriminations about replacements. I had always said that no matter how much you did for a voluntary organisation, the minute you reach the bottom step on the way out, most members will have forgotten your name.

I have no regrets about the way I went about affecting change within the surf club. I had to re-invent myself and play off a couple of people against each other, but I took it as a compliment when I was described once as the 'Master Puppeteer'. It gave me a feeling of great satisfaction even though I think it might have been offered with some cynicism.

I had a strong vision about what the surf club could achieve if they took the right direction and started moulding the future rather than rueing the past. I knew it would take a lot of hard work particularly fundraising which I knew many were frightened to do, but I knew the club was capable of having a lot more in the bank than they displayed. Success also took 'heart', and there was plenty of that within the club, but it had to be captured and massaged, manipulated even. Water finds its own level, however, and with a bit of creative thinking and some encouraging speeches about achievement, we kept generating new levels of success. New equipment meant new competitors, and President Gary Cain had driven himself to put a strong competitive side in the branch and state competitions. All of a sudden, we were attracting interest and calls from competitors from other clubs. We were considered competent enough to be asked to again, run state carnivals which we did two years in a row. We had been recognised. We were also attracting strong young minds to put their hand up to join the board. This involved management of the whole club, but effectively, they were responsible for the conduct of the licensed element of the club (bar, kitchen, etc).

I had acquired an 'impossible' loan to build a kitchen (which we did), which was critical to support our bar sales and gave the board hope that 'above-the-line' financial results were possible. The reason the loan was described as 'impossible' was because no one wanted to touch it. We were on State Crown Land administered by the Tweed Shire Council, and we therefore had no bricks and mortar that we could use as collateral even though we had bought and built the clubhouse ourselves. Effectively we had no assets.

The recent success of the club (twice winners of NSW Club of the Year Award) can be attributed to those who came after my time on the board. My sense of achievement comes from the stable platform that I helped provide for them to work from. I don't pretend that I did it alone, but I do know that when I first arrived back in the club, we seemed to have no clear direction as to where we were going, no defined vision, and seemingly little hope of establishing one. I sought and provided funds for a kitchen, a new veranda, a new training room, a new caretaker's residence, a new first-aid room, fireproof ceilings for most of the downstairs areas, a completed DA for our building committee to work from, and an amount of equipment for both competitors and our beach patrol. I felt satisfied that I had made a valuable contribution. The club repaid me with the 'Blue of Blues Award' twice and life membership. This was rewarding and said 'thanks' for the effort.

Whereas I stepped down from most positions in the surf club, I still attended the RSL because of the lack of available successors. I have spent some time encouraging young veterans to become involved and help change the direction of the aged organisation to a more modern, energetic one. Fortunately, I had some outstanding help in this region, particularly from Malcolm Smith our secretary/treasurer. Malcolm attended many of the important meetings at a state level and, with an accountancy background, assured any changes were not prejudicial to our day-to-day operations nor the future of the movement. He did this marvellously well.

My path through life, I feel, has been a rather tough one shared for most of it by Carole, my wife of fifty-three years. We only ever seemed to get on top of life for brief moments and then another obstacle would fall in our path. We saw many others who had not travelled an easy path so we always knew that we were not alone and similarly we saw many who, on the surface seemed to breeze through life with consummate ease. However, we have not had an unhappy life. We have two wonderful children, both who respect us as parents and friends, and four grandchildren who we find are always as pleased to see us as we are to see them. It is always a genuine pleasure to be in their company and share their stories, development, and achievements. We were fortunate in that for most of my service (except Vietnam), we were accompanied by our children, and even though they were too young to remember all of it, they both have fond memories of their good experiences, particularly Darwin and Brunei.

Life is what you make it, and we tried to take advantage of every opportunity presented to us and enjoy life to the fullest. Carole and I both undertook voluntary and community work in our retirement and found it to be wonderfully fulfilling and inwardly rewarding discovering the incredible hardworking people who make up regional communities and the commitment and dedication that they show to making other people's lives just a little better.

I have never been classified as one of 'those rich and successful baby boomers' even though I tried to work myself into that category and I would have willingly accepted the mantle if it had have been offered and I certainly tried. However, it has been a wonderful life, and I found out exactly what I was capable of and where my strengths and weaknesses lay. We lived in a superb era where the music was outstanding (unmatched in my opinion) and the opportunities boundless, but for the roll of a marble, I could have gone in a completely different direction. My lack of education was the biggest regret in my life, however, it was my choice (albeit a very immature one), and few of those who surrounded me in my formative years tried to persuade me otherwise. I am proud to have served in the

Queen's uniform, I am proud to be a Vietnam veteran, I am immensely proud of my family and I am proud to be quantified as a 'baby boomer'.

I have no difficulty in holding my head up high remembering often those words of US President Ronald Reagan when he said, 'Some people go through life wondering if they have made a difference. Veterans don't have that problem.'

Lest we forget.

Abbreviations

7GR	7th (Duke of Edinburgh's Own) Gurkha Rifles
AK	Kalashnikov (enemy preferred small arms weapon)
APC	Armoured Personnel Carrier (troop transport)
AWOL	Absent without leave (not granted a leave pass)
CASEVAC	Casualty Evacuation
CO	Commanding Officer (Battalion)
CPL	Corporal
CSM	Company Sergeant Major
DVA	Department of Veteran's Affairs
FOO	Forward Observation Officer (Mortar or Artillery Officer)
GOC	General Officer Commanding (Major General)
GPMG	General Purpose Machine Gun
LTCOL	Lieutenant Colonel (CO of a battalion)
LZ	Landing Zone (Helicopters)
NCO	Non – commissioned officer
OC	Officer Commanding (Company)
OR	Other Ranks (private soldiers)
QGO	Queen's Gurkha Officer
RAAF	Royal Australian Air Force
RAN	Royal Australian Navy
RAR	Royal Australian Regiment (1RAR, 2RAR, 3RAR etc)
RPG	Rocket Propelled Grenade (enemy weapon)
RSM	Regimental Sergeant Major
RV	Rendevous (Meeting point)
SAS/SASR	Special Air Service Regiment (Elite soldiers, highly trained)
SGT	Sergeant
VC	Viet Cong